ARM IN ARM

ARM IN ARM

THE GRIMKÉ SISTERS' FIGHT FOR ABOLITION AND WOMEN'S RIGHTS

ANGELICA SHIRLEY CARPENTER

ZEST BOOKS
MINNEAPOLIS

To Gaye

Text copyright © 2025 by Angelica Shirley Carpenter

All rights reserved. No part of this book may be reproduced, stored in a retrieval system, or transmitted in any form or by any means—electronic, mechanical, photocopying, recording, or otherwise—without the prior written permission of Lerner Publishing Group, Inc., except for the inclusion of brief quotations in an acknowledged review.

Zest Books™
An imprint of Lerner Publishing Group, Inc.
241 First Avenue North
Minneapolis, MN 55401 USA

For reading levels and more information, look up this title at www.lernerbooks.com.
Visit us at zestbooks.net.

Cover illustration by Chiara Fedele.

Designed by Athena Currier

Main body text set in Janson Text LT Std.
Typeface provided by Adobe Systems.

Library of Congress Cataloging-in-Publication Data

Names: Carpenter, Angelica Shirley, author.
Title: Arm in Arm / by Angelica Shirley Carpenter.
Description: Minneapolis, MN: Zest Books, [2024] | Includes bibliographical references and index. | Audience: Ages 11–18 | Audience: Grades 7–9 | Summary: "Born to a family of enslavers in the South, Sarah Grimké and Angelina Grimké Weld were some of the first women to speak out about abolition and women's rights in the United States" —Provided by publisher.
Identifiers: LCCN 2024012382 (print) | LCCN 2024012383 (ebook) |
  ISBN 9798765627426 (library binding) | ISBN 9798765627433 (paperback) |
  ISBN 9798765639085 (epub)
Subjects: LCSH: Grimké, Angelina Emily, 1805–1879—Juvenile literature. | Grimké, Sarah Moore, 1792–1873—Juvenile literature. | Women abolitionists—South Carolina—Biography—Juvenile literature. | Feminists—South Carolina—Biography—Juvenile literature. | Sisters—South Carolina—Biography—Juvenile literature. | Antislavery movements—United States—History—19th century—Juvenile literature. | Women's rights—United States—History—19th century—Juvenile literature.
Classification: LCC E449.G865 C37 2025 (print) | LCC E449.G865 (ebook) | DDC 326/.80922757—dc23/eng/20240620

LC record available at https://lccn.loc.gov/2024012382
LC ebook record available at https://lccn.loc.gov/2024012383

Manufactured in the United States of America
1-1010248-52128-4/30/2025

This book includes discussions of murder, sexual assault, torture, and forced breeding of enslaved people as well as descriptions of racial violence. It quotes shocking language from supporters of enslavement, including newspapers. Some content or language may be upsetting or stressful for some readers. The hope of this book is that people will learn from history and the methods used to change it for the better, bringing joy and safety to the world.

Contents

INTRODUCTION 9

CHAPTER 1: *Running Away* 11

CHAPTER 2: *Breaking the Law* 14

CHAPTER 3: *A Rod of Fear* 23

CHAPTER 4: *The Society of Friends* 30

CHAPTER 5: *To Philadelphia!* 41

CHAPTER 6: *Bound with Chains* 48

CHAPTER 7: *Quaker Ways* 55

CHAPTER 8: *What to Do?* 64

CHAPTER 9: *A Cause Worth Dying For* 75

CHAPTER 10: *Two Fanatical Women* 84

CHAPTER 11: *Woman's Sphere* 98

CHAPTER 12: *Turning the World Upside Down* 104

CHAPTER 13: *Two Halves Made Whole* 112

CHAPTER 14: *What Is a Mob?* 123

CHAPTER 15: *The Shadow of Our Own Roof* 135

CHAPTER 16: *Crushing the Viper* 143

CHAPTER 17: *The Woman Question* 154

CHAPTER 18: *The Whole Truth* 162

CHAPTER 19: *The Belleville School* 171

CHAPTER 20: *Splitting in Two* 182

CHAPTER 21: *Loyal Women* 191
CHAPTER 22: *Powerfully Impressive* 201
CHAPTER 23: *The Grimké Brothers* 211
CHAPTER 24: *One Grand Idea* 219
CHAPTER 25: *A Great Life Purpose* 227
CHAPTER 26: *Answering the Bugle Call* 234
AFTERWORD: *A History of the History of the Grimké Sisters* . . 242

Author's Note 250
Grimké Family Tree 254
Glossary 256
Source Notes 260
Selected Bibliography 287
Further Reading, Websites, Videos for Young Readers . . . 289
Index 290

The East Coast of the United States, circa early nineteenth century

INTRODUCTION

This book introduces Sarah and Angelina Grimké, two sisters who were nationally famous in the 1830s, but less well known today. It focuses on their lives, which shocked many, and also on the world and times in which they lived. It attempts to trace the way that life and myth interact, and to set the record straight.

The title, *Arm in Arm*, has three interpretations. First, Sarah and Angelina were sisters, working side by side all their lives. Second, at a time when mixed-race gatherings were considered scandalous, white women left meetings arm in arm with their Black colleagues, to protect them from pro-slavery mobs. Third, the title signifies the way the sisters considered the most important issues in their lives—human rights and women's rights—as unbreakably linked.

As you read this book about the past, consider, too, similar present-day issues and how they reflect history. And think about what we can do now, inspired by the example of two brave sisters.

CHAPTER 1
Running Away

1797

The first time Sarah Grimké ran away from home, she was only four or five years old.

She had to run, she said later, after coming upon a terrible scene at her house: anguished screams and the crack of a whip, cutting through the air to strike a helpless woman. Perhaps the enslaved servant had broken a plate or scorched her mistress's dress with an iron.

Whatever her misdeed, the woman had probably been stripped to the waist. Likely an enslaved man who had been ordered to punish her tied her hands above her head. Once she was secured, he lashed her with a "cowskin," a whip made from strips of untanned cowhide or oxhide twisted together into a handle at one end. The whip would have opened deep cuts on the woman's back, spattering blood each time it struck.

Sarah, who knew all the family servants, could not bear to stay while the woman suffered. Sobbing, she ran from her family's three-story townhouse, rushing along Church Street and then turning east, toward the docks.

Riders on horses along with carriages and heavily loaded wagons, driven by Black men, crowded the streets of Charleston, South Carolina. On that warm, humid day, Sarah smelled horse droppings but also sweet flowers, such as roses and jasmine. Their scents wafted from walled gardens behind wrought iron gates that lined the streets.

Vendors' calls rang out over creaking wheels. Horses' hooves kicked up clouds of sand and crushed oyster shells on the unpaved roads. Most of the pedestrians were people of color. They greeted one another with bows and curtsies, some pausing to chat. Many women wore bright, patterned scarves wound into turbans. Some balanced baskets of fruit or waterpots on their heads.

Charleston, South Carolina, was a major port. By 1800 its main export was cotton, grown by enslaved workers.

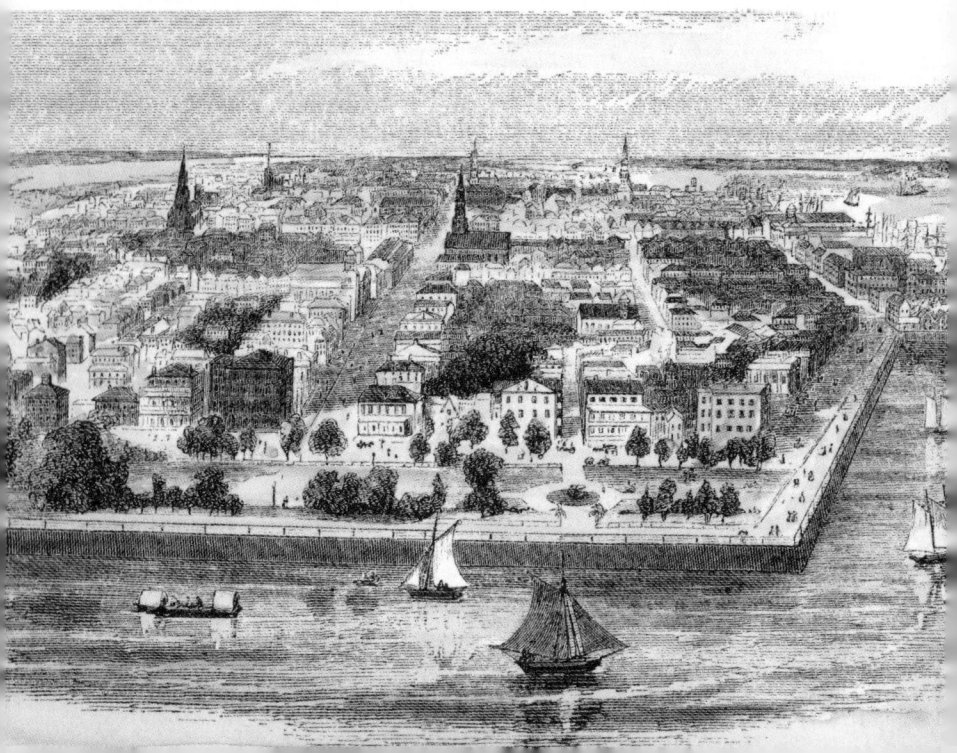

No one stopped Sarah as she hurried the few blocks to the wharf.

At the harbor, she found what she was looking for: dozens of schooners, sloops, and square-rigged vessels. Strong Black men and boys worked in teams, some singing and chanting as they unloaded barrels and boxes or filled ships' holds with bales of cotton and barrels of rice. On that bustling dock she went looking for a white man, someone who commanded a ship.

Spotting a sea captain at last, she begged him to help her. The captain must have been surprised to see a little girl, obviously wealthy, out on her own. He spoke kindly to her, but he could not grant her wish to take her away to a land where there were no whippings.

Sarah was still talking to the captain when her enslaved nursemaid found her on the dock and took her home.

CHAPTER 2
Breaking the Law

1798-1805

Sarah soon learned that her family thought cruel punishment was required to manage enslaved servants. All their servants were enslaved. Someday, her parents told her, Sarah would have to order whippings too. Controls had to be strict, they explained, as the enslaved Black workers outnumbered their white owners. If servants weren't forced to obey, they might band together and rebel.

Sarah Moore Grimké, nicknamed Sally, was her parent's sixth child, after four brothers and a sister. The Grimké (pronounced Grim key) household had more enslaved servants than family members. About seventeen cooks, laundresses, clothes pressers, chambermaids, waiters, seamstresses, shoemakers, coachmen, gardeners, stable hands, and their children lived on the upper floors of a row of work buildings, including the kitchen, which stood behind the main house. Chosen house servants slept on the bedroom floors of the white people to whom they were assigned. Some enslaved people who lived on the premises, worked elsewhere, and paid their wages to the Grimkés.

Sarah's father, John Faucheraud Grimké, was a judge. Born to a wealthy South Carolina family that owned plantations, he attended what later became Princeton University and then studied law in England. After returning to South Carolina, he fought against the British in the Revolutionary War (1775–1783). Later, he gained enormous wealth from the unpaid labor of hundreds of workers on his rice and cotton plantations. In 1784 he married Mary Smith, the beautiful daughter of a wealthy Charleston family of enslavers.

The Grimkés lived in Charleston each summer and spent their winters at Belmont, their country estate, two hundred miles northwest of the city. In Charleston, cool ocean breezes provided relief from summer heat and the dangers of disease. People especially feared yellow fever. In those days, they didn't know it was carried by mosquitoes, but they hated the swarms of insects, which were worse in the country than in town.

The Grimkés' Georgian style townhouse at 87 Church Street is now a museum. The family lived there from 1794 to 1803.

In 1803, when Sarah was ten, her family moved to a larger house in Charleston on what was then called Front Street. Outside the tall, boxy building, a graceful double staircase led visitors up to the front door. Inside were large, airy rooms—four on each of the two floors, divided by nine-foot-wide central halls. Many of the Grimkés' home furnishings were imported from Europe—carpets, sofas, game tables, bookcases, and sideboards filled with glass and fine china. A harpsichord provided music, as did an Italian music box that played a tinkling tune when the lid was opened. The house and its luxurious decorations were paid for by the labor of enslaved workers.

This miniature of John Faucheraud Grimké was painted in 1791 by John Trumbull, a prominent American artist.

The east windows of the new house looked out on Gadsden's Wharf. There slave ships docked, and enslaved Africans were washed, fed, clothed, and locked in pens until they could be sold at auction. From 1803 to 1807, more than forty thousand Africans were unloaded on this wharf. Slavery was big business in the fourth-largest city in the United States. Charleston had about twenty thousand residents, more than half of them Black. Of the Black residents, 90 percent were enslaved; the others were known as free people of color. Healthy enslaved workers sold for $500 or $600 each. Women of childbearing age brought higher prices, as they could produce additional workers. Enslaved people with a trade or skill such as sewing or carpentry sold for more than $1,000 each. Attractive young women with light skin tones brought the highest prices.

The white people of Charleston followed a strict code of manners and behavior, modeled on the society of wealthy British landowners but more extreme. The richest Charlestonians, those in "planter" families (who owned plantations) such as the Grimkés, entertained and visited one another constantly. Hospitality and lively, intelligent conversation were highly valued in their social circle.

As a mark of honor, the rich did no physical work. Sarah's mother did not permit her daughters to open windows themselves; instead, she called enslaved servants to do it. At meals, child servants wielded peacock fans to cool those at the table, while adult servers stood behind each family member to offer dishes as needed. The Grimkés would not think of passing plates themselves. In the evenings, enslaved children waited outside parlors to be called to snuff out candles or to pass tumblers of water from the sideboard. Sometimes they were allowed to sit down on the stairs while waiting, but usually they were required to stand.

Foreign visitors were not impressed by these habits. "The warmth of the climate," wrote a British guest, "induces great lassitude and indisposition to exertion. . . . This, which in England would be called laziness, is encouraged by the most trifling [jobs] being performed by slaves . . . the wives of men in affluent circumstances being in general like pampered children and suffering dreadfully from *ennui* [boredom]."

Another British visitor told him that "the females [in Charleston] are nurtured in indolence, and in seeking what they term a settlement, look more to the man's means than the likelihood of living happily with him. . . . Few girls would refuse a man who possessed a goodly number of slaves, though they were sure his affections would be shared by some of the best-looking of the females among them." A Southern wife, the

A slave auction in Charleston, South Carolina, in 1853 as depicted in *The Illustrated London News* on November 29, 1856.

English traveler concluded, if she is . . . furnished with dollars to "go shopping" apparently does not mind if her husband takes an enslaved mistress.

No evidence shows that Judge Grimké had mistresses, and Mrs. Grimke did not consider herself pampered. In her mind, she suffered dreadfully. She alone was in charge of the household. If enslaved people failed to do their jobs properly or spoke rudely, or sometimes if she just felt cross with them, she did engage in one form of physical labor: She hit them herself. She also assigned enslaved servants to be whipped at home or she paid a fee to have them punished in a city-run building called the workhouse.

Sarah learned to escape within her home when she heard that a servant would be flogged. Hiding herself away, she cried and prayed that the whipping would not take place.

Sarah's parents prayed too. At home they held morning services for both family and servants. Later in the day, some servants were punished in the same room where they had worshipped.

On Sundays the family walked or rode in carriages to St. Philip's Episcopal Church—the most fashionable church in Charleston. Sarah and her brothers and sister attended Sabbath school there.

On Sunday afternoons, girls from wealthy white families went to the "colored school," as it was known, where they taught Bible lessons to enslaved children. Only Sarah caused trouble. She loved spreading the word of God, but she had her own idea of how to do it. Instead of simply telling the Black children about Christianity, she wanted to teach them to read the Bible themselves. Absolutely not, she was told. Teaching enslaved people to read was against the law in South Carolina. Enslavers feared that reading would help their servants to forge passes allowing them to travel freely or to read maps or to communicate with other enslaved people in attempts to escape.

The same law applied at home. As the Grimké children outgrew the need for nursemaids, their parents "gave" to each son or daughter an enslaved child as a private "body servant"— someone to dress them, clean their rooms, and fan them on hot afternoons. Although Sarah was horrified at the thought of owning another person, when she was about eleven, her parents made her accept a girl anyway. But Hetty, who was about ten, became much more than a servant: She became Sarah's friend.

To Sarah, a friend needed to be able to read. "My great desire in the matter would not be totally suppressed," she wrote later, "and I took an almost malicious satisfaction in teaching my little waiting-maid at night, when she was supposed to be occupied in combing and brushing my long locks. The light was put out, the keyhole screened, and flat on our stomachs before the fire, with the spelling-book under our eyes, we defied the laws of South Carolina."

When Sarah's father caught the two girls reading together, Hetty barely escaped a whipping. Sarah got a stern talking-to, so loud that her siblings could hear it. She accepted this punishment as fair, but she could not believe that what she had done was wrong.

It's not clear what happened to Hetty. Most historians report that she died while still young and that Sarah grieved her loss, refusing to accept another girl as a servant. But in the 2023 book *The Grimkes: The Legacy of Slavery in an American Family*, author Kerri K. Greenidge says that John F. Grimké sold the girl, citing a bill of sale from 1828 (twenty-five years later) to prove that Hetty was still enslaved by another branch of the Grimké family.

Young Sarah continued to learn about managing servants one summer when her father took her on a trip to their country house. Proudly adopting the grown-up role of housekeeper, she inspected every cranny of the home. "Woe betide anything that did not come up to my idea of neat housekeeping," she said later.

During that summer trip, Judge Grimké had Sarah taught to spin and weave "negro cloth," a rough fabric used to make clothing for enslaved people. He assigned her other chores too. "I had to use my delicate fingers now and then to shell corn," she recalled, "a process which sometimes blistered them, and was sent into the field to pick cotton occasionally. Perhaps I am indebted partially to this for my life-long detestation of slavery, as it brought me in close contact with these unpaid toilers."

"Slavery was a millstone around my neck," she wrote later, "and marred my comfort from the time I can remember myself. My chief pleasure was riding on horseback daily. 'Hiram' was a gentle, spirited, beautiful creature. He was neither slave nor slave owner, and I loved and enjoyed him thoroughly."

Sarah longed to please her father. She took note of his favorite ideas. "Never lose an opportunity," he would say, "of learning what is useful. If you never need the knowledge, it will be no burden to have it; and if you should, you will be thankful to have it."

> "Slavery was a millstone around my neck and marred my comfort from the time I can remember myself."
> —SARAH GRIMKÉ

Judge Grimké wanted all his children to be well educated. Sarah attended a girls' school in Charleston, where she received a "polite education for ladies," in needlework, reading, writing, drawing, simple arithmetic, French, singing, piano playing, manners and, above all, obedience.

Sarah's father took a special interest in her education, likely because she was very bright. If only she had been a boy, he said, she would have made "the greatest jurist [expert on law] in the land." But colleges and universities at the time did not admit women.

Judge Grimké allowed Sarah to study with her second-oldest brother, Thomas, who was considered the smartest of the boys. Sarah felt closest to Thomas of all her family members, though he was six years her senior. She could talk to him about anything, including her unusual views on slavery. Their father let Sarah share her brother's studies in geography, history, natural science, and botany, and in exchange, Sarah helped Thomas study for tests. But when Sarah wanted to learn Latin with her brother, her father drew the line, contradicting his own belief that any knowledge acquired might someday prove useful.

"You are a girl," he told her. "What do you want of Latin and Greek and philosophy? You can never use them." When she told him she wanted to study law as Thomas planned to, he called her "unwomanly." And when she tried to learn Latin in secret, even Thomas laughed at her.

In early 1805, when Sarah was twelve, Thomas left for Yale College (later Yale University) to study to become a minister. Sarah wished she could go too. What was left for her at home? Her brothers John and Frederick were likely pursuing studies in Charleston. Her sister Mary was about to enter the life of a society belle. Her older brother Benjamin had died in 1794, at age six. Her parents named a second son, born in 1798, Benjamin; he was one of Sarah's five younger siblings. Except for Thomas, none of these older siblings spent much time with Sarah. He was, in many ways, her only serious teacher. What would she do without him?

CHAPTER 3
A Rod of Fear

1805–1818

On February 20, 1805, a few weeks after Thomas's departure, Sarah's mother gave birth to her fourteenth and last child, Angelina Emily. Sarah, thrilled to have a new girl in the family, asked to be her godmother, taking responsibility for Angelina's spiritual upbringing.

No, her parents said, twelve was too young to be a godmother. But Sarah insisted that she could take care of the baby. Angelina would have a nursemaid too, Sarah said, and by the time she was old enough for religious instruction, her big sister would be ready to teach her. Sarah begged and pleaded until her parents changed their minds. They may have hoped that caring for a baby would distract her from her strange ideas about slavery.

Joyfully, Sarah held the blue-eyed Angelina at her baptism. She prayed to God to make her worthy as a godmother. "Oh, how good I resolved to be," she wrote later, "how careful in all my conduct, that my life might be blessed to her!" Angelina became the cherished focus of her days. Sarah called the baby

"Nina," and when Angelina learned to talk, she called Sarah "Mother," which displeased their real mother.

The sisters' close attachment set them apart in their household, which was not a happy one. Mrs. Grimké had lost three children before giving birth to Angelina. She felt oppressed by the burden of managing both servants and children. Rich women had far more contact with enslaved servants than their husbands did. Judge Grimké spent time away from the house in his office or in court and later in the state legislature. Even at his plantations, he interacted chiefly with white overseers. They directed the enslaved "drivers," Black men who managed operations and field hands.

But whether in town or in the country, Mrs. Grimké assigned the servants' work daily, and she had to ensure it was done. Doling out provisions, which were stored under lock and key, she watched constantly to prevent theft of food or supplies.

"Only two meals a day are allowed the house slaves," Angelina wrote later, "*the first at twelve o'clock*. If they eat before this time, it is by stealth, and I am sure there must be a good deal of suffering among them from *hunger*, and particularly by children. Besides this, they are often kept from their meals by way of punishment."

Mrs. Grimké also had to keep an eye on the carriageway by the side of the house to make sure only authorized people came and went from the work area at the rear. With one opening for carriages, a high brick wall surrounded the backyard, cutting off the sight and sounds of neighboring households.

The more servants Mary Grimké acquired (enslaved women giving birth enlarged the household too), the more nervous, irritable, and tired she became. To her, enslaved people were lazy, stupid, and rude. Desperate for order and peace in her life,

In 1803 the Grimkés moved to a larger house to accommodate their growing family. This was their home for decades, until after the Civil War.

she punished them and shrieked at them and did the same to her sons and daughters. But the worse she treated them, the worse they all behaved.

The children did nothing to help their mother. Instead, they blamed her when the servants were ill-mannered and disobedient. As a child, Angelina felt alienated when her mother raged at her, but her strong sense of justice, like her sister Sarah's, helped her understand the problem. "Mother is perfectly blind as to the miserable manner in which she brought us up," she said later. "She rules slaves and children with a rod of fear!"

As she got older, Angelina tried to help. "I tried to convince them [her sisters Mary and Eliza]," she wrote in her diary, "that the servants were just what the family was, and that they were not at all more rude and selfish and disobliging than they themselves were. I gave one or two instances of the manner in which they treated mother and each other, and asked how they could expect the servants to behave in any other way when they had such examples continually before them." But her protest had no effect on her siblings. And although Angelina felt sorry for Mrs. Grimké, Sarah was the mother she loved.

Unlike Sarah, Angelina did not oppose the institution of

slavery during her childhood, but she did think that enslaved people should be treated kindly. Only the oldest servants had beds, which they had to build or scavenge for themselves. Angelina sympathized with the others, who had to sleep on bare floors with a sheet or blanket but no mosquito netting. She felt sad that servants weren't allowed to eat around a table and that they lacked basic equipment, such as towels, basins, firewood, furniture, and soap. Sometimes, after a servant was whipped, the little girl snuck out of the house at night to take the injured person healing oil to put on wounds.

"I saw *nothing* of slavery in its most vulgar and repulsive forms," she wrote later. "I never visited the *fields where the slaves were at work*, and knew almost nothing of their condition. I saw it in the *city*, among the fashionable and the honorable, where it was garnished by refinement, and decked out for show.

"I remember very well that when I was a child," she said, "our next door neighbor whipped a young woman so brutally, that in order to escape his blows she rushed through the drawing-room window in the second story, and fell upon the street pavement below and broke her hip. The circumstance produced no excitement or enquiry"—none of the neighbors seemed to care.

When Angelina was about eight years old, she walked by the workhouse. Originally built as a sugar mill, it was also called the sugar house, where owners had enslaved people "sweetened up." Its walls were topped with broken glass bottles to discourage escape attempts.

> *"I saw [slavery] in the city, among the fashionable and the honorable, where it was garnished by refinement, and decked out for show."*
> —ANGELINA GRIMKÉ

Harvesting cotton. The Grimké family's wealth came from the unpaid labor of more than three hundred enslaved men, women, and children.

Angelina knew the name of the building before she understood its function. As she grew older, she realized the workhouse was a punishment jail for enslaved people. Her mother and other mistresses sent their most disobedient servants there. Sometimes they sent people who had committed only minor offenses so as not to disturb the neighbors by whipping them at home. Other times they sent a servant for no reason at all.

In the workhouse, whippings were delivered by Black drivers and were limited to thirty-nine lashes a day. Many took place in a room with hollow walls filled with sand to deaden the sound of screams. Or victims were forced to climb on a huge staircaselike treadmill attached to a machine that ground corn, three minutes on and three minutes off, for eight hours a day. The servants were often maimed by these cruelties. Some did not survive.

"That house of blood," Angelina called it later. "When I was once obliged to pass it, the very sight smote [hit] me with such horror that my limbs could hardly sustain me. I felt as if I was passing the precincts of hell. A [child] friend of mine who lived in the neighborhood, told me she often heard the screams of the slaves under their torture."

Even at school, Angelina could not escape the cruelties of slavery. "When I was about thirteen years old," she wrote,

> *I attended a seminary [school], in Charleston, which was superintended by a man and his wife of superior education. They had under their instruction the daughters of nearly all the aristocracy. Their cruelty to their slaves, both male and female, I can never forget. I remember one day there was called into the school room to open a window, a boy whose head had been shaved in order to disgrace him, and he had been so dreadfully whipped that he could hardly walk. So horrible was the impression produced upon my mind by his heart-broken countenance [face] and crippled person that I fainted away.*

Under the overseer's whip, enslaved people power a "treadwheel" that could grind corn or sugar. This 1843 machine, from Jamaica, resembles the one in Charleston.

At home, Sarah comforted Angelina after this experience. Only Sarah, of all the family, understood or cared why her young sister was upset.

Angelina wrote later, "I used to say, 'Oh that I had the wings of a dove, that I might flee away and be at rest;' for I felt that there could be no rest for me in the midst of such outrages and pollutions."

Both sisters may have wondered at the discrepancy when, like other society women, Mrs. Grimké set off at least one day a week to devote herself to good deeds. Their mother felt relieved to have a change of scenery and to find uplifting duties outside her home, and she was known as "an active, efficient, *devoted* officer" of the Ladies Benevolent Society. The society, founded in 1813 by white, wealthy, mostly Episcopalian women, visited the sickbeds of poor women and the jail cells of "fallen" women (often prostitutes), bringing firewood, coal, coffee, sugar, blankets, and soap. Their primary focus was impoverished, uneducated white women. In the North, such women found work as servants, but in Charleston, all servants were enslaved. For her part in the society, Mary Grimké even helped a few free Black women who were ill, but only if they could produce "certificates signed by some respectable white persons, as to [their] character and necessities." Doing good deeds for the society probably made her view herself as a caring person.

CHAPTER 4
The Society of Friends

1818-1821

At thirteen, Angelina attended dancing school and children's balls. These events provided the training she would need, in three years, when she would join Sarah in a new kind of life as a society belle, eligible for marriage. Almost daily, embossed party invitations arrived for Sarah; they were displayed on a drawing room table. The more a young woman got (Sarah received a great many), the higher her social standing.

Both sisters loved beautiful things, especially fashionable clothes. Sarah had a collection of ball gowns, jewelry, soft gloves, and elegant fans and slippers befitting a wealthy young woman. By then she had finally accepted another enslaved girl to help her dress. Angelina must have enjoyed watching the servant prepare her big sister to go out.

At first, Sarah enjoyed society life. "Few have exceeded me," she wrote later, "in extravagance of every kind, and in the sinful indulgence of pride and vanity." While no one called Sarah pretty, she was smart, fashionable, jolly, and rich. Young men flirted with her, and she enjoyed the experience.

Rich women in Charleston followed European styles, as shown in this 1820 fashion plate.

Sarah's social life gave her more freedom but also exposed her to new atrocities. "As I was traveling in the lower country in South Carolina," she recalled, "my attention was suddenly arrested by an exclamation of horror from the coachman, who cried out, 'Look there, Miss Sarah, don't you see?'—I looked in the direction he pointed and saw a human head stuck high on a pole. On inquiry, I found that a runaway slave . . . had been shot there, his head severed from his body, and put upon a public highway, as a terror to deter slaves from running away."

Sarah's new mobility revealed abuses committed by "men and women of the highest respectability and of the first families in South Carolina." She felt shocked that "their cruelties did not in the slightest degree affect their standing in society."

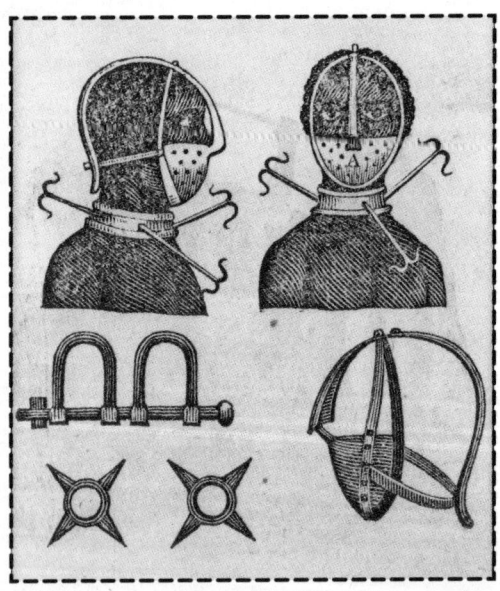

This 1807 illustration shows devices to restrain the enslaved: an iron mask, collar, leg shackles, and spurs.

In a house she visited frequently, she knew the family seamstress, a young woman who had run away again and again only to be recaptured. Despite whippings at the workhouse, she still tried to escape, so her enslaver developed an extreme remedy that Sarah described later: "A heavy iron collar, with three long prongs projecting from it, was placed round her neck, and a sound front tooth was extracted, to serve as a mark to describe her, in case of escape. Her sufferings at this time were agonizing; she could lie in no position but on her back, which was sore from scourgings, as I can testify from personal inspection."

> "Their cruelties did not in the slightest degree affect their standing in society."
> —SARAH GRIMKÉ

Her mistress, Sarah said, was considered a good Christian woman. But when the seamstress sat in her enslaver's chamber to sew, "with her lacerated and bleeding back, her mutilated mouth, and heavy iron collar," her mistress felt no compassion.

Sarah's experiences with slavery influenced her feelings about herself. "Often during this period have I returned home," she wrote, "sick of the frivolous beings I had been with, mortified at my own folly, and weary of the ball-room and its gilded toys." Repeatedly, she wished she could do something useful in society, something to alleviate the suffering of enslaved people.

She rejoiced when Thomas came home from Yale, full of new ideas to share with her. Their father had convinced him to study law, so he was preparing for the examination that would allow him to work as a lawyer. Sarah became his "amanuensis," taking dictation from him and copying documents. Thomas passed the test to become a lawyer in 1809 when Sarah was eighteen. His presence and his thoughtfulness made her think twice about the fun-loving men she met at parties.

By the time Sarah turned twenty-five, Thomas had wed and moved to his own home, and Sarah was considered by everyone, including herself, to be an "old maid." It is not known whether she had had a chance to marry. In that society, the only occupation for a rich single woman was to seek salvation by praying and doing good deeds. Sometimes, in an effort to be more religious, Sarah gave up parties and picnics, but this self-denial never lasted long.

One evening a friend invited her to attend a revival meeting, an event meant to reinspire Christians or attract new people to the faith. The leader was a charismatic Presbyterian minister. A year later, Sarah went to hear him again. She realized that when he warned of "a course of conduct which must eventually lead to everlasting punishment," he was talking about the society life she led with her friends. So Sarah tried harder to change, dressing plainly, giving up novels for religious books, attending prayer meetings and Bible classes instead of dances, and visiting the sick and needy. She also began attending services at the Presbyterian Church—embarrassing her mother because Charleston Episcopalians believed themselves to be superior to Presbyterians, who were seen as lower class.

While visiting friends in the country, Sarah met the young minister in a private home and talked with him for hours. She feared for her soul if, as he believed, people would go to hell for dancing. Episcopalians saw nothing wrong with her way of life (after all, she did not attend the theater, which would have shocked even them), but Presbyterians were stricter.

When Sarah's father fell ill, she believed his poor health was a punishment for her sinfulness, a sign from God, designed to save her from damnation. Withdrawing completely from her "butterfly life," she devoted herself to his care.

After a year of treatment, the doctors in Charleston could do no more for Judge Grimké. In 1819 they advised him to see a specialist in Philadelphia, Pennsylvania, and twenty-six-year-old Sarah sailed up the coast with him. They took no servants, expecting to be gone just a short time.

Sarah must have felt excited to visit the bustling, sophisticated city in springtime. Its red brick houses, trimmed in white, stood in a grid of wide cobblestone streets, raised sidewalks, and regularly spaced parks. Mixed crowds, mostly white, strolled past trees, fountains, and statues lining the public walkways. The City of Brotherly Love offered art and culture, but Sarah had no time to explore.

Caring for her father kept her busy. They boarded with a family of Quakers, members of the Religious Society of Friends. Sarah accompanied her father to the doctor's office, but the specialist could offer no help. When he told Sarah, "Your father's life is in the Lord's hands," she knew that his condition was grave.

The doctor sent them by chaise, a light, horse-drawn carriage, to Long Branch, a fishing village on the New Jersey shore. There Sarah rented an upstairs room in the Fish Tavern, a quiet boardinghouse. Propped up on pillows, her father watched the ocean waves from his bed. He took laudanum, a powerful medication made from opium, for his pain, which he hid by talking cheerfully. Sarah sometimes walked on the beach, where red and white flags indicated times when men and women could swim separately.

As days passed, father and daughter grew closer. "Do not indulge vain hopes, my child," he told her. "I no longer expect recovery nor do I desire it." After that, she refused to leave him, even when he tried to make her go out. She bathed him, fed him, changed his clothing and sheets, and prayed with him, as if she were the parent and he the child. She held his hand as he died in his sleep on August 8, 1819.

After arranging for his burial in New Jersey, Sarah returned to Philadelphia, where she boarded with a Quaker family for three months. She felt comforted by their simple lifestyle and

Quaker men and women sat separately at meetings, but women could speak, just like the men.

the peacefulness of their home. Quakers, or Friends, were little known in Charleston but prevalent in Philadelphia. Their plain dress made them easy to spot. Sarah, like other stylish women of the time, wore high-waisted dresses with puffed sleeves and elegant trims, often in bright colors, and she prided herself on following the latest fashions. Quaker women, on the other hand, wore styles that did not change: somber-colored dresses topped with shawls and, even indoors, white ruffled caps that hid their hair. Outside they wore bonnets over their caps.

Quakers used plain speech, avoiding honorific titles such as Mrs. and Dr. and using *thou* and *thee*—old-fashioned terms—to demonstrate their belief that all people were equal. Sarah learned that Friends were pacifists, thought that God existed in each person and, perhaps most encouraging, opposed slavery.

Still, Episcopalians, including her family, considered Quakers to be more extreme than Presbyterians, who at least followed similar religious rituals and services, so Sarah refused to attend Friends' meetings or to read their writings.

In November she sailed for home. There is no record that she traveled with a companion or maid, although it was unusual for a woman to journey alone at this time. On the seven-day voyage, she met more Quakers, including Israel Morris, a successful businessman and the head of a large family. After listening to her opinions, he gave her a book to take home with her: the memoirs of John Woolman, a Quaker minister. Sarah promised to read it and to write to Morris about her impressions.

Because slavery had been largely phased out in Philadelphia by this time, when Sarah returned to Charleston, she said the sight of it "burst on my mind with renewed horror." The family, still disorderly and troubled, suffered more than ever as they observed a season of mourning for their father. The servants despaired, too, facing uncontrollable change. Judge Grimké's will left the townhouse in Charleston to his son Henry, but it was to be used by Mrs. Grimké until she remarried or died. The judge also specified that his wife would receive "any five of my negroes whom she shall choose out of those belonging to me." The other house servants, including families, were sold or were divided among the Grimké children who had married and established separate households. More than three hundred enslaved workers on the judge's four plantations went, along with the plantations, to his sons. Sarah and her sisters each inherited £2,000 (pounds sterling, a kind of British money used in some parts of the United States then); each son received £1,000, with all the children to receive additional funds as property was sold. Seven Grimké siblings remained at home, including Sarah and Angelina.

By this time, their brother Thomas—a father, plantation owner, and enslaver—had begun to agree with Sarah that enslaved people would someday have to be freed. But he could not imagine how to change the system. All ideas seemed impractical when the economy of Charleston, and the entire South, depended on the unpaid labor of enslaved men, women, and children. And in the North, factories and stores needed products grown and processed by enslaved people to prosper. Enslaved people were the main resource of the United States.

Sarah thought separating people by race was un-Christian, but her family's attitude about slavery seemed unchangeable. Even her dear Angelina did not object to it if the enslaved

In the early 1800s, Philadelphia was the nation's second-largest city, after New York. The port city was filled with factories, warehouses, and workshops.

people were well treated. Sarah's brothers and sisters, and especially her mother, grew tired of her lectures on how slavery violated Christian concepts.

Facing her future, Sarah felt hopeless. Narrow Southern ideas about womanhood meant she could never play an active, useful role in society. Even her God seemed cruel and punitive. Sinking into depression, she brooded over her own trials and those of the enslaved "until they became like a canker," she said, "incessantly gnawing." Unable to help the enslaved, she said, "I was as one in bonds looking on their sufferings."

While she continued to perform good works and support her favorite charities, she focused increasingly on herself. "How dreadful did the state of my mind become!" she wrote later. "Nothing interested me; I fulfilled my duties without any feeling of satisfaction, in gloomy silence. . . . I felt as if my doom was irrevocably fixed, and I was destined to that fire which is never quenched. I have never experienced any feeling so terrific as the despair of salvation." She began to hear voices and claimed to have had mystical experiences. When she learned that her brother Benjamin had died in a shipwreck, she believed God was punishing her.

Eventually, she turned to the book that Israel Morris had given her. Like Sarah, Quaker author John Woolman had enjoyed an opulent life and had to fight with himself to give it up. Reading Woolman's work gave her hope for the first time in months. She began a lively correspondence with Israel Morris, asking him—as well as her brother Thomas—to supply her with additional reading about the Society of Friends.

She discussed Quaker philosophy with Thomas. "Thee had better turn Quaker, Sally," Thomas teased, using her childhood nickname as he handed her a book. "Thy long face would suit well their sober dress."

Sarah investigated other religious denominations too. She found Methodism lively at first but eventually unsatisfying. Finally, wearing her plainest clothes, she began attending the small Friends meeting in Charleston. Her mother felt disgraced—she despised Quakers as religious extremists. But Sarah felt at peace among them, as she had in Philadelphia.

Unlike Episcopalians, Presbyterians, and Methodists, Quakers did not have ministers who led ritual meetings. Instead, they sat quietly until moved to speak. In other churches, women were forbidden to speak during religious services. But at Friends meetings, women were encouraged to voice their opinions. Sarah did not care to reveal her private feelings in public, even to a small group. She felt guilty because she could not make herself do it. Still she stayed, praying and listening.

She begged God to show her a sign or speak directly to her, telling her what to do. And one day, she believed that he did. "Go North," she heard, and she knew that she should go back to Philadelphia.

CHAPTER 5
To Philadelphia!

1821-1828

Sarah, then twenty-eight, sailed back to Philadelphia in May 1821, accompanied by her sister Anna Grimké Frost. Anna, the widow of an Episcopal clergyman, was considered an appropriate chaperone for Sarah (single women were not supposed to travel alone), even though Sarah was three years older. On the weeklong voyage, Sarah helped with her sister's baby, Mary Anna. She was glad that Anna had decided to raise her daughter away from slavery.

Anna planned to support herself by starting a small school. The idea would have been shocking in Charleston, where people recognized her as a woman from a prominent family. But in Philadelphia, no one knew her, and as a widow, she had more freedom to work and live an independent life than a never-married woman such as Sarah. Sarah helped Anna rent a house with servants' quarters in the backyard. Then, with the Frosts settled, Sarah went to stay with the Morris family as planned.

Israel Morris was now a widower; his wife had died a year earlier, in 1820. Their nine children, born between 1800 and

1815, graciously welcomed Sarah to Pennsylvania. Details are lacking, but he surely took care to see that she was properly chaperoned in his home.

The Israel Morris family lived west of the city on a country estate, Green Hill. Their large stone house, built in 1695, was known as the Old Homestead. Sarah, who loved to walk outdoors, enjoyed exploring the grounds. June in Pennsylvania felt fresh and cool after the heat of Charleston, and many plants were new to her. Magnificent trees made shady groves. Elegant gardens invited strolling, and green lawns led to old barns, a bathhouse, fields and meadows, an orchard, and a raspberry patch.

The Morrises frequently took Sarah to town, where they attended worship meetings at the Arch Street Meeting House of the Society of Friends. In that simple red brick building, filled with sunshine and wooden pews, Sarah found comfort in the women's section, sitting silently in the company of people who seemed like herself. Israel Morris's unmarried forty-nine-year-old sister, Catherine Wistar Morris, always greeted her warmly, and they soon became friends.

As months passed, Sarah felt a growing attraction to Israel, which he seemed to return. After a year, perhaps because of her feelings for him, she moved to town to live with Catherine in the Morris parental home, a three-and-a-half-story double townhouse at 225 South Eighth Street. She could walk to Friends meetings and to many other places in the bustling city. By this time, Sarah felt like a Morris family member, frequently visiting Green Hill and sometimes caring for the children when they were ill.

Glad to be free from the daily horrors of slavery and constraints imposed by her mother, Sarah began remaking her life within the Society of Friends, but one practice—speaking

The Old Homestead was Israel Morris's home on the Green Hill estate in Pennsylvania.

aloud at meetings—seemed impossible to her. Quakers believed that men and women were equal in the eyes of God, but Sarah had been taught that women were inferior, and that they could never speak in church. Uncertain and timid, Sarah disappointed the members of the Arch Street Meeting. The first time she applied to join, they advised her to wait. Eventually, on May 29, 1823, they admitted her as a member.

Sarah had enough money from her inheritance to live modestly, especially as a guest in others' homes. (And society decreed that respectable single women could not live alone then.) Sarah longed for meaningful work and the ability to support herself, but there were few suitable jobs for women of her social standing. "Oh! had I received the education I desired,"

Sarah Moore Grimké, 1792–1873, shown in a wood engraving from the 1830s

she wrote, "had I been bred to the profession of the law, I might have been a useful member of society, and instead of myself and my property being taken care of, I might have been a protector of the helpless, a pleader for the poor and unfortunate."

Teaching, one of two viable career options for single Quaker women, did not appeal to Sarah, so she turned to the other choice, available to either single or married women: becoming a minister. The goal was appealing but not the means of achieving it: speaking spontaneously at meetings. Feeling shy and unworthy, Sarah tried to make herself speak up. She modeled her behavior on that of Lucretia Mott, another congregant at Arch Street. Mott, who was just Sarah's age, was married, with a growing family. An accomplished speaker, she had been a minister for five years, and she encouraged Sarah. Soon the two became close friends.

Other aspects of Quaker life also presented challenges. Sarah, who had always loved fashion, tried to dress plainly but found it hard to give up perfectly good clothing. "Can it be of any consequence in the sight of God whether I wear a black dress or not?" she asked. (It was difficult and costly to dye fabric black at this time, and so black dresses were often both expensive and fashionable.) Then Sarah answered herself: "The evidence was clear . . . that self-will was the cause of my continuing to do it." Realizing that stylish clothes made her new friends uncomfortable, she adopted full Quaker attire: drab dresses in gray or brown, an untrimmed kerchief at the neck, and a brimmed bonnet with a white ruffled cap underneath.

On September 16, 1826, Israel Morris proposed marriage to Sarah. She turned him down, even though she loved him. "I struggle against feelings and temptations I blush to think of," she wrote in her diary. Historians have offered varying explanations for her decision. Self-sacrifice, which she believed God demanded, was by this time a way of life for her, easier than happiness. She also felt a duty to dedicate herself to some still unknown godly work, which she could control only if she remained single. In marriage, which she called "the snare of Satan," the husband was in charge.

"That was a day," she wrote of the proposal, "for solemn heartfelt supplication [prayer] that nothing would intervene between me and my God." It was hard for her to give Morris up, but she did. Whatever her reason for declining, they decided to remain friends.

A month after the proposal, in October, Sarah returned to Charleston. Her mother met her with tears of pleasure, and her siblings joyfully welcomed her back. When they argued with her about religion, Sarah answered gently. When they teased her about her new style of dressing, she didn't mind. She knew they loved her, even if they could not understand that wearing plain clothes made her feel peaceful and confident.

Angelina, her dear "Nina," supported her older sister in every way. Now twenty-one years old, she was searching for her own purpose in life. Bolder than Sarah and more decisive, she could be counted upon to speak her mind. At thirteen she had refused to be confirmed at St. Philip's Episcopal Church, telling the bishop that she could not promise the commitment to the church which was required in the ceremony. As an adult, she left the church entirely, saying she was "starving on the cold water of Episcopacy."

Episcopalians, who knelt to pray, considered themselves more religious than other Protestants, who did not. The Grimkés' church emphasized formal, traditional rituals and priestly authority, strongly resembling the practices of Roman Catholics. Critical that Episcopalians, including her mother, seemed to exalt themselves above other Christians, Angelina turned to the more austere Presbyterian Church, which had simpler rituals. And to broaden her horizons, she formed an all-woman, interfaith prayer group with local Baptists, Methodists, Congregationalists, and Presbyterians. Her mother was shocked, as was her sister Mary, who said that Methodists and Baptists were "quite beyond the pale."

Sarah inspired her younger sister to observe new religious habits. "My attention has lately been called," Angelina wrote in her diary, "to the duty of Christians' dressing quite plain."

"We must not sanction sin in others," Sarah wrote, "by giving them what we had put away ourselves." So instead of passing on their beautiful clothes, the sisters cut them up, using the scraps to stuff pillows and an ottoman, and making a rag carpet of lace veils, flounces, trimmings, and caps.

"My hat," Angelina wrote, "I untrimmed & have just nothing but a band of ribbon round it & taken the lace out of the inside. I do want if I am a Christian to look like one." She also tore up her novels (Quakers considered them sinful), horrifying her mother.

Sarah resumed visiting the sick, bringing supplies to those in need, and supporting charities in the city. She prayed constantly for guidance about what to do next. After a year and a half in Charleston, she wrote in her diary, "The subject of returning to Philadelphia has been revived before me [by God, she believed]. It seems like a fresh trial, and if, did my Master permit, here I would stay, and in the bosom of my family be content to dwell, but if He orders it otherwise, great as will be the struggle, may I submit in humble faith."

Then, finally, "Go," she said God told her, "and I will be with thee." In April 1828 she returned to the Philadelphia home of Catherine Morris.

CHAPTER 6

Bound with Chains

1828-1829

Left in Charleston, without Sarah to guide her, Angelina continued her new way of life. She began to doubt the Presbyterian Church. "The Spirit whispers," she wrote, "'Come out from among them.'" She left her prayer group too. "My mind is composed," she wrote, "and I cannot but feel astonished at the total change which has passed over me in the last six months. . . . I find that every stream from which I drank the waters of salvation is dry and I have been led to the fountain itself."

For her, the fountain of salvation was Quakerism. "I feel that He who is Head of all things," she wrote, "has called me to follow Him into that little silent meeting which [is] in this city."

Her family had been shocked when she joined the Presbyterians. But all of Charleston society reeled when she began attending the city's Quaker meeting. Unlike the large Quaker community Sarah had found in Philadelphia, the Friends' membership in Charleston consisted of just two old men. For months Angelina met with them—unchaperoned—scandalizing family and friends and confirming their belief that the religion was not respectable.

At her wit's end, Mrs. Grimké suggested that she visit her sisters in Philadelphia. Angelina readily agreed, but four months in the Northern city changed nothing. She came back determined to save herself, her family, and her friends from sin. And unlike her sister Sarah, who spoke kindly, even when criticizing, Angelina was confrontational and direct.

Angelina also had received an inheritance from her father, and she wanted to support herself. As Sarah had done on her last visit to Charleston, Angelina insisted on paying her mother five dollars a week for meals. The practice upset some of their siblings who still lived at home (which was typical for rich families at the time), "several of whom," a friend wrote later, "were living in idleness on their mother, doing nothing and paying nothing." Angelina berated her brother Charles for being jobless and drinking to excess.

She complained about her mother's elaborate meals. "It is true that I can always take the plainest food, and this I do generally," she wrote. "But it is not only the food I eat at mother's, but the whole style of living that is a direct departure from the simplicity that is in Christ." When her mother had a sitting room painted and decorated with new wallpaper, at a cost of twenty-six dollars (about seven hundred dollars in 2024), Angelina deemed the room too fine to use. She refused to sit in it, even when friends visited. Angelina wrote,

> *[Mother] said it was very hard that she could not give her children what food she chose, or have a room papered, without being found fault with; indeed, she was weary of being continually blamed about everything she did, she*

> *wished she could be left alone for she saw no sin in those things. . . . She again very ungenerously (as she frequently does) alluded to my turning* Quaker *& it was because I was a* Quaker *that I disapproved of a great many things that no body but Quakers could see any harm in. I was a good deal roused at this & said with a good deal of energy, [dear] Mother what but the* power *of God could ever have made* me *change my sentiments?*

The power of God, Angelina believed, forced her to intervene when her mother mistreated enslaved people. Having refused to own servants herself, Angelina made an exception when Mrs. Grimké repeatedly punished a woman named Kitty. Following some "very painful conversation," Angelina accepted ownership of Kitty—for long enough to find her a job in another household. But Kitty had no right to the wages she earned there; they had to be paid to her enslaver. Angelina soon transferred ownership back to her mother, as she did not want to receive payment for another person's labor.

Angelina clashed with her brother Henry too. He was a lawyer and, as the oldest brother still at the family home, the head of the household. Angelina loved him and liked his young wife, who came to live with them. But Henry was known for his hot temper and his violent treatment of enslaved people, having broken a large stick over one servant's back and an ivory handle of a long coach whip over the head of another. When one of Henry's servants ran away to avoid a beating, Angelina spoke up.

"No wonder poor John ran away at the threat of a flogging," she wrote after arguing with her brother, "when [Henry] has told me more than once that [after he last whipped John, he was himself] in pain for a week afterwards. I don't know how the boy must have felt, but I know that that night was one of agony to me; for it was not only dreadful to hear the blows, but the oaths & curses H. uttered went like daggers to my heart."

She wrote in her diary that Henry "said rather than suffer the continual condemnation of his conduct by me he would leave mother's house." But he did not leave and, surprisingly, when the servant John returned, Henry told him to go about his work without punishment.

Angelina got along better with her unmarried sisters, though she refused to go shopping or to sew with them, not wanting to help them commit the sin of "excessive ornamentation."

Often they felt tolerant of her critiques. "Though we considered her views entirely irrational," one sister said, "yet so absolute was her sense of duty, her superiority to public sentiment, and her moral courage, that she seemed to us almost like one inspired, and we all came to look upon her with a feeling of awe."

Despite disagreements between daughter and mother, they spent many happy hours together, Angelina reading aloud or sitting on the floor with her head in her mother's

Angelina Emily Grimké, 1805–1879, shown in a wood engraving from the 1830s

lap while Mrs. Grimké stroked her hair. Angelina felt torn: How could she help improve the lives of the oppressed? Should she stay in Charleston and keep trying to change the family she loved?

On April 23, 1829, while walking home from the Quaker meeting, she saw "a colored woman who in much distress was [begging for mercy from] two white boys, one about eighteen and the other fifteen, who walked on each side of her." They were taking her to the workhouse.

"As I approached," Angelina wrote later, "the younger said to her, 'I will have you tied up.' My knees smote together and my heart sank within me. As I passed them she exclaimed 'Missis!' But I felt all I [could] do was to suffer a pain of seeing her. . . . How long O Lord, how long wilt thou [allow] the foot of the oppressor to stand on the neck of the Slave." She could not stop picturing the woman and the other victims at the workhouse. "Night & day they were before me," she wrote, "& yet my hands were bound as with chains of iron."

"When shall I be released from this land of Slavery!" she asked in her diary. "But if my suffering for them can at all [relieve] their condition, surely I ought to be quite willing" to stay in Charleston. She made a little progress with her mother, who tried to treat the servants better and who sometimes admitted that slavery might have to end someday. To please her daughter, Mrs. Grimké even started, in the Quaker tradition, to sit in silence for a few minutes before the evening meal.

> "O Lord, how long wilt thou [allow] the foot of the oppressor to stand on the neck of the Slave."
> —ANGELINA GRIMKÉ

But Angelina could not resign herself to life with slavery.

As her mother often reminded her, she had benefited from it herself when young. Though she had not collected payment directly from the unpaid labor of enslaved people, the money she lived on, her inheritance from her father, had been made in that way. Once Angelina had believed that enslaved people were less than human, although she could not bear to see them hurt. Now, Angelina had changed her beliefs, and her mother seemed to be softening, but the institution of slavery remained entrenched in their family and in all of Charleston and the South. The local Presbyterian minister told Angelina that although he prayed slavery would end, he feared to speak out against it in church. Angelina had little power to change things in her hometown.

The North seemed like the promised land to her, a land of freedom, but she could not decide by herself to leave. Then a letter came from Sarah. Catherine Morris, she wrote, had invited Angelina to come live with them. Angelina, who had stayed with Catherine and Sarah on her visit to Philadelphia, made up her mind to go.

One problem remained: Women were not supposed to travel alone. How could a twenty-four-year-old single woman live for nine days on a ship where she might well be the only female? Sarah and Angelina previously had traveled back and forth, but details of those trips are lacking. "My soul sometimes faints at the idea of going only under the Captain's care," Angelina wrote as she faced the voyage, but still she planned to sail.

Then Sarah wrote again. She had taken the problem to the Quaker elders in Philadelphia, and they had given permission for the trip.

Leaving Charleston was hard. "I had a very satisfactory conversation with dear Mother on several subjects," Angelina wrote, "& feel considerably relieved. . . . I found her views far more correct than I had supposed." She told Mrs. Grimké that she wanted her to come to Philadelphia someday.

Despite their disagreements, Angelina had grown close to her mother. Mary Grimké sobbed as they said goodbye. "I have parted with other of my children," she told her youngest, "but never felt as I now do, sometimes I think I should never see you again." Her words were prophetic—she never did.

CHAPTER 7
Quaker Ways

1829-1833

Angelina arrived in Philadelphia in October 1829. She liked living with Catherine Morris and Sarah. "Very often do I contrast the sweet, unbroken quiet of the home I now enjoy," she wrote, "with the uncongenial one I was taken from."

Catherine, now fifty-eight, mothered both sisters and taught them Quaker customs. Quakers objected to the names of months and days because they were not Christian in origin. For example, January is named for the Roman god Janus. Monday is named for the moon. So the sisters learned to write "1st month, 2nd day" instead of "Monday, January 2."

Another change came in their way of speaking, using *thou* and *thee* instead of *you*. In the seventeenth century, when Quakerism began, the English language referred to one person as *thou* or *thee*, as in "*Thou* (subject) likest apples, I see," and "I have some apples for *thee*" (object). The term *you* was plural then, referring to more than one person. By the 1830s, most Americans had given up using *thou* and *thee*, saying *you* for both singular and plural, but Quakers continued the distinction.

Sarah and Angelina had no trouble adapting to this old-fashioned language, which also appeared in their Bibles. But they could not bring themselves to speak ungrammatically, which they thought Philadelphia Quakers did when they used *thee* instead of *thou* as a subject of a sentence. To some, their use of proper grammar made the sisters seem stuck up.

"Too independent," Quaker elders pronounced after hearing the Grimkés talk. "Too different," they complained, when the sisters sewed fur inside their bonnets to keep their ears warm in winter. Sarah, some said, spoke either too quickly or unclearly or without enough religious spirit. Once, when she did manage to speak forcefully, they said her talk sounded memorized instead of spontaneous—an unpardonable offense for someone who wanted to become a Quaker minister.

Sarah kept trying, "feeling as if I were condemned already," she said, "whenever I arise." Although Sarah did eventually succeed in becoming a minister, Angelina bristled at the unfairness shown her sister.

Meanwhile, Philadelphia Quakers were dividing themselves into two groups. The Arch Street Meeting was led by Orthodox, or traditional, Friends, including the Morris family. The wealthiest of the Quakers, they believed in strict enforcement of narrow rules, emphasizing biblical authority and making up for their sins by sacrificing pleasures or privileges. They believed that humans were sinful by nature. More liberal groups, called Hicksites (named for Elias Hicks, their leader) believed that individuals had the power within themselves to guide their own consciences. They believed that sin consisted of turning away from God's will. They also believed in abolition—the outlawing of slavery. Hicksites, who were outnumbered by the Orthodox in Philadelphia, challenged wealthy Quakers on the use of products made with the labor of enslaved people.

Friends still meet at the Arch Street Meeting House, designed in 1803–1804 by Quaker master builder Owen Biddle Jr. The Georgian style building stands at Fourth and Arch Streets.

Despite some misgivings about the uncompromising rules, Angelina applied to join Arch Street; the meeting sent representatives to interview her. She was surprised when the examining overseer, a friend, Jane Bettle, told her that her neglect of her mother—leaving Mrs. Grimké in Charleston—would make it hard to recommend her for membership.

"I sobbed aloud." Angelina wrote in her diary. "As soon as I could command myself I remarked . . . that she [Mary Grimké] was in excellent health & had other daughters with her & that I believed that circumstances must be very peculiar which would render it binding on anyone who had embraced the principles of Friends to live in Slave country."

To Angelina, the Quaker attitude toward slavery was beyond peculiar. After Pennsylvania outlawed slavery in 1780, individual Friends freed their enslaved servants, but the Society of Friends took no group action to join the growing Northern movement opposing slavery. Angelina could not understand. What her new colleagues saw as a nonreligious matter, she believed was a sin that needed correcting.

Quakers judged theaters, dancing, and sports to be sinful and saw music as frivolous. Orthodox Quakers opposed interfering in secular (nonreligious) matters, and they forbade excited discussion, which the topic of slavery always aroused. Forbidden to mix with people of other religions—even Hicksites—Orthodox Quakers were prohibited from reading secular or "public" newspapers, and some of these papers campaigned against slavery. *The Friend,* an Orthodox Quaker journal the sisters read, reported on religious matters, interpreted Bible verses, and criticized Hicksites for supporting the abolition of slavery. Curious to know what was happening in the outside world, Angelina asked her brother Thomas to send her political news.

After six months, the Arch Street Meeting accepted Angelina as a member. Like her sister, she began to prepare for the ministry. But Quakerism seemed less appealing to her than to Sarah, who liked living by specific rules. When Angelina chafed under Friends' restrictions, Sarah wrote in her diary, "O Lord, be pleased, I beseech Thee, to preserve my precious sister from moving in her own will, or under the deceitful reasonings of Satan. Strengthen her, I beseech Thee, to be *still.*"

Angelina also believed that Satan might be trying to tempt her away from Quakerism. She fought against the urge to leave the faith by reading the Bible and studying religious texts. The sisters attended assigned meetings, led prayer sessions in prisons, and visited hospitals and houses for the poor. Sarah did not question these traditional duties, though they bored her, but Angelina hoped to find a more creative way to make a difference in the world. Unlike Sarah, she felt drawn to teaching.

Meanwhile, the two enjoyed a quiet life in the elegant

city, learning the names of unfamiliar plants and relishing the change of seasons. They made new friends and, with their sister Anna, welcomed visits from their brothers Henry in March 1830 and Thomas the following June, when he was on his way to Yale to receive an honorary law degree.

For both sisters, marriage remained possible. Israel Morris had proposed again to Sarah in 1829, but she again turned him down, this time more convincingly. Then Edward Bettle, a young widower whose parents, Jane and Samuel Bettle, were important elders at Arch Street, began to call on Angelina. The sisters learned that by Quaker standards, such visits meant the couple was engaged.

Angelina liked Edward, but she was interested in a career, an impossible accomplishment for a married woman. A stint of teaching in the Quaker school for young children made her think she might prefer working with older students. She also tried helping her sister Anna, who taught girls in her home in what was known as a dame school. But Anna and Angelina, lacking formal education, had to work hard to stay ahead of their students. If Angelina was going to teach, she decided, she wanted to be educated and trained for the job.

Learning of the famous Hartford Female Seminary in Connecticut, which since 1823 had been known for training teachers, Angelina wrote to the principal, Catharine Beecher, requesting information. When Beecher came to Philadelphia, she arranged to meet Angelina and then invited her to visit the school herself. Sarah was away on a monthslong visit to Charleston when Angelina decided to go.

On July 4, 1831, Angelina sailed on a steamboat with some Quaker friends—John Whitall and his daughter Sarah—bound for New England. All the sights were new to Angelina: New York Harbor, its wharves—"far inferior to those of Phila[delphia]"; the

Battery (an area she called "a moving mass of gayity & fashion"); and the ride up beautiful Broadway to their lodgings. Another steamboat took them to New Haven, Connecticut, where they visited Yale. Finally, they reached Hartford by coach.

Angelina and Sarah Whitall stayed in Hartford at the home of Beecher's sister, Mary Beecher Perkins, where Catharine Beecher, her younger sister Harriet, and twelve students boarded. The Beecher sisters came from a prestigious New England family; their father was one of the best-known Presbyterian ministers in the United States. Harriet, a teacher who had graduated from the seminary, was especially friendly to Angelina. No one guessed that the work of these two young women would someday change the nation. (Harriet Beecher Stowe would publish *Uncle Tom's Cabin* in 1852.)

Harriet Beecher Stowe, about 1852. She and her husband hid escaped freedom seekers in their Maine home.

Angelina enjoyed her visit. The twelve teenaged boarders, who had never met Quakers before, were surprised by their appearance and by some of their practices—for example, Quakers sat when others stood for prayers. Nonetheless, the girls behaved politely.

Catharine Beecher was unusual in believing that teaching, then a man's job, could become a profession run by women. She wanted her students to make a difference in the world as teachers. "A lady should study," she said, "not to *shine*, but to *act*."

Angelina attended Beecher's school on several occasions, participating in regular exercises, such as drawing maps, and going on a school picnic. She toured local sites known in those days as the "reformed" state prison (presumably more humane than other prisons), the "deaf and dumb asylum" (for those who could not hear or speak), and the "insane" retreat (for mental health patients). She also visited a wool-carding factory, where eighteen machines brushed wool, all powered by five large dogs who ran on wheels. At the end of her twelve-day stay, Angelina took the seminary's entrance examination, passing easily. Catharine Beecher said she could train her to be a teacher within six months.

Catharine Beecher, about 1860. She believed that women could influence society as mothers and teachers but did not think they should have the right to vote.

Beecher accompanied Angelina and the Whitalls part of the way on their return trip to Pennsylvania. Traveling by coach, they visited pretty towns in Massachusetts and a waterfall in the Catskill Mountains. Sometimes they stayed in hotels, where Angelina's tall stature, chestnut curls, blue eyes, and fair complexion drew male attention. One young man offered her wine, which she declined. Later, he sent a message to her room, asking for one of her caps to send to a milliner to use as a pattern to make a cap for a friend.

Angelina was amused by his interest. "We had many jokes & conjectures about the strange request during the afternoon & I wondered what I should do if I met him at tea tables," she wrote. When they went downstairs for tea, he came in and sat by her: "It was utterly impossible to contain myself," she wrote, "indeed both C[atharine] & S[arah] joined me in a fit of laughter which lasted a full five minutes."

Back in Philadelphia, at the Arch Street Meeting, Angelina's happiness faded. "When I told dear J[ane] B[ettle] about my prospect of going to Hartford to prepare myself to become a Teacher," Angelina wrote, "she could not see it at all, [Jane Bettle thought] there was great danger in my throwing myself so entirely among Presbyterians. . . . It seems that they [everyone at Arch Street, including Edward Bettle] were all tried at my going away instead of staying home to receive his visits."

Offended, he stopped calling. "How humbling to any woman," Angelina wrote in her diary, "to feel that her affections are fixed on one who no longer pays her any attention." Blaming herself for losing him, she filled her evenings with studying. But three months later, in October 1831, he slowly resumed his visits.

As their romance grew, Sarah went on another long visit to Charleston. Angelina moved then to live with her sister Anna. "This was my right place," she wrote, "not only because my board would be a help to Sister A[nna] but because I should be receiving visits [which] must either deprive dear Catherine [Morris] of her parlor or make her feel like an intruder in her own house."

Recognizing family obligations, the Arch Street leaders did not object to this living arrangement, even though Anna was an Episcopalian who subscribed to a secular newspaper. Angelina enjoyed the more liberal atmosphere at Anna's, and Edward

Bettle's visits continued. "My heart is becoming more and more attached to E," Angelina wrote in June. They had serious conversations. "I cannot but admire & approve that candor," Angelina wrote, "which induces him to throw open his character to me by the free expression of his opinion on a variety of subjects—he seems to do it very designedly & thus to wish to show me what he really is." It is not clear whether Bettle knew or cared what Angelina really was. Despite their deep conversations, she still felt torn between marriage and teaching.

Then a cholera epidemic gripped the city. Edward Bettle caught what seemed to be a light case but died suddenly in September 1832. His parents, believing Angelina had made him unhappy, refused to let her attend his funeral. After his death, and the rejection by his family, Angelina fell ill. "I was most tenderly cared for by my dear Sisters & niece," she said.

"I am grieved that your young man died," her mother wrote from Charleston: "It is hard to accept these things, but our Heavenly Father knows best. I am sure you will accept this as His will. . . . I have prayed fervently for your happiness and will continue to do so for both you and dear Sarah. . . . We enjoyed Sarah's visit very much. Do you plan to visit us any time? You would be most welcome."

Her mother also wrote about the Grimké family's enslaved servants: "Last week Charles [Angelina's brother] was here to take Bertha and Ellen back to care for Ella; she is quite old and ill. I sent Mark with them, too. We don't need all those servants now. Emma has three children. I have given Amos and Patsy to Henry. The increase of our servants presents many problems. If we don't sell them, what are we to do with them? Your devoted mother, Mary Grimké."

CHAPTER 8
What to Do?

1834-1835

As time passed, Angelina began to take more interest in life again, especially the anti-slavery movement. "Five months have elapsed since I wrote in this diary," she said on May 12, 1834, "since which time I have become deeply interested in the subject of abolition. I had long regarded this cause as utterly hopeless, but since I have examined anti-slavery principles I find them so full of the power of truth, that I am confident not many years will roll by before the horrible traffic in human beings will be destroyed."

A year and a half after Edward Bettle's death, her sorrow had given way to a new feeling of independence. She pored over abolitionist newspapers and anti-slavery pamphlets, and what she read amazed her. For four years, while she had lived a sheltered Quaker life in Philadelphia, Americans had been fighting and dying over the issue of slavery. In 1831 rebellions by enslaved people demanding their freedom in Virginia and Jamaica killed dozens of white people, including women and children. In past decades, white people had ruthlessly murdered thousands of

> In 1831 Nat Turner, an enslaved Virginia preacher, led the nation's largest slave revolt, killing fifty-five white men, women, and children, including his "owners." In retribution, white people killed many more Black people, even some who had not rebelled, then caught and executed Turner.

enslaved people, and in the backlash to these insurrections, they executed hundreds of Black people, some of them free men and women who had not been involved in the uprisings.

In the United States, news of the revolts terrified white Southerners and Northerners alike. Many states enacted new, harsher laws controlling enslaved and free Black people. Meanwhile, the rebellions also attracted new supporters to the antislavery movement.

When her sister read these accounts, Sarah reported, "[Angelina] found to her surprise that [the abolitionists'] principles were her principles, and that they were men and women with whom she could work for the slave."

Catherine Morris reprimanded Angelina for taking an interest in "matters entirely outside of the Society." When Angelina asked another elder why the Friends did not take action against the terrible sin of slavery, she was told that these issues were handled by the Quaker Meeting of Suffering committee and that individuals ought not to concern themselves with such matters.

But Angelina kept reading. She learned that the British Parliament had passed the Slavery Abolition Act, outlawing the practice in British colonies. The new British law helped to inspire a meeting in the United States five months later, on December 4, 1833, when sixty-four men from ten free states (where enslavement and the trade in human beings were illegal) met in Philadelphia to organize the American Anti-Slavery Society.

Reformers, such as William Lloyd Garrison, a newspaper editor from Boston, Massachusetts, led the convention, calling slavery "a heinous crime in the sight of God." Garrison held what was considered to be a radical position on enslavement because he wanted "its immediate abandonment, without expatriation." Expatriation was the goal of another, more conservative organization, the American Colonization Society. Believing that Black and white people could never live together in an integrated society, and that abolition should happen gradually, the American Colonization Society planned to purchase enslaved people, free them, pay for their transportation (and that of other free Black people) to the west coast of Africa, and provide financial assistance to establish them in a colony there. This back-to-Africa idea did not appeal to enslaved people, many of whose families had lived in the United States for six generations.

Philadelphia had a strong, wealthy free Black society that had worked for decades to fight slavery. Some free Black men attended the organizational meeting of the American Anti-Slavery Society, but the leaders elected were all white men. Four women came too. Lucretia Mott, now a Hicksite minister and a well-known activist for abolition and women's rights, was even invited to speak to the convention. But women were denied membership and voting rights in the new group. The men urged women to form their own anti-slavery societies.

Lucretia Mott was one of the founders of the Philadelphia Female Anti-Slavery Society and was a leader in the women's rights movement.

Days later, a mixed group of white and Black women gathered, in what is now considered one of the earliest women's rights meetings, to form the Philadelphia Female Anti-Slavery Society. A female society seemed controversial to many people because women were supposed to stay at home, not join clubs. Mott pushed ahead, saying she was "so thoroughly imbued with women's rights that it was the most important question of my life from an early day."

Free Black women had organized in Philadelphia years before to promote abolition, and now they joined the new group too. Black charter members included Grace Bustill Douglass, a prominent milliner, and her daughter, Sarah Mapps Douglass, a young teacher. Four women joined from the prominent Forten family: Charlotte Vandine Forten, whose husband, James, was a wealthy sailmaker, and her daughters Margaretta, Sarah, and Harriet. Sarah Forten was married to Robert Purvis, another prominent Black abolitionist leader; later his brother Joseph married Harriet Forten.

White women, who made up the majority of the new organization, included two Mott daughters (Anna Mott Hopper and Maria Mott Davis), Abba Alcott (whose daughter Louisa May Alcott would later write *Little Women*), and two Quaker women who ran "free produce" stores, selling only goods that were not produced by enslaved labor. The society used members' dues to pay for subscriptions to abolitionist newspapers such as *The Emancipator*, the official publication of the men's society, and *The Liberator*, which was edited by William Lloyd Garrison. The Fortens and Sarah Mapps Douglass led a successful effort to fund a school for Black children.

The women's society drew criticism from many men. If women wanted independence for Black people, these men worried, might they not someday demand it for themselves? One newspaper advised the women to return home to their own "sphere," where more useful work awaited them.

Angelina wondered if she should collaborate with women from differing religious sects, writing in her diary, "Is it right for me to unite with other denominations in the benevolent operations of the day?" Most white founders of the women's group were Hicksite Quakers, and according to Arch Street rules, she was not supposed to mix with them. But she joined anyway, becoming close friends with twenty-eight-year-old Sarah Mapps Douglass and her mother.

Angelina introduced the Douglasses to her sister Sarah, and the four women bonded over their shared opinions. All opposed the effort to send Black people to Africa. This country

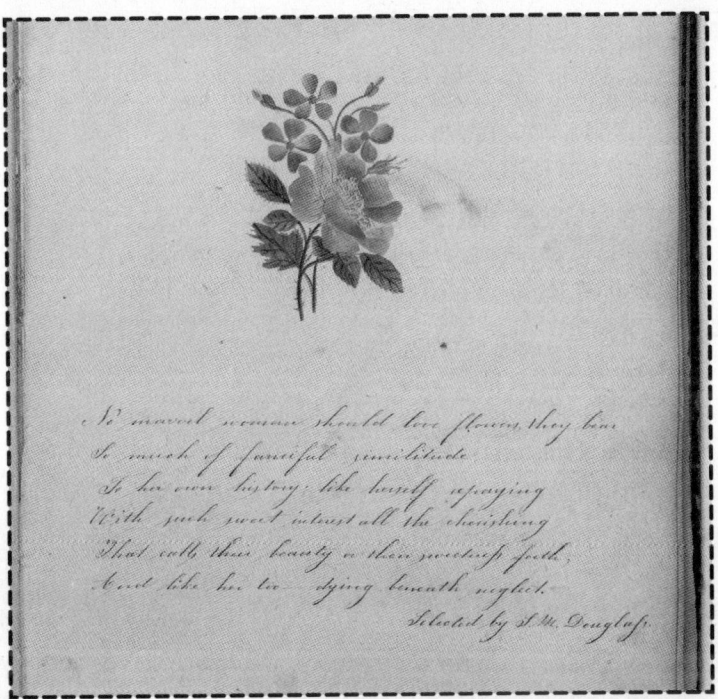

Sarah Mapps Douglass painted flowers and wrote and transcribed poems, which were compiled into a friendship album by her friend Amy Matilda Cassey. They are the earliest-surviving artwork signed by an African American woman.

"is my own, my native land," Sarah Mapps Douglass wrote in *The Liberator*, even though the United States "unkindly strives to throw me from her bosom."

The Douglasses followed Quaker beliefs, although Black people were not allowed to become members of the Society of Friends. They could attend meetings, however. At Arch Street and other meetings, African Americans had to sit in "the negro seat," which was often under the stairs or stuck in a corner. The Grimkés were alarmed to realize that Catherine Morris approved of this discriminatory practice. White people were not supposed to sit with Black people, but the Grimké sisters did anyway in solidarity. The insult to African Americans reflected the Friends' feelings on a related issue: Quakers still refused to take an official stand against slavery.

"If Friends take no part in the great moral reformation of the day," Angelina asked her diary, "will it not be right to [leave] them?"

Sarah, who did not want to leave the Quakers, nevertheless developed doubts about the Arch Street Meeting. "Satan is tempting me strongly," she wrote, "with increased dissatisfaction with Friends; but I know if I am to be of any use it is in my own Society."

In 1834 another controversy over slavery, this time in Ohio, rocked the nation. Frederick Grimké, who was a judge in Columbus, wrote to his sister Angelina about a debate at the Lane Seminary in Cincinnati, and she read about it in newspapers too. The debate in question: whether Southern states should abolish slavery immediately or work toward colonization by sending freed Black people "back to Africa." Theodore Weld, a thirty-year-old student at Lane, led the debate's winning argument for immediate emancipation without colonization. The school's trustees, afraid the decision would upset Southern financial backers, censured Weld and banned future debate on the topic. Weld, his friend Henry Stanton, and other supporters—a majority of the student body—resigned from the seminary. Nicknamed the Lane Rebels, they began traveling the Northern and Western states, lecturing on the need for abolition.

"The Great Debate" attracted attention to the anti-slavery movement. Many white Northerners favored slavery for the same reason Southerners did: money. Enslavers considered their unpaid workers to be property, the country's most valuable resource. Enslaved laborers grew crops, built infrastructure, and kept money flowing to the rich men at the top of society. The country was expanding rapidly to the west, displacing Indigenous people to make room for white settlers. New territories formed and eventually sought admission to the Union as states. In both the North and South, pro-slavery advocates worked to protect enslavement where it already existed and to make it legal in the new territories and states.

After the debate, mobs of white Northern men, who considered themselves patriots protecting the American way of life, attacked abolitionist speakers—some of them called Weldites. In a letter to his sisters, Frederick called Theodore Weld "a tremendously forceful speaker, a giant of a man of courage who has withstood such abuse and dangerous situations when he goes to speak against slavery in this free state." Frederick added, "I find this astonishing. . . . I would have thought in Ohio, all people were against slavery. It seems that the lower classes fear job competition [from free Black people qualifying for jobs formerly limited to white workers]. It is not just race prejudice."

Frederick admired Weld's nonviolent resistance. "[He] stands with arms folded before the mobs who come to heckle and abuse him," he wrote. "They become intimidated or curious to see what kind of man it is who can withstand their treatment with such courage. However, he and his followers are often beaten and stoned. His life has been in danger several times. He does not give up and only leaves a town after having made several converts to his cause. He must be a most remarkable man."

Then violence struck in Philadelphia. In August 1834, white people and Black people fought over seats on a merry-go-round known as the flying horses. The carousel was destroyed, and over the next two days, white mobs tore down a Black church and sacked another, destroyed thirty homes, and beat any Black people they could find on the streets.

Soon after, Thomas Grimké came from Charleston to visit his sisters for a week. Still an enslaver, he had also become a colonialist, though he admitted that the plan to send Black people to Africa seemed unlikely to succeed.

"We often conversed on the subject of slavery," Sarah wrote, "and never did I hear from his lips an approval of it." Sarah and Angelina argued strongly against the institution of slavery. "He had never examined the subject," Sarah wrote, "he regarded it as a duty to do it, and he intended devoting the powers of his mind to it the next year of his life, and asked us to get ready for him all the abolition works worth studying."

At this point, Thomas was a nationally known politician and educator. He was on his way to Ohio to give a speech at a teachers' college and to visit their brother Frederick, and he planned to pick up literature from his sisters on the way home to Charleston. Instead, he caught cholera in Ohio and died suddenly there. Sarah and Angelina wrote a memorial to their favorite brother and sent it south to their hometown. When Arch Street members ignored their loss, offering no condolences, both sisters questioned the meeting's relevance.

Their doubts about Quakerism increased as Angelina broadened her circle of colleagues. When the Philadelphia Female Anti-Slavery Society sponsored a speech by George Thompson, a British abolitionist, Angelina went to hear him at a Presbyterian church, despite the disapproval of Sarah and Catherine Morris. To protect Thompson from a mob attack, there was no public announcement of his talk. Still, more than a thousand people gathered to listen to him, and Sarah was certainly interested to hear what he had said.

Angelina spent the summer of 1835 with Quaker friends Margaret and James Parker in Shrewsbury, New Jersey. She had hoped to reflect there about what she should do, but upsetting articles in newspapers, especially *The Liberator*, made clear thought impossible. Mobs were murdering Black people in New York and Philadelphia. Angelina feared for the safety of the Douglasses, the Fortens, and her other Black friends.

In Charleston, she read, public officials had burned mail sacks filled with anti-slavery pamphlets in the street. A cheering crowd of three thousand people hanged dummies representing famous abolitionists, including William Lloyd Garrison. In the North and West, rioters attacked abolitionists—especially the Lane Rebels—with rotten eggs, sticks, bricks, and manure. Some anti-slavery speakers were thrown out of windows or tarred and feathered. Pro-slavery activists offered rewards for kidnapping or even assassinating abolitionists.

"New method of assorting the mail as practiced by Southern slave-holders, or attack on the post office, Charleston, S.C." is the caption of this 1835 cartoon. In the picture, a sign on the wall offers a reward, "$20,000 for Tappan," likely Arthur Tappan, a New York abolitionist.

"What to do? What to do?" Angelina asked herself. How could she honor and encourage the bravery and pacifism of the abolitionists? Then, in *The Liberator*, she read Garrison's appeal to the citizens of Boston to stop attacking anti-slavery speakers. He wrote:

> *Abolitionists have never, in any of our addresses or, uttered a publications more dangerous . . . or incendiary sentiment than that which was unanimously adopted BY THE SIGNERS OF THE DECLARATION OF INDEPENDENCE . . . —to wit—We hold these truths to be SELF EVIDENT: that all men are created equal. . . . We view the system of slavery in this country as a system of irresponsible and despotic power on the one hand, and of unprotected and suffering humanity on the other . . . a system that transforms more than TWO MILLIONS OF AMERICAN CITIZENS into BRUTES to be branded, maimed, lacerated, plundered, driven, tasked, or murdered, as their proprietors may elect! . . . We believe, therefore, that slaveholding, or claiming human beings as property, is in all cases an atrocious SIN AGAINST GOD; and hence, that it can and ought to be abandoned at once and forever. We have a moral and constitutional right to cherish and utter this belief. . . . WE SHALL NOT YIELD AN INCH.*

What to do? Angelina sat down to write a letter.

CHAPTER 9
A Cause Worth Dying For

1835-1836

"Respected Friend," Angelina's letter to William Lloyd Garrison began:

> I can hardly express to thee the deep and solemn interest with which I have viewed the violent proceedings of the last few weeks. . . . I was afraid of even opening one of thy papers, lest I should see some indications of compromise, some surrender. . . . [After reading] thy Appeal to the Citizens of Boston . . . I thanked God, and took courage, earnestly desiring that thousands may adopt thy language, and be prepared to meet the Martyr's doom, rather than give up the principle [of nonviolence] you have adopted. The ground upon which you stand is holy ground; never—never surrender it. . . . If we call upon the slaveholder to suffer the loss of what he calls property, then let us show him we make this demand from a deep sense of duty, by being ourselves willing to suffer the loss of character, property—yea, and life itself.
>
> My mind has been especially turned toward those, who

are standing in the forefront of the battle. . . . If persecution is the means which God has ordained for the accomplishment of this great end, EMANCIPATION, then. . . . I feel as if I could say, LET IT COME. . . . This is a cause worth dying for.

Her last line was a quote from Theodore Weld, whom Angelina had come to admire.

Garrison printed Angelina's letter in his newspaper, along with her name, though it was considered disgraceful for a respectable woman's name to be published. "The following epistle is from a sister of the departed GRIMKÉ," Garrison wrote in his introduction, referring to Thomas. "[The letter] comes to us as the voice of an angel," he said. "We publish it, especially, that female abolitionists may derive support and comfort from its perusal, in the midst of danger and distress."

The letter shocked many people, including Angelina herself. "I had some idea it might be published," she wrote in her diary, "but . . . I had no idea that, if it was, my name would be attached to it. . . . Oh! the extreme pain of extravagant praise! To be held up as a saint in a public newspaper, before thousands of people, when I felt

William Lloyd Garrison, portrait from 1833. "Wherever there is a human being," he said, "I see God-given rights in that being, whatever may be the sex or the complexion."

I was the chief of sinners. . . . Then, again, to have my name, not so much my name, as the name of Grimké, associated with that of the despised Garrison, seemed like bringing disgrace upon my *family*, not myself alone."

Sarah wrote disapprovingly in her own diary, "The suffering which my precious sister has brought on herself, by her connection with the anti slavery society . . . is another proof of how dangerous it is to slight the clear convictions of Truth, but like myself she listened to the voice of the tempter. . . . [May she] learn obedience by the things that she suffers."

Lucretia Mott cheered Angelina on, but Catherine Morris and other conservative Quakers were scandalized. Arch Street elder Samuel Bettle visited Angelina, asking her to reexamine the letter and take back parts of it. She refused.

The letter was reprinted widely in newspapers, and Garrison published it in a pamphlet: *Slavery and the Boston Riot.* The pamphlet told how, soon after Angelina wrote to him, Garrison had been dragged by a pro-slavery lynch mob through the streets of Boston. The city's mayor saved his life by putting him in jail. When the pamphlet reached readers, Garrison's name and Angelina's became firmly linked.

In the winter of 1835–1836, violence against abolitionists increased, spreading from Ohio through Pennsylvania to New York. Angelina read about how Theodore Weld trained other anti-slavery speakers to react as he did, with nonviolence. When he arrived in new towns, he faced hostile mobs that he would stare down, standing straight, arms crossed on his chest. Usually, his courage and calm prevented violence, but sometimes the crowds threw stones, pieces of brick, eggs, and sticks. Weld remained peaceful, trying again the next night, until people wondered what cause made him so brave. Finally, they let him speak, and his arguments usually converted a small number.

By the time he moved on to another town, he left behind a few supporters to spread anti-slavery information.

Angelina made a more private effort to help enslaved people. Her sister-in-law, Thomas's widow, now owned Kitty (the enslaved servant Angelina had helped before), and Angelina offered to buy the woman and her children so she could free them. But the widow never responded to the request.

When Sarah and Angelina learned their mother was making a will, they wrote to her, asking her to leave them enslaved servants they could then free.

In February 1836, Angelina and Sarah accepted an invitation to visit some Quaker meetings in Rhode Island. There they met liberal Friends, many of whom admired Angelina's letter to Garrison. On several occasions, she was invited to speak, but she declined, feeling unprepared to talk publicly about her opinions on abolition.

While on this trip, the sisters concluded they could no longer live with Catherine Morris. She had been wonderful to them, and Sarah felt especially close to her. But her Orthodox views remained strong, even as the Grimkés loosened their ties with the Society of Friends. Lately, Catherine had criticized Sarah's habits of kneeling to pray and praying aloud, which she did only when alone. Horrified by Angelina's published letter, Catherine urged Angelina to give up abolition work to start a school in Philadelphia. As differences mounted between her and the sisters, they decided to leave her home.

Sarah went to stay with friends in Burlington, New Jersey, where she filled her diary with page after page of anguish and self-doubt. She prayed she could love the Quaker elders who criticized her unfairly. She begged God to forgive her for kneeling to pray and praying aloud. She prayed for release from her self-confessed sins of laziness and wanting to have her own way; she prayed for patience, resignation, stillness, obedience, and humility. She thanked Jesus for making her feel ashamed of herself. The words in her diary are so extreme that a modern reader might suspect severe depression or mental illness or, at the very least, the lack of anything meaningful to do. Uncertain of how she and Angelina could afford to live on their own, Sarah still hoped they might work things out with the Arch Street Meeting.

Angelina, who was visiting the Parkers in Shrewsbury, New Jersey, had no such hope. "My mind is fully made up not to spend next winter in Philadelphia, if I can help it," she wrote to Sarah. She, too, felt sad. "I feel no openness among Friends," she said. "My spirt is oppressed and heavy laden, and shut up in prison. What am I to do? The only relief I experience is in writing letters and pieces for the peace and anti-slavery causes."

One night, Margaret Parker heard Angelina sobbing in the guest room. After some time, she went in to comfort her. She found her friend lying on the carpet, her wet face buried in a pillow. Angelina apologized sincerely for disturbing her.

The next morning, Margaret reported, Angelina entered the breakfast room a changed woman. "It has all come to me," Angelina said, beaming; "God has shown me what I can do; I can write an appeal to Southern women, one which, thus inspired, will touch their hearts and lead them to use their influence with their husbands and brothers. I will speak to them in such tones that they *must* hear me, and through me, the voice of justice and humanity."

> *"I will speak to them in such tones that they must hear me, and through me, the voice of justice and humanity."*
> —ANGELINA GRIMKÉ

A Cause Worth Dying For

That day she began, using a conversational tone, to write an *Appeal to the Christian Women of the South*. This time, she planned to publish her work, proudly, under her name. She addressed her appeal to personal friends and strangers, whom she called "Sisters in Christ." Southern women were extremely religious, so Angelina based her arguments on the Bible and on her own belief that slavery was a sin. By owning slaves, she said, Southerners condemned themselves as sinners. She wrote:

> *I know you do not make the laws, but I also know that* you are the wives and mothers, the sisters and daughters of those who do; *and if you really suppose you can do nothing to overthrow slavery, you are greatly mistaken. You can do much in every way: four things will I name. 1st. You can read on this subject. 2d. You can pray over this subject. 3d. You can speak on this subject. 4th You can act on this subject. . . . Some of you* own *slaves yourselves. If you believe slavery is* sinful, *set them at liberty.*

On the day Angelina began to write, she received a letter from Elizur Wright, the secretary of the American Anti-Slavery Society. Wright invited her to come to New York to speak against slavery to women in private parlors there. In turmoil she wrote to Sarah for advice. "Now dearest," she asked her sister, "what dost thou think of it?"

If Angelina thought it right to go, Sarah replied, she would agree to the plan. But she doubted that Angelina could make a living by writing, especially in a new place. "My beloved sister does indeed need the prayers of all who know her," she wrote to Sarah Mapps Douglass. "Perhaps the Lord may be pleased to cast our lot somewhere together. If so, I feel as if I could ask no more in this world."

In addition to his abolitionist activities, Elizur Wright invented a water valve and a calculating machine and led a successful campaign to end dishonest and unsound practices in the insurance industry.

Two weeks later, Angelina sent her finished piece to New York. "I have just finished reading your Appeal," Elizur Wright responded, "and not with a dry eye. I do not feel the slightest doubt that the committee will publish it."

While Angelina was writing, Sarah endured a new trial of her own. In nine years as a Quaker minister, she had never overcome her fear of speaking in public. One day, she felt the Lord required her to rise in a meeting. She recalled after, "As I was speaking . . . the Friend who rules in our Yearly Meeting rose in the meeting and desired me to desist [speaking]. I of course instantly resumed my seat . . . and the conviction then arose that my bonds were broken. The act on the part of this Elder was entirely unprecedented and unsanctioned by our Discipline but his power is undisputed."

The presiding elder, Jonathan Evans, was known for his dictatorial style. Having long disliked Sarah, he intended his interruption as an insult. He had not followed Quaker rules, which were to let speakers go on until they finished. Why then, she wondered, should she try to observe the religion's strict regulations? The incident ended by relieving her, she said later, as it "has proved the means of releasing me from those bonds which almost destroyed my mind." At last she felt free to reject the harsh requirements she had followed faithfully, even when she disagreed with them.

When Angelina heard what had happened, she asked Sarah to join her in Shrewsbury. "Language cannot express to thee the shock thy letter was to my feelings," Angelina wrote. "I will break your bonds & set you free."

Angelina's *Appeal*, published in October 1836, made a stunning impact. A Southern woman author was an anomaly. The idea that women could impact politics and society was radical. Though it was widely read across the North, her pamphlet did not generally reach Southern readers. Postmasters and other government officials burned copies in Charleston; confiscated them in New Orleans, Louisiana; and suppressed them in Richmond, Virginia, and in other cities. The mayor of Charleston called on Mrs. Grimké to tell her that if Angelina ever returned, she would not be allowed to set foot on land. If she managed to get off the steamer that brought her, he said, she would be arrested and sent back north.

What to do after her publication? Angelina did not want to teach. She wrote to the Rhode Island Quakers, offering to work for them, but they had no use for an outsider abolitionist. If she accepted

Angelina's *Appeal* drew ire from Southerners who opposed abolition and Northerners who thought women had no right to write or speak about slavery.

the invitation to go speak in parlors in New York, she would have to interact with strangers, a daunting prospect. The city had a much smaller proportion of Friends than Philadelphia, so her Quaker clothing would draw attention. Fashions for women had changed from the simple elegance of Angelina's youth to elaborate dresses with huge "leg-o-mutton" puffed sleeves, nipped-in waists, wide skirts, and hats that were "startling in color and size."

In New York her Quaker way of talking would seem unusual too. Furthermore, speaking in public, even to female audiences, was unthinkable for a woman. Both sisters feared that if Angelina went anywhere without permission from the Society of Friends (which certainly would not be granted), the Quakers would formally disown her. Angelina did not care about the potential consequences for herself, but she also did not want to bring more disgrace on her family.

Angelina decided to go to New York anyway, and she asked Sarah to go with her. Sarah hesitated until her mother wrote her a letter. Stay with your sister, Mary Grimké urged, don't let her go to a new place alone. "It was like a voice from the Lord," Sarah wrote, "and I instantly resolved to do so." She told Angelina of her decision in biblical terms: "Where thou goest, I will go; thy God shall be my God, thy people my people. What thou doest, I will, to my utmost, aid thee in doing. We have wept and prayed together, we will go and work together."

CHAPTER 10
Two Fanatical Women

1836–1837

The Grimkés paid their own travel expenses to New York, staying there at the home of an officer in the American Anti-Slavery Society. Both sisters attended training sessions at the society's offices at 143 Nassau Street, although only Angelina had been invited. The organizers welcomed Sarah, too, pleased to have another woman and to know that Angelina would be chaperoned when she began public speaking. "A *single* female travelling in a public conveyance *must* have a protector," an official told them. "Two friends together can protect each other."

Many well-known anti-slavery activists came to the training meetings. William Lloyd Garrison, the most hated abolitionist in America, turned out to be soft-spoken, cheerful, and the same age as Angelina, thirty-one. The sisters met Henry Stanton, a Lane Rebel turned lecturer; Quaker poet John Greenleaf Whittier; James G. Birney, a former enslaver who had converted to the abolitionist cause; and brothers Arthur and Lewis Tappan, wealthy merchants who funded the American Anti-Slavery Society to a considerable extent. The society had Black members, too, such as founder Theodore S. Wright, a Presbyterian minister. But overall, the leaders were white men.

The sisters were pleased to learn that Theodore Weld would be the main teacher. Elizur Wright had invited him many times to work for the society, but Weld thought a backwoodsman like himself would feel out of place in the city. But after rioters injured him in Troy, New York, and the mayor there ordered him out of town, Weld at last agreed to come. Two years of constant lecturing had strained his voice badly, so office work seemed appealing.

Wright was delighted to have Weld's help in leading the organization in a new direction. To carry their ideas into small towns across the North, Wright planned to recruit seventy "Apostles," or messengers, basing that number on a Bible passage. (Luke 10, 1: "After these things the Lord appointed another seventy also, and sent them two and two before his face into every city and place, whither he himself would come.") About forty men and the Grimkés attended the first training meeting.

In 1836 Theodore Weld considered himself a backwoodsman. He began his abolitionist career in Ohio, which at that time was considered the frontier.

Wright told Weld that he had called the meeting of agents "for the purpose of kindling, warming, 'combustionizing' and in short getting the whole mass to a *welding* heat.'"

He wanted them prepared for all possible problems; Wright said, "It is wisdom to look before you leap—especially if you are going to leap among rattlesnakes or steel traps."

Tall, thin, and rough-looking, Theodore Weld, "the thunderer of the West," wore a linsey-woolsey coat—made of flax and wool—and cowhide shoes. His unruly brown hair matched his shag overcoat, and sometimes he neglected to shave. In a letter, Angelina described him to her Philadelphia friend Jane Smith. "Perhaps now," Angelina wrote, "thou will now want [to] know how this lion of the tribe Abolition looks. Well, at first sight there was nothing remarkable to me in his appearance, and I wondered whether he was really as great as I had heard. But as soon as his countenance became animated by speaking, I found it was one which portrayed the noblest qualities of the heart and hand, beaming with intelligence, benevolence, and frankness."

With Weld's guidance and the Grimkés' help, Wright planned to start women's anti-slavery societies too. In the North, like the South, white women led constricted lives, controlled by their fathers and husbands. They were banned from higher education and most professions, and they were not allowed to vote, testify in court, or serve on juries. Married women could not sign contracts or own property; their husbands could beat them or imprison them for almost any reason, or no reason at all. A husband could turn his wife out with nothing, even without her clothes or money that she had inherited or earned. If a marriage ended, the father always got custody of the children. Forbidden to speak publicly in churches or meetings, most women did not attend public events on their own. Wright hoped to reach them by organizing parlor meetings for women in people's homes—gatherings that focused on women's issues. Sarah and Angelina, still nervous about public speaking, were glad to learn these sessions would be private.

The women's issues to be addressed were beyond grim. Harriet Jacobs, author of *Incidents in the Life of a Slave Girl: Written by Herself* (1861), said, "Slavery is terrible for men; but it is far more terrible for women. Superadded to the burden common to all, *they* have wrongs, and sufferings, and mortifications peculiarly their own."

Jacobs was talking about the many enslavers who raped their female servants and enslaved the mixed-race children who resulted from such sexual violence. Specific terms defined the mix: *mulatto* for one who was half Black, *quadroon* for a quarter, and *octoroon* for an eighth. Even "one drop" of Black blood was considered enough to make a person Black. Unlike white children, who inherited their standing in society from their fathers, babies born to enslaved women shared the status of their mothers. Many enslavers sold these, their own children. Wives did not like to see the mixed-race offspring of their husbands, who often resembled their fathers. Many white children must have felt bad when their young half brothers or sisters, often looking like them, were sold away to strangers. As Angelina said, the sale of any enslaved person broke human hearts by separating families.

Enslavers also "bred" enslaved women like livestock, regardless of their feelings, choosing Black male partners for them who seemed likely to produce healthy children. Enslaved couples were not allowed to marry; if they held their own ceremony, it had no legal standing. The more children a woman had, the richer the enslaver became from gaining new "properties" or the profits from selling them. Even while pregnant, enslaved women were expected to work hard and to endure whippings. One formerly enslaved woman said, "When woman was with child, they'd dig a hole in the groun' and put their stomach in the hole, and then beat them."

White women were expected to find fulfillment in their love for their families. The Anti-Slavery Society believed that if Northern women understood that slavery destroyed family bonds, both Black and white, they would influence their male relatives toward abolition. The society also suggested that women boycott products made with the labor of enslaved people and that they sign petitions opposing slavery.

From November 8 to 27, 1836, the agents met for daily training from nine to one, three to five, and seven to nine. "It is so good to be here," Sarah wrote. "We sit all day and are never tired."

In December the sisters, refusing payment from the society, began speaking in Manhattan homes. Sarah focused on religious and moral issues; she was writing *An Epistle to the Clergy of the Southern States*. In this pamphlet, Sarah asked Southern ministers to oppose slavery. She criticized them for teaching the Bible while forbidding enslaved people to read it. She said white men took advantage of Black women in a sin "we cannot name." This publication, like Angelina's *Appeal*, would be censored in the South but widely read in the North.

Angelina focused her speeches on the politics of slavery. Speaking dramatically, waving her hands, sometimes making her audience cry, she insisted that Northerners had to give up racial prejudice. Women who attended the sisters' talks left so inspired that soon each parlor Sarah and Angelina visited was filled to overflowing.

Theodore Weld, who, like the sisters, declined payment for his work, stayed on at the Anti-Slavery Society, doing editorial and administrative jobs. He boarded with an African American brother and sister, chopping wood for his fireplace and carrying it up to his attic room. Each morning he walked two miles south to work in the society office, taking meals with a Black family who lived nearby. Frequently, he visited the sisters.

Sarah and Angelina spent the winter of 1836–1837 in New York with the family of Henry Ludlow, a Presbyterian minister. Two years before, his house and church had been partially destroyed by anti-abolition rioters, but he rebuilt, sticking to the cause. By 1836 a few other Protestant churches were beginning to support abolition; another liberal minister invited the sisters to speak in a meeting room at his Baptist church.

But most people, whether for slavery or against it, thought it sinful for women to speak in public, even in church. They cited St. Paul, who wrote in 1 Corinthians 14:34–35, "Let your women keep silence in the churches, for it is not permitted unto them to speak, but *they are commanded* to be under obedience, as also saith the law. And if they will learn anything, let them ask their husbands at home: for it is a shame for women to speak in the church."

New York Quakers, who did permit women to speak in their meetings, still fumed when they read handbills promoting a meeting of the Female Anti-Slavery Society at the Baptist church and mentioning the sisters by name. Angelina, upset by the controversy, was ready to back out, but Weld encouraged her to go ahead with her speech.

At that first church gathering, the sisters found three hundred women waiting to hear them. Henry Ludlow stood guard to keep men out; if the idea of women speaking in public was outrageous, speaking to a "promiscuous" group (a mixed group of women and men) was unthinkable. As it was, this meeting marked the first time in the United States that women had spoken in public to a large assembly of other women who were not Quakers.

After the meeting, the sisters and their new friend Theodore Weld went to tea at the home of Lewis Tappan. Tappan's daughter Julia told them that a male abolitionist had tried to attend their talk, only to be turned away by Ludlow. "How supremely ridiculous," said Weld, "to think of a man's being shouldered out of a meeting, for fear he should hear a woman speak!"

In early 1837, the sisters expanded their range, traveling to New Jersey and northern New York State. Both spoke, but Angelina had a special talent for moving audiences. In Poughkeepsie, New York, she addressed a mixed group of men and women for the first time, proud to lecture to three hundred people in an African American church.

By spring, as their audiences grew, men regularly attended the sisters' talks. Angelina and Sarah quickly became the biggest draw of all abolitionist speakers of the time. Their words, as women and Southerners, brought up to be enslavers, proved unique and powerful. Their passion was obvious; their topics were sensational: the sin of slavery, the sexual exploitation it allowed, and the physical horrors they had witnessed firsthand.

Sarah and Angelina created a list of fifteen "sins of the north," including the internal slave trade (the sale of enslaved people within the United States), the admission of seven new slave states to the Union, banks that loaned money using enslaved workers as collateral, and racial prejudice. They wanted Northerners to stop using products created by unpaid labor. They also asked Northern churches to refuse communion, a religious sacrament, to enslavers, whom they considered to be sinners.

Newspapers published articles against the sisters. "The Richmond papers call us the two 'fanatical women,'" Sarah wrote to Sarah Mapps Douglass. The same paper called their audiences "idle and curious women."

"Why are all the old hens [unmarried women] abolitionists?" asked the *Boston Morning Post*. "Because not being able to obtain husbands they think they may stand some chance for a negro, if they can only make amalgamation [race-mixing] fashionable."

An open letter to a Connecticut newspaper asked the

sisters to stop preaching in the North about slavery. "Ladies, what would you have us do?" the writer asked. Pastors warned women in their churches to stay away from the immodest, unnatural, unwomanly, and evil Grimkés.

"They think to frighten us from the field of duty," Sarah said, "but they do not move us. God is our shield and we do not fear what man can do unto us."

Sarah had a new outlook on life. She wrote to her mother: "Thou remember the dissatisfied, unhappy little girl, Sally Grimké. How deprived I felt when I could not study Latin with Frederick. How disappointed that I could not become a lawyer. How much more superior is what I am doing now."

The sisters helped organize the Anti-Slavery Convention of American Women, held May 9 to 12, 1837, at the Free Church in Greenwich Village, New York. To avoid protesters, the conference organizers did not send announcements to newspapers. Accounts vary, but at least seventy and perhaps as many as two hundred women from seven to ten states attended this first women's political meeting in the United States. Hicksites such as Lucretia Mott, Grace Douglass, and Sarah Mapps Douglass represented Philadelphia. Author Lydia Maria Child and

Lydia Maria Child, who wrote the poem "Over the River and Through the Wood," published the first American magazine for children. It failed when parents canceled subscriptions after she wrote a book demanding immediate abolition.

abolitionist Maria Weston Chapman, both white women from Boston, also attended.

Ten percent of the women who came were Black. Sarah and Angelina had made a special effort to recruit them, knowing that even abolitionists discriminated against people of color. To prevent prejudice in the convention, they invited not just the integrated women's anti-slavery societies from New England and Philadelphia but also Black women's groups from New York, including the Colored Ladies Literary Society and the Rising Daughters of Abyssinia. The convention was one of the first to be well integrated.

Sarah spoke first, stating "that the object of the Convention was to interest women in the subject of anti-slavery, and establish a system of operations throughout every town and village in the free states, that would exert a powerful influence in the abolition of American slavery."

The convention included committee appointments, debates, speeches, and resolutions. Angelina offered one of these resolutions: "Resolved, That as certain rights and duties are common to all moral beings, the time has come for woman to move in that sphere which Providence has assigned her." Women should not be satisfied, she went on, with the limited roles men imposed on them. The men had created corrupt customs, which they justified by perverting the Bible. At the end, the resolution turned to abolition: "It is the duty of woman, and the province of woman, to plead the cause of the oppressed in our land, and to do all that she can by her voice, her pen, and her purse, and influence of her example, to overthrow the horrible system of American slavery."

After some debate, the resolution was adopted, but twelve women who believed that the proper role of women should be silence and submission asked that the minutes make it clear they did not approve of this declaration of independence for women.

Women of color kept a low profile at first, though they took to the floor to protest "the dreadful effects of the scheme of expatriation" proposed by the American Colonization Society. No one believed that it would be possible to round up and ship off to Africa every Black person in the United States. The cost alone would be prohibitive (some colonizationists wanted to reimburse enslavers for the loss of their workers), and the whole idea was, in fact, ridiculous.

> *"It is the duty of woman . . . to plead the cause of the oppressed in our land, and to do all that she can by her voice, her pen, and her purse, and influence of her example, to overthrow the horrible system of American slavery."*
> —ANGELINA GRIMKÉ

Though Black women were respected within the convention, outside, racism continued as usual. While in New York, Grace Douglass attended a Quaker meeting, where a white woman asked her to sit upstairs "because Friends do not like to sit by persons of thy color."

"I believe they despise us for our color," her daughter Sarah Mapps Douglass wrote later to a friend. Soon the two Sarahs—Douglass and Grimké—began to collaborate on what they could do to eliminate prejudice within the Society of Friends.

The American Convention of Anti-Slavery Women met when Theodore Weld was traveling away from New York. After it ended, Sarah wrote to him, "Angelina has given me so saucy a message to insert I hardly know how to write it, but *she says it must be done*. . . . She says, 'Tell brother Weld I am much obliged to him for his hypocritical offer to serve us and then taking care to go so far that we cannot get him to do anything.'"

Angelina wrote to Weld later, sending him a message that she said came from a convention secretary (she was one herself): "Tell Mr. Weld that when the women got together, they found they had *minds* of their own, and could transact their business *without* his directions."

The convention published Sarah's essay *An Address to Free Colored Americans* and Angelina's *An Appeal to the Women of the Nominally Free States*. Angelina wrote:

> *The female slaves are our countrywomen, our sisters, they have the right to look at us as women for sympathy with their sorrows and for effort at their rescue. Nothing in the North is open to them except in the capacity as servants. We refuse to eat with them, to walk with them, to allow them in our schools. . . . We women should feel a special sympathy for the colored race for we, as women, have been accused of mental inferiority and denied the privileges of a liberal education.*

New York newspapers called the convention a "farce." The *New-York Commercial Advertiser*, for example, sarcastically berated women who neglected their traditional feminine roles in favor of political involvement, saying:

> *Yes, most unbelieving reader, it is a fact of most ludicrous solemnity, that "our female brethren" have been lifting up their voices. . . . The spinster has thrown aside her distaff— the blooming beauty her guitar—the matron her darning*

> needle—*the sweet novelist her crow-quill [pen]; the young mother has left her baby to nestle alone in the cradle—and the kitchen maid her pots and frying pans—to discuss the weighty matters of state—to decide upon intricate questions of international policy.*

Despite the negative stories in mainstream newspapers, speaking invitations poured in from many states after the convention. The sisters decided to start a lecture tour of New England. Staying in the homes of supporters, Sarah and Angelina gave five to six talks a week, moving often and traveling by coach six to eight miles one way to meetings. Both caught colds doing the exhausting work, but they kept on, aware that some in their audiences walked long distances to hear them speak.

Then opposition arose from a surprising source: Catharine Beecher, former head of the Hartford Female Seminary, published an open letter to Angelina. "My Dear Friend," it began, "Your public address to Christian females at the South has reached me, and I have been urged to aid in circulating it in the North." But Beecher had no intention of helping. Instead, in 152 pages of advice, later published as *An Essay on Slavery and Abolitionism, with Reference to the Duty of American Females*, Beecher opposed Angelina on many subjects. Northerners, she said, had no right to tell Southerners what to do. Gradual emancipation (with colonization to Africa), she insisted, would end slavery more efficiently than immediate freedom in the states. Women were made by God, she said, to be subordinate to men in society, and God had given women different ways of gaining power and influence. Women should achieve their goals, she advised, "in the domestic and social circle," not by speaking in public or signing petitions.

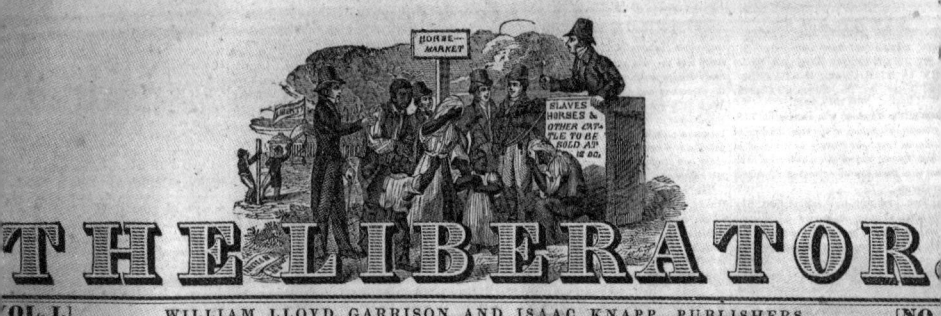

The Liberator newspaper's first illustrated masthead depicted a horse market where enslaved Black people were being sold at auction. This was one of three mastheads over the newspaper's history, all of which were intended to show the horrors of slavery.

Angelina responded with thirteen letters published in *The Liberator*. "The great fundamental principal of Abolitionists," she wrote, "is that man cannot rightfully hold his fellow man as property." Slaveholding, she insisted, was a national sin that violated the Constitution. As for colonization, she said, "I have never yet been able to learn, how our hatred to our colored brother is to be destroyed by driving him away from us. . . . I want them to stay in this country; and in order to make it a happy home to them . . . we must dig up the weed [of racial prejudice] by the roots out of each of our hearts." Refuting Beecher's claim that men were superior, she stated, "I recognize no rights but human rights. . . . I believe it is a woman's right to have a voice in all the laws and regulations by which she is to be governed, whether in Church or State."

Theodore Weld praised Angelina's response in a letter. "Your letters to Catharine Beecher I like greatly," he wrote, "and yet I wish they were *better*." He cited specific ways he thought she could have improved them.

"I thank thee for thy strictures [criticisms] on my letters to C. E. B[eecher]," Angelina replied, "but should have thanked thee still more if *before* they were republished in *the Emancipator* [the Anti-Slavery Society newspaper he edited] thou hadst been so *kind a brother as to have corrected them* for me. *Didst* thou do as thou wouldst have been done by?"

Angelina could handle criticism from Weld, but public censure from Beecher saddened her deeply. And then came the most outrageous attack of all.

CHAPTER 11
Woman's Sphere

1837

In the summer of 1837, the General Association of Congregational Ministers of Massachusetts issued a pastoral letter (one offering spiritual advice) to all parishes, warning against the sisters.

> We invite your attention to the dangers which at present seem to threaten the female character with wide spread and permanent injury.... The power of woman is in her dependence, flowing from the consciousness of that weakness which God has given her for her protection.... But when she assumes the place and tone of a man as a public reformer... her character becomes unnatural.... We especially deplore the intimate acquaintance and promiscuous conversation of females with regard to things 'which ought not to be named;' by which... the way [is] opened... for degeneracy and ruin.

The letter, which was reprinted and published in newspapers in many states, did not mention Angelina and Sarah by name, but it was clearly a response to their New England tour. This document roused supporters of the Grimkés in addition to opponents. Their new friend Maria Weston Chapman, a Boston abolitionist, poked fun at it with her poem "The Times That Try Men's Souls":

Confusion has seized us, and all things go wrong,
The women have leaped from "their spheres,"
And, instead of fixed stars, shoot as comets along,
And are setting the world by the ears!

Mary S. Parker, president of the Boston Female Anti-Slavery Society, suggested to the editor of *The New England Spectator*, an abolitionist newspaper, that the Grimké sisters be asked to write a rebuttal to the letter. When he agreed, Sarah took on the task.

Her series of essays, "Letters on the Province of Woman," appeared as fifteen open letters to Parker starting in July 1837. In 1838 they were published as a book called *Letters on the Equality of the Sexes, and the Condition of Woman*. Today it is regarded as a landmark text, the first complete feminist statement written by an American woman.

Maria Weston Chapman started the Boston Female Anti-Slavery Society in 1832 with twelve other women. Chapman served as William Lloyd Garrison's chief assistant and helped him run the Massachusetts Anti-Slavery Society and edit *The Liberator*.

Sarah, who believed that God had created both men and women in his image, explained that biblical ideas urging restrictions on women were due to incorrect translations of the Scriptures made by men. "I am inclined to think," she wrote, "when we [women] are admitted to the honor of studying Greek and Hebrew, we shall produce some various readings of the Bible a little different from those we now have."

The Bible said that God had created Adam and Eve, the first man and woman in the world, and given them a Garden of Eden to live in. They could eat any fruit from the garden except fruit from the tree of knowledge of good and evil. But Eve, tempted by Satan, who was disguised as a serpent, ate the fruit and gave some to Adam. Christians believed that by doing so, she had brought sin into the world, and that her evil act made women inferior to men. Sarah said that Adam and Eve, created as equal companions, had committed the same sin of eating the forbidden fruit. Sarah wrote:

> *Even admitting that Eve was the greater sinner, it seems to me man might be satisfied with the dominion he has claimed and exercised for nearly six thousand years. . . . All history attests that man has subjected woman to his will, used her as a means to promote his selfish gratification, to minister to his sensual pleasures, to be instrumental in promoting his comfort; but never has he desired to elevate her to that rank she was created to fill. He has done all he could to debase and enslave her mind; and now he looks triumphantly on the ruin he has wrought, and says, the being he has thus deeply injured is his inferior.*

Sarah stated that when one group of people had power over another, the first group benefited and the second was exploited. "Intellect is not sexed," she said, ". . . strength of mind is not sexed; and . . . our views about the duties of men and the duties of women, the sphere of man and the sphere of woman, are mere arbitrary opinions, differing in different ages and countries, and dependent solely on the will and judgment of erring mortals."

Radically for the time, she called for legal rights for married women and better educational and economic opportunities for all women, along with equal pay for equal work and equal rights of citizenship. She urged women to take action against the oppressive social structure.

"I ask no favors for my sex," she said, in what became her most famous quotation. ". . . All I ask of our brethren is, that they will take their feet from off our necks, and permit us to stand upright on that ground which God designed us to occupy."

As Sarah's letters were published, and as Angelina and Sarah continued to advocate for equal rights for all, the public began to connect the two movements promoting abolition and women's rights. Hostility toward the sisters increased. Hate mail poured in. Notices of the Grimkés' meetings were ripped from walls and poles. Increasingly, they had to find unusual venues, at one point addressing 150 people in a *"barn* beautifully fitted out with green boughs."

The poet John Greenleaf Whittier wrote a poem in their defense:

> *So this is all! the utmost reach*
> *Of priestly power the mind to fetter,*
> *When laymen* think, *when women* preach,
> *A war of words, a "Pastoral Letter!"*

But Whittier himself questioned their choice to speak out for women instead of focusing solely on abolition. He asked Sarah and Angelina in a letter:

> *Why is it necessary for you to enter the lists as controversial writers on this question? Does it not look, dear sisters, like abandoning in some degree the cause of the poor and miserable slave, sighing from the cotton plantations of the Mississippi, and whose cries and groans are forever sounding in our ears, for the purpose of arguing and disputing about some trifling oppression, political or social, which we may ourselves suffer?*

John Greenleaf Whittier worked as an editor for multiple magazines and newspapers. But he was best known for his poetry, which often featured the politics of the time and called for the emancipation of enslaved people.

Most male abolitionists objected to the Grimkés' crusade for women's rights, including Theodore Weld. He wrote to them:

> *I do most deeply regret that you have begun a series of articles in the Papers on the rights of woman. Why, my dear sisters, the best possible advocacy which you can make is just what you* are *making day by day. Thousands hear you every week who have all their lives held that woman must not speak in public. . . . Besides you are Southerners, have been slaveholders; your dearest friends are all in the sin and shame and peril. All these things give you great access to northern*

mind, great sway over it. . . . You can do more at convincing the north than twenty northern females, tho' they could speak as well as you. Now this peculiar advantage you lose the moment you take another subject. . . . Let us all first wake up the nation to lift millions of slaves of both sexes from the dust, and turn them into MEN and then when we all have our hand in, it will be an easy matter to take millions of females from their knees and set them on their feet, or in other words transform them from babies into women.

Angelina fired back:

"What is the matter with thee?"
One would really suppose that we had actually abandoned the anti-slavery cause and were roving the country, preaching nothing but woman's rights, when, in fact, I can truly say that whenever I lecture, I forget everything but the slave. HE is all in all for the time being. And what is the reason I am to be scolded because sister writes letters in the Spectator? Please let every woman bear her own burdens. Indeed I should like to know what I have done yet. And dost thou really think in my answer to C.E. Beecher's absurd views of woman that I had better suppress my own?

"Why dear child!" Weld replied, "What is the matter with you? Patience! Rally yourself." But the sisters, having no idea of when or even if slavery could be defeated, did not feel inclined to wait patiently for women's rights until that unlikely goal had been accomplished.

CHAPTER 12
Turning the World Upside Down

1837-1838

For weeks Angelina and Sarah argued with Weld in letters about whether the sisters should promote women's rights in addition to abolition. Gradually, the tension between them eased, but the sisters felt betrayed, especially when Weld told them that the Executive Committee of the Anti-Slavery Society had declared they were just helpers, not official society agents. Of all the prominent society members, only William Lloyd Garrison stood entirely for full equality for women.

Meanwhile, their lecture tour continued. Despite criticisms from the popular press, or perhaps because of it, they drew considerable crowds. In Woonsocket Falls, Rhode Island, a thousand people gathered to hear them speak at a local church—such a large audience that the building nearly collapsed. Sarah wrote to Sarah Mapps Douglass: "The [church] was crowded to overflowing and soon after I commenced speaking I noticed a slight crack, which produced some bustle. Soon after a voice from the gallery assured the congregation there was no danger. I had not proceeded far however the second time before I was requested to stop and a person near the pulpit said . . . that one of the beams had given way and he did not think it safe for the whole congregation to remain."

Lectures were the most popular kind of public entertainment at this time. Crowding at the sisters' speeches became typical; their growing fame attracted both supporters and detractors, as well as some people who simply wanted to gape at the unusual sight of women speaking in public. At another event, spectators who could not fit into the building placed ladders at all the windows, standing on them precariously to hear.

In November the tour ended. In twenty-three weeks, at eighty-eight meetings in sixty-seven towns, the sisters had addressed more than forty thousand people. The spread of newspapers and magazines, made possible by new printing technology and new steam-powered railroads and riverboats, ensured that their written sentiments reached many more.

The Grimkés spent the winter at the "delightful farm" of their friends Samuel and Eliza Philbrick in Brookline, outside Boston. When they arrived, both were ill—Angelina with typhoid fever and Sarah with bronchitis. From New York, Theodore Weld wrote letters filled with concern for their health. As the sisters recovered, the three friends resumed a friendly correspondence. Angelina scolded Weld for his hard-to-read handwriting, which she called "scratchifications."

He teased the sisters about their Quaker traits: "theeing and thouing," "tight crimped caps," and the dull hues of their clothing: "that impenetrable drab that defieth utterly all amalgamation of colors!"

By December Angelina and Sarah felt well enough to accompany their host Samuel Philbrick to the first public debate ever held about women's rights in the United States. Fifteen hundred people attended the event at the Boston Lyceum.

Established in 1830, the Boston Lyceum was a popular stop on the lecture circuit. Run by a civic association, it offered classes, lectures, discussions, writing contests, and exhibitions.

Angelina and Sarah addressed the crowd on the question, "Would the condition of women and of society be improved by placing the two sexes on an equality in respect to civil rights and duties?" Later, Angelina said the discussion "was conducted with respect, delicacy, and dignity, and many minds no doubt were roused to reflection, though I must not forget to say it was decided against us by acclamation, our enemies [men] themselves being judges. It was like a meeting of slave-holders deciding that the slaves are happier in their present condition than they would be freed."

On February 8, Theodore Weld sent Angelina a letter marked "Private." It said:

> *I know it will surprise and even amaze you, Angelina, when I say to you as I now do, that for a long time* you have had my whole heart.
>
> *. . . Your letter to Wm. Lloyd Garrison formed an era in my feelings and a crisis in my history that drew my spirit toward yours by irrepressible affinities.*
>
> *. . . I have no expectation and almost no hope that my feelings are in any degree* RECIPROCATED BY YOU. *If . . . your heart, Angelina, does not reciprocate my love, I charge you . . . not to shirk for a moment thro[ugh] fear of giving me pain from declaring to me the* whole truth.

He added a P.S. saying she could show the letter to Sarah if she wanted to.

Angelina wrote back:

> *Your letter was indeed a great surprise, My Brother, and yet it was no surprise at all. It was a surprise because you have so mastered your feelings as never to betray them; it was no surprise because in the depths of my own heart* there was found a response *which I could not but believe was produced there by an undefinable feeling in yours.*
>
> *. . . I feel my Theodore that we are the two halves of one whole, a twain one, two bodies animated by one soul and that the Lord has given us to each other.*

Sarah added a note to Angelina's response: "Thy letter to my precious sister was not unexpected to me. . . . Since our first meeting I have felt as if you were kindred spirits."

"My heart is full!" Theodore wrote to Angelina. "THAT LETTER found me four days ago!" He had felt too overwhelmed to write back immediately.

Now that Theodore and Angelina had confided their love for each other, Angelina longed to see him, but she had just a few days left to prepare for her biggest speech to date. Henry Stanton had invited her to address a special committee of the Massachusetts State Legislature that had been appointed to consider petitions from anti-slavery groups. Many petitions against slavery had been signed by women; petitions were the only way women could formally address legislators on political issues. Stanton suggested that Angelina could present women's petitions at the state capitol. Some historians think he may have been joking; no woman had ever before addressed a legislative body in the United States. The all-male Massachusetts Anti-Slavery Society opposed the idea and so did the Executive Committee of the American Anti-Slavery Society. But after Stanton got the special committee chairman to approve, Angelina decided to go ahead.

Both sisters were scheduled to speak, but Sarah was ill on that cold February 21, 1838, so Angelina spoke alone. On the streets of Boston, vendors were selling insulting caricatures of her and of William Lloyd Garrison. Arriving by carriage with her friend Maria Weston Chapman, the so-called "brazen Miss Grimke" pushed toward the capitol through crowds of people, some applauding and others yelling insults. All one thousand seats in the Hall of Representatives were filled, mostly with white men, though some white women and Black people also attended.

Henry Stanton, born in 1805, was a lawyer and abolitionist orator. He and Theodore Weld were two of the forty Lane Rebels who left Lane Theological Seminary in Cincinnati to protest a gag order on abolition discussions.

Angelina felt nervous, but "the Lord was my Helper," she wrote later to Sarah Mapps Douglass. "The feeble, trembling knees were made strong and I was enabled to lift my voice once more like a trumpet."

She said:

> *Mr. Chairman . . . I stand before you as a citizen, on behalf of the 20,000 women of Massachusetts whose names are enrolled on petitions which have been submitted to the Legislature. . . . These petitions relate to the great and solemn subject of slavery. . . . And because it is a political subject, it has often tauntingly been said, that women had nothing to do with it. Are we aliens, because we are women? Are we bereft of citizenship because we are mothers, wives and daughters of a mighty people? Have women no country—no interests staked in public weal—no liabilities in common peril—no partnership in a nation's guilt and shame?"*
>
> *. . . I stand before you as a southerner, exiled from the land of my birth by the sound of the lash and the piteous cry of the slave. I stand before you as a repentant slaveholder. I stand before you as a moral being and as a moral being I feel that I owe it to the suffering slave and to the deluded master, to my country and to the world to do all that I can to overturn a system of complicated crimes, built upon the broken hearts and prostrate bodies of my countrymen in chains and cemented by the blood, sweat and tears of my sisters in bonds.*

The hall was so packed that some feared the balconies might collapse from the weight of the audience. Angelina asked for a chance to speak again on a second day. The session ended in good humor when a legislator proposed that "a committee be appointed to examine the foundations of the State

The roof of the Massachusetts State House, designed by American architect Charles Bulfinch, is gilded with gold and topped with a pine cone, as a symbol of the forests that made it possible for early white settlers to survive.

House of Massachusetts to see whether it will bear another lecture from Miss Grimké."

Newspaper reactions to her speech were mixed. *The Burlington (VT) Free Press* admired Angelina's passionate way of speaking. "Clothed in a dark dress," the newspaper said, "with a simple fancy neck-cloth, she stood up before that immense audience, unabashed; and over her smoothly combed hair, a quaker cap, neatly crimped border, was placed." Although the paper admired her openness and said her cause was just, it criticized her "delusion," saying that, as a woman, "she was beyond the province of her sex—out of that sphere which custom and propriety and even the Apostles assigned to woman."

The *Boston Globe* said, "She exhibited considerable talent for a female, and as an orator; appeared not at all abashed in exhibiting herself in a position so unsuitable to her sex, totally disregarding the doctrine of St. Paul, who says, 'Is it not a shame for a woman to speak in public?' . . . She belabored the slaveholders and beat the air like all possessed."

One sign of her effect, said Angelina's friend Lydia Maria Child, was that "the sound part of the community (as they consider themselves) . . . give vent to their vexation by calling her Devil-ina instead of Angelina. . . . Another sign is that we have succeeded in obtaining the Odeon, one of the largest, most central halls for her to speak in, and it is the first time such a place has been obtained for anti-slavery in this city."

Sarah felt well enough to join Angelina for her second appearance at the State House, where the crowds were even larger than before. "The hall was jambed to such success," Angelina wrote to Sarah Mapps Douglass, "that it was with great difficulty we were squeezed in, and then [we] were compelled to walk over the seats in order to reach the place assigned us. As soon as we entered we were received by clapping. . . . After the bustle was over I rose to speak and was greeted by *hisses* from the doorway."

The chairman stopped Angelina's speech three times to quiet the crowd, and then he moved her to the speaker's desk, so that people could hear her better. Sarah sat beside her in the speaker's chair. Nothing rattled Angelina. "I never felt more perfectly calm in my life," she wrote to Theodore later. Impassioned, she spoke out against racial prejudice, which she argued was the real basis for slavery. Even emancipation would not overcome this problem, she said, which also existed in the North.

Tired but happy after her second speech, Angelina wrote to Sarah Mapps Douglass, "What the effect of these meetings is to be, I know not, nor do I feel that *I* have anything to do with it. This I know, that the chairman was in tears almost the whole time that I was speaking. . . . We abolition women are turning the world upside down."

CHAPTER 13
Two Halves Made Whole

1838

In March 1838, when the sisters had a short break in their lecture schedule, Theodore came to visit them in Brookline at the Philbrick farm. He had not seen Angelina since declaring his love, but in long, almost daily letters they shared many of their activities, histories, and beliefs. Theodore had been born in 1803 in Hampton, Connecticut, and had grown up on a farm. The son and grandson of Congregational ministers, he considered himself a Presbyterian. He worried that his longing for Angelina might be a sin.

"I will be with you on Saturday evening," he wrote. "And now my love grant me this boon—I know you will—when I meet you, let me meet you ALONE. For a little while I MUST be *alone* with you."

The Philbricks were agreeable. When Weld arrived, he ate supper with Sarah and their hosts while Angelina dined in her room. Then the Philbricks and Sarah left to attend a lecture in Boston, and Angelina came down to the parlor, where Theodore waited. He looked thinner, having lost 10 pounds, and she seemed different too. Her cap was gone, so, probably for the first time, he saw her wavy chestnut hair, loosely arranged around her face. A pretty, non-Quaker shawl reflected her deep blue eyes.

For the next four days, walking hand in hand, the couple made plans for their wedding and their new lives together. Theodore was so happy that sometimes he had to rush away from his fiancée to gain control of himself, "keeping an extinguisher" on his desires.

Angelina wrote to her sister Anna, asking if she would host the wedding in Philadelphia. They made a list of eighty guests to invite. After checking with the Weld family, they set the wedding date for mid-May, when Angelina, Theodore, Sarah, and many of their friends would be in the city to attend a women's anti-slavery convention. The couple also invited Sarah to live with them after the wedding.

Theodore would look for a house to rent near New York, they decided, as he planned to keep working at the American Anti-Slavery Society. His throat seemed permanently damaged from overuse, so he could not go back on the lecture circuit.

In Brookline, the sisters worked on sewing Angelina's trousseau using "free" cotton that had not been grown by enslaved workers. They gave some thought to housekeeping, which neither sister, nor Weld, had done before. "I cant see what we should want a girl [servant] for," Angelina told Theodore, "if we live in the simplicity we expect to. . . . What dost thou think of my getting dear Jane Smith to go home with me to *teach* me my duty? I could learn in one or two weeks. If we put out our washing and ironing, I think certainly [we] could do the rest of the work."

Theodore planned to grow vegetables. "I could easily," he told Angelina, "by working three hours a day raise enough with my own hands to pay the whole rent; for you must know that you are going to marry a *farmer*. When but fourteen years old I had the entire charge of a farm of near one hundred acres."

His visit ended as the sisters began a lecture series at the Odeon, the largest meeting hall in Boston. Newspapers anticipated the event by calling them "old maids who wanted to attack society," "abnormal creatures," and "'crack pots, cranks, and freaks,' unworthy of imitation by decent women."

Nevertheless, Sarah gave the first talk to a packed house. On the ground floor, she stood before five hundred red upholstered seats arranged in a circular pattern. Three galleries above seated another eight hundred people. When she started to speak, every chair and the aisles were full. Despite some hissing from the audience, she spoke against slavery for two hours.

The next day, Theodore, who had not attended the lecture, took the train for Connecticut, to tell relatives there about his engagement. From Hartford he wrote to Sarah, "My dear sister will you let me take a brother's liberty with you? . . . On board

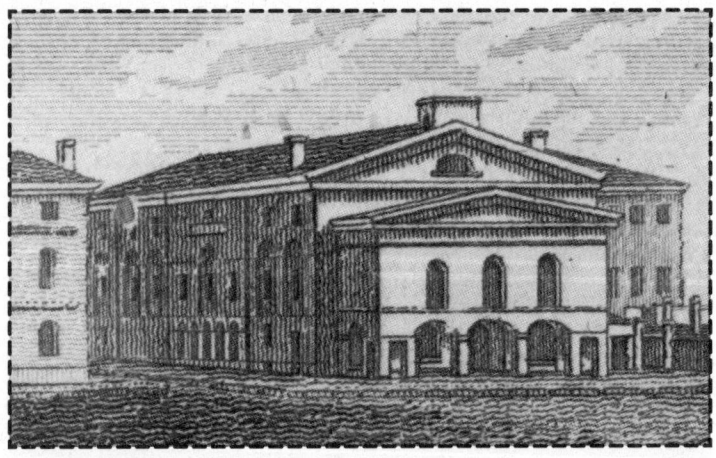

The Boston Odeon—also known as the Boston Theatre—was a 1,300-seat lecture and concert hall.

the cars ... were a number of abolitionists ... and a number of strong pro-slavery folks.... *All* agreed, pro slavery and anti slavery, that Angelina's lectures before the legislature had done more for the abolition cause in Massachusetts than any or *all other measures together* for the whole season."

But, he said, the abolitionists did not respond well to Sarah's speaking, which they found less compelling than Angelina's. "I found the abolitionists distressed," he wrote, "about the first meeting in the Odeon. They said that the crowd went there to hear Angelina, that they waited patiently as they saw her there and presumed she would speak, and therefore did not leave, but they would have done so ... if they had supposed she was not to speak. The *anti* abolitionists were rejoiced that you spoke instead of A." He added, "They all said that the lack of interest in your lecture was not at all for lack of excellent matter, but for lack of an interesting and happy manner of speaking; that your manner is monotonous and heavy."

Then he asked Sarah to let her sister deliver the rest of the Odeon lectures, as Angelina was proving to be the more gifted orator. "If you can make any excuse to Angelina for not letting her see this letter or know what it contains," he wrote, "... I think you had better do it."

"She read it all out to me," Angelina wrote to Theodore. "O! that thou hadst written *Private* over it. I can't tell thee how I feel about it. I love thee unutterably for such fait[h]fulness to her and yet beloved it pained me more than words can tell." She was upset by his words to her sister, but she also understood that feelings among three people who were so close had ups and downs over time.

Sarah resigned from the series, and Angelina gave the remaining five talks. Sarah, apparently still on good terms with Theodore, praised her sister's performances. "The end crowned all," Sarah wrote to him. John Tappan, she told him, a major supporter of the Anti-Slavery Society, had come from New York. "He said a fire had been kindled which would never go out."

By letter, the engaged couple continued their daily revelations, confessing even their bad habits to each other. Theodore sent Angelina a list of his views and feelings, inviting her to compare it to hers:

> *1st. Persons who contemplate uniting . . . should STUDY EACH OTHER PROFOUNDLY and know each other perfectly. . . . 2nd. They should . . . converse together on* all the responsibilities involved in the marriage relation, on the mutual relation of husband and wife, the sphere of each. . . . *3. They should fix upon plans of life, modes of employment, the system by which to regulate their household, its order, rules, mode of living, dress, equipage, furniture, diet, regimen . . . exercise, family habits, hours, time and seasons, etc. 4.* Rules of intercourse with others, *neighbors, visitors, laws of hospitality, action on the community at large, relations to the civil government, to religious denominations, principles on which charities and benefactions [donations] are to be regulated.*

Angelina, who had a more relaxed view of life, described wedding presents she had received from friends: twelve silver teaspoons and a large lump of beet sugar (grown in the North, so not by enslaved workers). She reminded Theodore that Sarah would need a room with a fireplace.

During the sisters' last week at Brookline, Angelina received a letter from their mother. "I feel assured," Mary Grimké wrote, "that my dear daughter will marry no one who is not equal to her in every sense of the word; and from the description given of your lover by Sarah and yourself, he seems to be suitable to you in all respects. . . . After you become a Matron [married woman], I hope you will feel that retir[e]ment is best suited to your station."

Theodore wrote that his family, too, approved of the wedding. He had rented a midsize house in Fort Lee, New Jersey, on the Hudson River, where a steamboat would let him commute to New York. "I . . . go up there [to New Jersey] this afternoon," he wrote, "to plough up the ground for our garden and field. It will probably take me two days. . . . [Not far from the house] is a very excellent colored family who will be very glad to do our washing and will as I find by inquiry in the neighborhood do it very well. They will also be ready to help us in whatever we want done that we cant do ourselves."

The house would be replastered and painted inside before they arrived. "By the way," he wrote, "we shall find one part of [moving in] very difficult, that is to find *plain* furniture. Everything is so tricked out and covered with carved work or bedizzened and *gew gawed* and gilded and tipt off with variegated colors."

At the end of April, the sisters left Boston for New York. Theodore took them for a quick viewing of the new house and then saw them off on the boat for Philadelphia. Sarah stayed with their friend Jane Smith, and Angelina stayed with Anna. There she wrote invitations on abolitionist stationery, which showed, at the top, an engraving of a young, enslaved man kneeling in chains:

> *Wilt thou grant us thy presence, sympathy & prayers on the occasion of our marriage which (the Lord permitting) will take place at 8 o'clock on the evening of the 14th. . . at Anna H. Frost's No 3 Bellmont Place. Pray for us that our dear*

> *Master may be present with us, and spread before us all who meet on that solemn occasion a spiritual feast.*
> Angelina E. Grimké
> Theodore D. Weld
> May 1st

Angelina's nineteen-year-old niece helped with the preparations. "M[ary] A[nna Frost] has paid very dearly for our having sealed our letters in the parlor," Angelina wrote to Theodore, "for the scent of the sealing wax killed both her little fish; however [a friend] promises to give her two more, so her grief is assuaged."

In another letter she wrote, "I mean to get our cake, etc., made by a *colored* confectioner who has just set up a shop, and makes every thing of free sugar."

Theodore was so excited he could barely keep his mind on antislavery business. "Do pray tell me what you have to suggest about my wedding suit," he wrote. "I am just as great an ignoramus about what would be suitable as can be conceived.... I suppose there is such a thing as *propriety* in dress, varied by *occasions*. Now I want to know *what that is*. During my

Angelina and Theodore wrote their wedding invitations on abolitionist stationery bearing the image of a kneeling enslaved man.

whole life, as you know dearest, dress has occupied my thoughts I can almost say *not at all*."

The ceremony itself needed to be decided upon as well. Following Quaker tradition, Angelina did not want a minister to preside. Sarah consulted a lawyer to find out what was required; she learned that in Pennsylvania, marriage was a civil contract. If made before witnesses, the contract did not require the presence or signature of a civil official.

So the bride and groom decided to stage their own ceremony, with no authority presiding. "Now for thy wedding suit," Angelina wrote. "We have talked the matter over and here are our preferences; a brown coat—*frock if thou likest it*—white cravat (Sister Anna volunteers to tie it for thee, as we told her we presumed thou hadst never done such a thing before), white waistcoat and white or light colored pantaloons, white stockings, and shoes, *lower* on the instep than those thou generally wearest, *nothing* high priced."

"*White* vest and pantaloons," Theodore wrote back, "strike me as a little *buckish* and *dandyish* as tho[ugh] they were put on to attract attention." Nonetheless, he decided to wear them, and Angelina chose a brown dress to match his coat.

As friends and relatives received invitations, well-wishes poured in. Some recalled that both Theodore and his friend John Greenleaf Whittier had vowed never to marry until slavery was abolished. Whittier noted Theodore's change of mind in his poem, "On Leaving Me and Taking a Wife," in which he jokingly called marriage "the enemy":

> *Alack and Alas! that a brother of mine,*
> *A bachelor sworn on celibacy's altar,*
> *Should leave me alone at the desolate shrine*
> *And stoop his own neck to the enemy's halter!*

On Monday morning, May 14—the day of the wedding—abolitionists from several states gathered in Philadelphia to dedicate a new building: Pennsylvania Hall. It had been designed to provide free speech opportunities to abolitionists and for any other purpose "not of an immoral character." Two thousand people, including many women, had bought $20 shares to help raise $40,000 for construction.

At the hall's grand opening, protesters gathered outside, taunting a seemingly white man who helped a Black woman follow him out of his carriage. The crowd didn't recognize these members of a prominent Black Philadelphia family: Robert Purvis, the light-skinned son of a white father and a mixed-race mother, could easily be taken for white. He chose to identify as Black. The woman he was escorting was his wife, Harriet Forten Purvis, also of mixed race but with a darker skin tone. The crowd yelled at another Black man escorting two "pretty white girls," who turned out, similarly, to be mixed race. They, too, were leaders in the Black community.

That evening, many of the same people who had attended the hall opening walked the few blocks to the wedding, where forty guests formed a group remarkably diverse for the time. They included William Lloyd Garrison, Henry Stanton, Maria Weston Chapman and her sister Anne Weston, Samuel Philbrick, and the Tappan brothers. Betsy Dawson and her daughter attended; they were former enslaved servants of Angelina's father and had moved to Philadelphia after being "given" to Anna Grimké Frost, who freed them. The sisters' friends Jane Smith, Sarah Mapps Douglass, and her mother, Grace, were there, along with Theodore's siblings Lewis and Cornelia.

No one from the Grimkés' Charleston family attended; it is not clear whether Angelina invited them. They would not have wanted to attend a mixed-race social gathering, and they would not have wanted to meet Quakers, whom they considered to be extremists, although they tolerated Angelina and Sarah.

Some Quakers, such as Lucretia Mott, sent regrets and good wishes, not wanting to be banned from their own meetings for attending a marriage between a Quaker and a Presbyterian. John Greenleaf Whittier came, but he stepped outside during the actual ceremony for the same reason. (Individual Quakers interpreted the rules in their own ways.)

The bride and groom, age thirty-three and thirty-four, respectively, spoke no formal vows. "I here promise," said Theodore, "before God, his angels, and this [abolitionist] assembly, to take Miss Angelina Grimke for my wife, as an equal, and I waive all claims to that obedience which is usually claimed in the marriage ceremony."

Sarah wrote later to a friend, "Angelina's address to him was brief but comprehensive, containing a promise to honor him, to prefer him above herself, to love him with a pure heart fervently. . . . A colored Presbyterian minister then prayed, and was followed by a white one. . . . The certificate was then read by William Lloyd Garrison and was signed by the company."

Abby Kelley, a rising young Quaker abolitionist from Massachusetts, was the first to sign the wedding certificate, followed by Garrison and Stanton. Maria Westman Chapman's signature was largest and boldest. "A more interesting service it never was my fortune to witness," she said later. "It was an abolitionist wedding."

The sisters knew that the Society of Friends would formally disown them, Angelina for marrying a Presbyterian and Sarah for attending the wedding. But "we feel no regret," Sarah said. Nothing could spoil their happiness as the bride and groom celebrated with family and friends.

Practical Amalgamation (The Wedding), an 1839 print by Philadelphia artist Edward W. Clay, whose pictures often featured buffoonish Black characters trying to improve their status by imitating white middle-class customs and by marrying across racial lines.

Later, all were saddened to learn of vicious, racist rumors about the ceremony. One made-up charge, that there were six white bridesmaids and six Black groomsmen, led to threats of violence against the so-called "amalgamationists." Philadelphia slavery supporters believed that abolitionists, especially those from Boston, such as Garrison, were dangerous, subversive, and unpatriotic. They thought these radical wedding guests were determined to overturn all public institutions and to eliminate slavery in favor of only one possible alternative: "miscegenation," or sexual relationships or marriage between people considered to be from two different races.

The wedding attendees would try hard to change their minds.

CHAPTER 14
What Is a Mob?

1838

Angelina and Theodore spent their wedding night at the home of Jane Smith, while Sarah stayed with Anna Grimké Frost, who also hosted Theodore's sister Cornelia. On May 15, the newlyweds took time off from abolition work for a one-day honeymoon.

That same morning, across Philadelphia, women set out for the newly opened Pennsylvania Hall to attend the second Anti-Slavery Convention of American Women. Three hundred delegates and correspondents were expected to attend the convention from Pennsylvania, New York, and New England. Approaching the hall in the heart of the city, the women saw placards posted which read: "Whereas a convention for the avowed purpose of effecting the immediate emancipation of slavery in the Union is now in session in this city, it behooves all citizens entertaining a proper respect for the right of property, and the preservation of the Constitution of the United States, to interfere, *forcibly*, if they *must*, and prevent the violation of these pledges, heretofore held sacred."

The biracial Philadelphia Female Anti-Slavery Society played a large role in raising funds to build Pennsylvania Hall. Black and white donors gave generously to create a place where even the most radical abolitionists could speak.

In other words, slaves were property, and freeing them would violate the Constitution.

"We would therefore," the signs continued, "propose to all persons, so disposed, to assemble at the Pennsylvania Hall in 6th street, between Arch and Race, on to-morrow morning (Wednesday 16th May) at 11 o'clock, and demand the immediate dispersion of said convention. —May 15, 1838."

Hall managers removed placards as they found them, but not before many people had read them. The threat of violence proposed for Wednesday did not stop the women who gathered that Tuesday, including Sarah Grimké and many other participants from the first convention. At 10 a.m., they settled in a meeting room on the hall's first floor, which also held offices, a free produce store, and an abolitionist bookstore.

Mary S. Parker was elected convention president; vice presidents included Lucretia Mott, Sarah Grimké, and two Black women, Susan Paul and Martha Ball. Sarah Mapps Douglass was made treasurer. In the afternoon meeting, African American Hetty Burr was appointed to the business committee, as was Angelina, despite her absence.

The morning group planned a large public gathering for the following evening, but some present disapproved of women speaking to "promiscuous" assemblies. So they decided the event would not be an official convention function. Instead, it would be managed by abolitionists working as a team of individuals.

New signs went up around the city advertising the Wednesday meeting, promoting a speech by Angelina Grimké Weld. In response, copies of the original, anti-abolitionist placards were posted again.

At 11 a.m. on Wednesday, May 16, fifty or sixty pro-slavery agitators gathered outside the hall. They rattled the locked doors trying to enter the building and inspected the gas pipes, hoping they could use the gas to burn the place down. The crowd grew quickly by hundreds, then thousands. The men hissed and hooted as well-dressed people arrived throughout the afternoon and evening to hear the speeches. Later, a newspaper disparagingly reported on the "petticoat convention" at "Agitation Hall," and on the attendees' "incendiary" looks: "white dandies with spectacles, and black wenches,—and black dandies and white wenches."

Angelina, Theodore, and Jane Smith arrived in a coach belonging to their friends the Chapmans. Sarah rode in another carriage with Anna and Mary Anna Frost, and Cornelia Weld. They must have come early; the building managers reported that by 3 p.m. "the hall was *thronged*; and hundreds, if not thousands, went away, unable to obtain access."

The second-floor auditorium, called the Saloon, was a huge room with balconies overlooking it. On an arch at the west end, large gold letters spelled out "Virtue, Liberty, and Independence."

A speaker's platform held furniture made of Pennsylvania walnut, upholstered in rich blue silk and damask. At the center of the high ceiling was a nine-foot vent decorated with a huge sunflower; the flower's center was a concave mirror that sparkled at night. Four additional air shafts in the corners allowed fresh air to pass through while the windows remained closed.

Inside the gas-lit Saloon, Angelina and Maria Weston Chapman went up on the stage, joining William Lloyd Garrison, Lucretia Mott, and Abby Kelley. Sarah took one of three thousand seats in the auditorium, while Theodore watched from the wings; surprisingly, this would be his first time watching Angelina speak.

"An audience promiscuously mixed up," a newspaper described it later, "of blacks and whites, sitting together in amalgamated ease. One pretty woman (white) was seen seated between two black fellows with woolly heads."

Later, the hall's official report said, "Frequent vollies of stones were thrown against the windows, and some disorganizers within made repeated attempts to frighten the audience."

By starting time, the aisles were packed with people both for and against slavery, with even more crowding outside. Garrison, the most radical, and therefore the most hated

Abby Kelley gave up her teaching career to become an abolitionist speaker and leader. She considered Sarah and Angelina to be role models and asked their advice about speaking.

of all abolitionists, gave the opening speech to hisses and groans. "When he took his seat," the official report said, "the rioters within the building made great efforts to create confusion and break up the meeting."

Then Maria Weston Chapman, another radical abolitionist from Boston, stood before the crowd, wearing a crimson shawl. She had spoken for women's groups in the past, but never to men and women together. Waving her hand to quiet the audience, she introduced Angelina, who wore her brown wedding dress.

"Men, brethren, and brothers," Angelina said, "—mothers, daughters, and sisters, what came ye out to see? . . . Is it curiosity merely, or a deep sympathy with the perishing slave, that has brought this large audience together?"

The mob outside, who could not hear her, gave a huge yell. She continued:

Those voices without tell us that the spirit of slavery is here.

This opposition shows that slavery has done its deadliest work in the hearts of our citizens. Do you ask, then, "what has the North to do?" I answer, cast out first the spirit of slavery from your own hearts, and then lend your aid to convert the South. . . . The great men of this country will not do this work; the church will never do it. A desire to please the world, to keep the favor of all parties and of all conditions, makes them dumb on this and every other unpopular subject.

Roars from outside grew louder as she went on:

As a Southerner I feel it is my duty to stand up here to-night and bear testimony against slavery. I have seen it—I have seen it. I know it has horrors that can never be described.

I was brought up under its wing. I witnessed for many years its demoralizing influence and its destructiveness to human happiness. It is admitted by some that the slave is not happy under the worst forms of slavery. But I have never seen a happy slave. I have seen him dance in his chains, it is true, but he was not happy. There is a wide difference between happiness and mirth. . . . The slaves, sometimes, are mirthful. When hope is extinguished, they say, "let us eat and drink, for to-morrow we die."

At that point, stones thrown by the rioters outside began to shatter the windows. Strong venetian blinds drawn inside the building kept the debris from raining down on the crowd.

Nothing stopped Angelina. "Her eloquence kindled, her eye flashed, and her cheeks glowed," Garrison said later.

When the glass started crashing down, two of the hall's managers went to the police station to ask for help. The mayor, who had charge of the police, was not there, but the receptionist told them four officers had been dispatched. Meanwhile, Angelina continued her oration.

"What is a mob?" she asked. "What would the breaking of every window be? What would the levelling of this Hall be? Any evidence that we are wrong, or that slavery is a good and wholesome institution? What if the mob should now burst in upon us, break up our meeting and commit violence upon our persons—would that be anything compared with what the slaves endure?"

The audience, looking nervously around, murmured and shifted in their seats. Angelina called them back to attention. "All this disturbance," she said, "is but an evidence that our efforts are the best that could have been adopted, or else the friends of slavery would not care for what we say or do."

Ending her hour-long speech with an appeal to the women of Philadelphia, Angelina yielded the floor to Abby Kelley. The young Massachusetts Quaker, who had been inspired by Garrison and the Grimké sisters, gave her first public address. Lucretia Mott closed the meeting, stating that the mixed gathering was not an official meeting of the Anti-Slavery Convention of American Women, as many considered it improper for women to address audiences of both sexes. She hoped that "such false notions of delicacy and propriety would not long obtain [last] in this enlightened country."

> "I have *never seen* a *happy slave.*"
> —ANGELINA GRIMKÉ

Afterward, Theodore came to congratulate the speakers. He urged Kelley to become an anti-slavery lecturer. "Abby," he said, "if you don't, God will smite you!"

As the audience left the hall, the mob drew back to let them pass, perhaps because half were women. A letter from a spectator to a Georgia newspaper later described the crowd filing out: "Pairs and trios of different hues, from 'jetty black to snowy white,' arm in arm . . . the descendant of . . . Africa, linked, side by side, with some of the fairest and wealthiest daughters of Philadelphia."

But not everyone was allowed to pass without issue. The official report said that "a number of colored persons, as they came out, were brutally assaulted, and one, at least, was severely injured."

The next day, as Angelina and Sarah returned to the Saloon for a convention meeting—this time of five hundred women—another pro-slavery mob waited outside. Some had been there all night.

The hall managers visited Mayor John Swift, presenting him with a letter about the vandalism committed the day before: "We call upon thee, as Chief Magistrate of the city, to protect us and our property, in the exercise of our constitutional right to assemble and discuss any issue of general interest."

The mayor replied, "There are always two sides to a question—it is *public opinion makes mobs!*—and ninety-nine out of a hundred of those with whom *I* converse are against you." To him, the mob's actions were justified by the scandalous goings-on inside the hall. He said that the city solicitor had given orders that none of the protesters from the night before should be arrested. Offering to address the mob later, he suggested banning people of color from future meetings, as their presence was particularly upsetting to the protesters.

Next, the hall managers turned to the sheriff, who replied that trouble such as this was the mayor's business. The mayor had a force of 160 men, while the sheriff had only 4. He did not want to interfere with the mayor's decision.

The Thursday morning meeting included a speech by Sarah. "Miss Grimké was very eloquent in behalf of the colored race," reported Laura H. Lovell, a white audience member. "She was grieved to see the prejudice against them existing in the free states."

At their afternoon meeting, the convention adopted a motion proposed by the business committee: "We are told that it is not within the 'province of women' to discuss the subject of slavery; that it is a 'political question,' and we are 'stepping out of our sphere' when we take part in its discussion. It is not true that it is merely a *political* question—it is likewise a question of justice, of humanity, of morality, of religion."

Lucretia Mott read a message from the hall managers, asking the convention members to recommend to "their colored sisters" not to attend the evening meeting as the mayor had advised. Mott did not agree with the mayor, and she expressed her own opinion as well, which was that "our colored friends should not absent themselves from the meeting this evening."

In late afternoon they adjourned. "Mrs. Weld," Lovell wrote, "proposed that we should, as far as possible, protect our colored sisters while going out, by taking each one of them by the arm." At a time when most white people would not even consider touching a Black person, Angelina was suggesting a tactic that the abolitionists had used the night before and at an earlier meeting in Boston. "We passed out through a mob of two or three thousand, fierce, vile-looking men, and large boys," Lovell said. "They allowed us just room to walk, two abreast."

By the time the women filed out, the mob was estimated at ten to fifteen thousand strong. The hall managers decided to cancel the evening meeting, but the crowd remained outside. When the mayor arrived, about sunset, he asked for and received the keys to the building. Then he made a speech to the mob:

> Fellow Citizens: . . . *There will be no meeting here this evening. This house has been given up to me. The Managers had the right to hold their meeting; but as good citizens they have, at my request, suspended their meeting for this evening.*
>
> We never call out the military here! *We do not need such measures. Indeed, I would, fellow citizens, look upon you as my police, and I trust you will abide by the laws and keep order. I now bid you farewell for the night.*

"Three cheers for the mayor!" the crowd yelled, and they continued to cheer as they began breaking down the hall doors with battering rams, crowbars, and hatchets. Storming the bookstore, they threw some abolitionist titles into the street and carried others up to the Saloon. They tore down the window blinds, piling them together with books and furniture on the speaker's platform. After dousing the heap with tar and turpentine and lighting them on fire, they wrenched the gas pipes loose and aimed gas at the flames.

The convention's executive committee had moved its evening meeting to a private home. As the meeting disbanded, someone brought news of the blaze. Angelina and others saw the night sky lit "ruddy crimson" for miles around. From atop Independence Hall, the Liberty Bell rang an alarm.

Fire engines soon arrived by the burning building, but the fire crews sprayed water only to protect neighboring structures.

> The destruction of Philadelphia Hall upset people on both sides of the abolition issue. "We are decidedly opposed to any mingling of the two races," wrote *The Philadelphia Ledger*, "[but] we should prefer as companions, moral, peaceful and orderly blacks, to profligate and disorderly whites."

When the hall's zinc roof caught fire in a blue blaze, a triumphant cry rose from the crowd, and all the floors collapsed at once.

Satisfied with their work, the mob turned to other targets. The rioters tried to find the Mott house, but to save their home, a friend gave them the wrong directions. The well-known Philadelphia Black abolitionists James Forten, his son Robert, and Robert Purvis had to smuggle William Lloyd Garrison out of town in the Fortens' carriage. It was the same way that these Philadelphia leaders helped other Black people escape slavery. They moved freedom seekers via the Underground Railroad, a network of people, shelters, and escape plans to aid runaways. Later, Garrison would describe what happened to Pennsylvania Hall as "a legal lynching."

The next day, convention women held the final meeting at the school of Sarah Pugh, an abolitionist teacher. Sarah Grimké proposed a resolution denouncing racial prejudice. It was the duty of abolitionists, she said, to identify themselves with Black people "by sitting with them in places of worship, by appearing with them in our streets, by giving them countenance [support] in steamboats and stages, by visiting them at their homes and encouraging them to visit us, receiving them as we do our white fellow citizens." Her resolution passed, but not unanimously—even some abolitionists harbored racial prejudices.

Over the next two days, many Black people were attacked in Philadelphia. A mob set fire to a Quaker shelter for children of color and a Black church.

The fire at Pennsylvania Hall made headlines across the nation. "A white woman," a St. Louis paper wrote, "hanging to the arm of a negro, was sufficiently insulting to people of good taste, to justify the demolition of the unholy temple of the abolitionist lecturers."

The 1851 board members of the Pennsylvania Anti-Slavery Society. *Standing (left to right):* Mary Grew, Edward M. Davis, Haworth Wetherald, Abby Kimber, J. Miller McKim, and Sarah Pugh. *Seated (left to right):* Oliver Johnson, Margaret Jones Burleigh, Benjamin C. Bacon, Robert Purvis, Lucretia Mott, and James Mott.

A New Orleans paper said that the mob's urge to burn the hall, "though contrary to the spirit of the law, was called for by a firm conviction that the efforts and purposes of the vile abolition faction tended to destroy the Union!"

Another account of the fire said:

> *Least of all have American females cause to complain of the position custom has assigned them. The kindness and attention they receive—the gallantry universally shown them—not the least worthy for being often uncouth—should teach them one and all to appreciate their social position without looking for immoderate or strange privileges or applauding and running after public Reformers from their own sex. Instead of attending useless discussions and listening to itinerant lecturers, let them read at home.*

CHAPTER 15
The Shadow of Our Own Roof

1838

As they began their new life with Theodore, Angelina and Sarah faced three problems: They had no idea how to keep house, they did not know how to cook, and many people, including abolitionists, wanted Angelina to fail.

Theodore worried more about the last issue than the sisters did. "Probably no female in the country is so extensively known or so much the subject of remark everywhere as *you*," he had written to Angelina a month before their wedding. "Your being so generally known as a public lecturer to promiscuous assemblies, and especially as having addressed the legislature, all eyes are upon you. . . . Nine tenths of the community verily believe that you are utterly spoiled for domestic life." Thousands and thousands, he supposed, would await her failure with "a Satanic eagerness." Despite these predictions, the sisters proceeded cheerfully.

Sarah and Angelina had always lived in houses with servants, first in their childhood homes in South Carolina, then as guests in Philadelphia and New York, and on the lecture circuit. Usually, servants cleaned rooms when the wealthy occupants were absent, so the sisters had no idea of what procedures to follow. Someone would need to haul water for cleaning and cooking, they realized. Commercial soapmaking had just begun; they could probably buy it in New York instead of making it themselves. But when to use it? Or vinegar? Lye? Oil? Ammonia? Bluing? Blacking? Chalk? And wouldn't those things be hard on their hands?

They pored over an advice and recipe manual: *The Young House-Keeper or Thoughts on Food and Cookery*, by William A. Alcott. Alcott considered housekeeping to be an honorable profession, a science worthy of study since it had a powerful influence on every citizen of the nation. He advised women to make a plan for household work, to stick to a strict schedule, and to train their husbands and children to help. In this way, he said, women could have time for self-improvement.

The new family traveled, probably by stagecoach, to Manlius, a small village in central New York where Theodore's parents lived on a farm. Ludovicus and Elizabeth Weld, who had been unable to attend the wedding, received the sisters warmly, despite Ludovicus Weld's doubts about Quakers and women who spoke in public. The countryside offered views of rolling green hills, but the sisters spent their week in the farmhouse kitchen, taking cooking lessons from Theodore's mother and his sister Cornelia.

From Manlius, they continued to their new home in Fort Lee, New Jersey. It stood on the Palisades, a picturesque line of steep cliffs three hundred feet tall, overlooking the Hudson River. Across the water they could see Manhattan. Their grounds included orchards with apples and pears already forming, and land Theodore had plowed in April to create a field and large garden.

Freshly plastered inside, the house looked bright and welcoming. They ordered furniture from a local cabinetmaker:

simple in design (no gew gaws) and made from cherry wood, a frugal choice. Sarah made curtains for the windows.

Over the mantelpiece, they hung a large picture of a kneeling slave, sent to Angelina by Elizabeth Pease, a British abolitionist. "It is just such a speaking monument of suffering as we want in our parlor," Angelina wrote to her. "We want those who come into our house to see at a glance that we are on the side of the oppressed and the poor."

Designed by the British potter Josiah Wedgwood in 1787, the image of a kneeling enslaved man and the accompanying slogan were reproduced on medallions and in print.

Angelina, who loved flowers, decided that growing them would require time she could spend more profitably on antislavery activities. But the trio admired wildflowers and sunsets during "rambles," and they climbed rocks for better views, read books in the woods, and enjoyed picnics atop the Palisades, always returning home to their "dear little No. 3," as they called the house.

It would be hard to overestimate what this home meant to them. Sarah, at forty-five, had felt uncomfortable growing up in her parents' houses and rootless during "years of tossing and buffeting" since leaving Charleston in 1821. During his lecture tours, Theodore, now thirty-four, had stayed wherever he could, sometimes in rough conditions. Angelina, who was thirty-three, missed the good parts of her South Carolina homes—comfort and family.

"Oh, Jane," Sarah wrote to Jane Smith, "words cannot tell the goodness of the Lord to us since we have sat down under the shadow of our own roof, and gathered round our humble board [table].... I confess I do not love public work."

Their mother was astonished by reports of their simple living arrangements. "Pray, have you no servants?" she wrote to Angelina. "And you mean [to do all the housework yourself]? This, my daughter, is like some of your other strange notions."

They could have afforded a servant but did not want a stranger to intrude on their newfound privacy. Sarah paid the Welds a small monthly sum for rent and food. Both sisters still had modest incomes from their inheritances, and Theodore had begun accepting pay for his part-time job at the Anti-Slavery Society, earning $1,000 a year. Their combined resources, along with Theodore's crops, which he sold to markets, allowed them to live frugally, without want.

The house stood near a ferry landing, with daily service by *The Echo* to Manhattan. Commuting into town several times a week, Theodore supervised society publications, wrote many himself, and helped to develop and lead the organization.

Sometimes the sisters waited in front of the house when it was time for him to come home. From there, they could watch the boat approaching the Jersey shore. When Angelina heard its engine, she blew a whistle. If Theodore was on board, he blew an answer, and when his response came "merrily over the water," she ran down to the dock to meet him. In the evenings, the newlyweds took moonlit walks along the river.

In July an official letter arrived, disowning the sisters as Quakers as they had expected: Angelina for marrying outside the faith, Sarah for attending the wedding. Unperturbed, they responded in a joint letter: "It is our joy that we have committed no offense for which Christ Jesus will disown us as members of the household of faith. If you regret that we have valued our right of membership so little; we equally regret that our Society should have adopted a discipline which has no foundation in the Bible or in reason."

From then on, they dressed simply but no longer followed the strict Quaker dress code, and they gave up much of their plain speech, though they continued to use *thou* and *thee*. The sisters remained devout, but they did not attach themselves to any other religious organization. Occasionally, they attended Black churches in Manhattan with Theodore.

Their friend Jane Smith came for a weeklong visit, providing additional lessons in housekeeping and cookery, and soon the sisters had established routines that pleased them all. They followed the popular and frugal "Graham diet," which Theodore had eaten for two years and Angelina adopted before their wedding. That summer Sarah decided to follow it, too, glad they could all be of "one heart and mind." Invented by a minister, Sylvester Graham, the diet was the first to win a national audience. Pamphlets, newspaper and magazine articles, and books, produced on new steam-powered printing presses, expounded

Sylvester Graham was famous for his health-oriented diet; his legacy lives on in the graham cracker.

his theories. In Boston both sisters had attended lectures on this revolutionary way of eating.

Graham criticized the typical American diet, which he thought consisted of too much meat and grease, not enough fruit and vegetables, and unwholesome bread made from highly processed flour. Recommending vegetarian alternatives, he allowed milk and eggs but discouraged the consumption of butter, meat, fish, and highly seasoned foods. The basis of his diet was whole wheat bread. To make it, cooks had to grind whole wheat kernels at home, but as the number of Grahamites increased, healthful flour became available in stores.

The sisters took turns cooking, each time preparing enough food to last the family for seven days. "We can make good bread," Sarah wrote to Jane Smith, "and this with milk is an excellent meal. This week I am cook and am writing this while my beans are boiling and pears stewing for dinner. We use no tea or coffee [or sugar; all slave-grown products] and take our food cool." Cool food was another Graham idea; he thought hot food and spicy flavors were overstimulating.

"It so happens," Angelina wrote to Smith, "that labor (planting a garden) gives Theodore such an appetite that everything is sweet to him, so that my rice and asparagus, potatoes, mush, and Indian bread [made of rye and cornmeal] all taste well, though some might think them not fit to eat." Even when she burned a pot of apples, Theodore insisted they were good. Their guests, however, found the menus somewhat lacking.

Sarah wrote to Smith about two visitors who arrived from the city just as the little family sat down for a simple meal of rice and molasses. "With bread and milk," Sarah said, "and pie without shortening, and hominy, we contrived to give them enough and as they were pretty hungry they partook of it with tolerable appetite."

Sarah Mapps Douglass visited, staying just one night. Her thank-you letter, mentioning their hospitality and "Christian conduct"—as though they were fulfilling an obligation rather than welcoming a friend—upset both sisters. "It seemed to me thy proposal 'to spend a day' with us," Sarah Grimké said, "was made under a little feeling something like this: 'Well, after all, I am not quite certain I [as an African American] shall be an acceptable visitor.'"

Angelina wrote that both she and Theodore were surprised and disappointed with just one day's stay and that she hoped Douglass would bring her mother for the next visit and stay for a week. After that reassurance, the Douglasses and the sisters visited each other's homes frequently.

When they weren't working or entertaining, the new family wrote numerous letters, and the sisters helped Theodore revise his pamphlet *The Bible Against Slavery*. Sarah, who much preferred writing to speaking, worked on women's rights essays. The trio read newspapers, too, and letters from friends, learning that the Pennsylvania Hall fire in Philadelphia had increased support for the abolitionist movement. Even pro-slavery supporters had been shocked by the blaze and the accompanying violence, which made some of them rethink the violence of slavery.

Throughout the summer, all three received invitations from anti-slavery organizations to reenter the lecture field. Theodore declined, as his throat seemed permanently damaged. He could talk quietly but, in this time before microphones, could no longer project his voice to an audience. The sisters also turned down the requests. "Great disappointment," a friend wrote, "was felt by all who had once listened to them that they should have retired from public work."

But the sisters did not consider themselves to be permanently retired from the lecture circuit. "I cannot tell thee how I love this private life," Angelina wrote to a friend. She was willing to enter public life again, she said, if the Lord called her to it. And her husband would help, she felt sure. "My dear Theodore entertains the noblest views on the rights and responsibilities of woman, and will never lay a straw in the way of my lecturing," she said.

But her new life came first. "We keep no help," she wrote to another friend, "& therefore are filling up the appropriate 'sphere of woman' to admiration, in the kitchen with baking pans & pots & steamers, &c, & in the parlor and chambers with the broom & the duster. Indeed, I think our enemies w[ou]ld rejoice, could they only look in on us from day to day & see us in our domestic life, instead of lecturing to *promiscuous* audiences."

Sarah was glad that the Lord had not, so far, called her back to a public role. "It looks like almost too great a blessing for us three to be together in some quiet, humble habitation," she wrote to Jane Smith, "living to the glory of God . . . to be spiritually united, and to be pursuing with increasing zeal the great work of the abolition of slavery."

And indeed, their next abolitionist project would require great zeal.

CHAPTER 16
Crushing the Viper

1838–1839

"I do not think we ever labored more assiduously for the slave than we have done this fall and winter," Sarah wrote to a friend. "... We have been almost too busy to look out on the beautiful winter landscape, and have been wrought up by our daily researches to a frenzy of justice, intolerance, and enthusiasm to crush the viper that is eating out the vitals of the nation."

The viper was slavery, and the plan to crush it took the form of a new project from the activist family of three: a documentary study of the institution as it existed in the United States. To be published as a book-length pamphlet, *American Slavery as It Is: Testimony of a Thousand Witnesses* was designed to make the South "condemn itself" through the printed word.

"Reader," Theodore wrote in the introduction: "you are [seated] as a juror to try a plain case and bring in an honest verdict. The question of issue is not one of law, but of fact—'What is the actual condition of the slaves in the United States?'... TWENTY-SEVEN HUNDRED THOUSAND PERSONS in this country, men, women, and children, are in

SLAVERY. Is slavery, as a condition for human beings, good, bad, or indifferent?"

To answer that question, he sent lithographed (lithography was a new printing method) letters to abolitionists across the country, asking them to request reports from ministers, teachers, lawyers, physicians, and other respected people who could provide "facts and testimony respecting the condition of slaves, in *all respects* . . . their food, (kinds, quality, and quantity,) clothing, lodging, dwellings, hours of labor and rest, kinds of labor, with the mode of exaction, supervision &c.—the number and time of meals each day, treatment when sick, regulations respecting their social intercourse, marriage and domestic ties, the system of torture to which they are subjected . . . and *in detail*, their *intellectual* and *moral* condition."

Some people did write, but much of the information Theodore used came from Southern newspapers collected by the New York Commercial Society Reading Room. The library kept these publications for a month, then sold them for scrap. Theodore bought the 1837–1839 back issues of daily papers from many Southern cities. Then Angelina and Sarah took over, glad to have a project to work on at home, on their kitchen table. "Those dear souls," Theodore wrote later, "spent six months, averaging more than six hours a day, in searching through thousands upon thousands of Southern newspapers, marking and cutting out facts of slave-holding disclosures for the book."

"We will prove," Theodore wrote in the introduction, "that the slaves in the United States are treated with barbarous inhumanity." Two of the

> *"We will prove that the slaves in the United States are treated with barbarous inhumanity."*
> —THEODORE WELD

thousand witnesses he quoted in the book were Sarah and Angelina, who provided descriptions of their experiences with slavery when they lived in South Carolina.

Sarah told of a woman, a member of "one of the first families in Charleston," who bragged to her of improving the already dreaded torture, often imposed upon enslaved people, of standing on one foot and holding the other foot in the hand. This woman added a strap, "contrived to fasten around the ankle and pass around the neck; so that the least weight of the foot resting on the strap would choke the person. The pain occasioned by this unnatural position was great; and when continued, as it sometimes was, for an hour or more, produced intense agony."

Angelina told of visiting a Charleston woman and hearing "her daughters disputing, whether their mother did right or wrong, to send the slave *children*, (whom she sent out to sweep chimneys) to the work house to be whipped if they did not bring in their wages regularly. This woman moved in the most fashionable circle of Charleston. The income of her family was derived mostly from the hire [renting out for their wages] of their slaves, about one hundred in number. Their luxuries were blood-bought luxuries indeed."

Angelina also wrote about her family, disguising identities but giving accounts that match entries in her diary, where she named names. She told of a religious society member [her mother] who "used to keep cowhides [whips], or small paddles (called 'pancake sticks,') in four different apartments in her house; so that when she wished to punish, or to have punished, any of her slaves, she might not have the trouble of sending for an instrument of torture." Often, Angelina said, her slaves "were flogged *every day*; particularly the young slaves about the house, whose faces were slapped, or their hands beat with the 'pancake stick,' for every trifling offence—and often for no fault

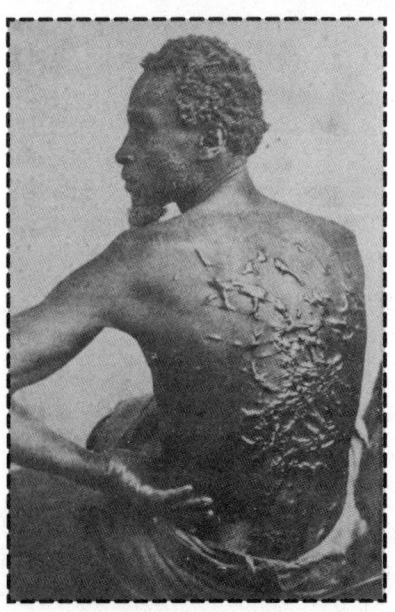

Photographer Mathew Brady took this 1863 picture of a man known only as "Peter" who escaped enslavement in Louisiana and enlisted in a Black Union regiment. The photo, reprinted on cards and in magazines, caused a sensation as visual proof of the brutality of slavery.

at all." This woman whipped her slaves, Angelina explained, in the same room where she prayed at the family altar.

American Slavery as It Is described many methods of torturing enslaved people: branding; flogging; having wounds rubbed with red pepper, salt, and turpentine; being made to wear iron collars, chains, fetters, and handcuffs; amputations; knocking out eyes and teeth; being placed in stocks or torn to pieces by dogs; or being burned alive, starved, or shot to death.

Some newspaper advertisements seeking runaways were reprinted in the book. One from Alabama offered "Ten dollars reward for my woman Siby, *very much scarred about the neck and ears by whipping.*"

Others sought to return runaways to their enslavers. In Mississippi a sheriff wrote: "Was committed to jail a negro man, says his name is Josiah, his back very much scarred by the whip, and *branded on the thigh and hips in three or four places, thus (J.M.) the rim of his right ear has been bit or cut off.*"

Others advertised enslaved workers who could be hired (and their wages paid to white enslavers). A Virginia paper printed, "NEGRO HIRINGS. Will be offered for hire, at Captain

Long's Hotel, a number of SLAVES—men, women, boys and girls—belonging to the orphans of George Ash, deceased."

Still others offered individuals. A New Orleans advertisement read: "NEGROES FOR SALE.—A negro woman, 24 years of age, and has two children, one eight and the other three years. Said negroes will be sold SEPARATELY or together as *desired*. The woman is a good seamstress. She will be sold low for cash, or *exchanged for* groceries."

Several Charleston newspapers offered group sales, such as this one:

> *120 Negroes for Sale—The subscriber has* just arrived from Petersburg, Virginia, *with one hundred twenty* likely young negroes *of both sexes and every description, which he offers for sale on the most reasonable terms.*
>
> *The lot now on hand consists of plough boys, several likely and well-qualified house servants of both sexes, several* women with children, small girls *suitable for nurses, and several small boys without their mothers. Planters and traders are earnestly requested to give the subscriber a call previously to making purchases elsewhere, as he is enabled and will sell as cheap, or cheaper, than can be sold by any other person in the trade.*

After Sarah and Angelina sorted the materials into categories, Theodore put them together, writing commentary to link the different topics. Angelina recopied the manuscript from Theodore's poor handwriting into her more proper penmanship. She may have edited the text too. It's hard to know who did what, since Theodore, who never sought personal fame, insisted on publishing the book anonymously, but the creators' identities were well known in the abolitionist community.

"After the work was finished," Theodore wrote to a friend, "we were curious to know how many newspapers had been examined. So we went up to our attic and took an inventory of bundles, as they were packed heap upon heap. When our count had reached *twenty thousand* newspapers, we said: 'There, let that suffice.'" Eventually, he moved the papers to the Anti-Slavery Society offices, where, as advertised at the front of the book, "Those who think the atrocities, which [these newspaper articles] describe, incredible, are invited to [visit] and read for themselves."

Published in the summer of 1839, *American Slavery as It Is* sold for thirty-seven and a half cents a copy. Most Northerners, including abolitionists, had never heard such gruesome details as those described in the book. Mainstream newspapers found it too shocking and divisive to cover, or perhaps too damaging to their readers who benefited from unpaid labor. If the book had been about slavery in other countries, the *New York American* said, it would have received wide publicity, "but when the South struts menacingly before their vision, how many editors, even those of religious journals . . . have the courage of a kitten to cry *mew*?"

Theodore sent copies of the book to the Southern newspapers quoted in it, with their names marked. In *The Emancipator*, the newspaper of the American Anti-Slavery Society, he urged people to buy the book. It would demolish arguments, he said, "that American slavery is mild, and the slaves well treated, and well off. Let our southern visitors meet it wherever they go. Many of them will, doubtless, be surprised to find their own names and deeds recorded in its faithful pages."

Despite limited reviews, *American Slavery as It Is* sold more than one hundred thousand copies within a year in the United States and Britain, and it has kept selling ever since. *American Slavery as It Is* and *Uncle Tom's Cabin*, published more than a decade later in 1852, became known as the twin bibles of the abolitionist crusade.

Not everyone welcomed the controversial book. Mrs. Mary Grimké died at the age of seventy-five just as *American Slavery as It Is* was published. "Our beloved mother . . . is *dead*," Theodore wrote to a fellow abolitionist, "died a *slaveholder*, obdurate [stubborn] to the last. Dear A. and S. are deep in anguish, but are sweetly upstaid by Jesus." Mary's will left $1,000 to each of her sons and family keepsakes to her daughters, with more money to be divided among the children after the estate was settled.

American Slavery as It Is outraged Sarah and Angelina's siblings, who recognized family incidents in it. Anna, who had gone to Charleston to help care for their mother, wrote to Angelina with details of the death (now lost), adding that she was glad Mary had been spared by not knowing about this "last infamous publication."

But their mother did know of the forthcoming book and of their testimonies in it; Sarah had written to her about it before it was published. "I am indeed sorry," Angelina wrote to Anna, "for thee if thou canst for one moment believe that in writing these testimonies we aimed any 'envenomed shafts' at the Mother who bore us—No! No! We wrote them to show the awful havoc which arbitrary power makes in human hearts and to excite a holy

> *"We wrote them to show the awful havoc which arbitrary power makes in human hearts and to excite a holy indignation against an institution which degrades the oppressor as well as the oppressed."*
> —ANGELINA GRIMKÉ

indignation against an *institution* which degrades the *oppressor* as well as the oppressed."

She felt sad that her other sisters had not written to her too. "I am very glad to hear Mother left me her watch," she told Anna, "and hope Sisters will be careful to send it to me by some *safe* opportunity. I knew she intended doing so, for *she knew* I loved and honored her as a parent tho' I felt bound in Christian and filial faithfulness to pursue the course I have, and to rebuke, exhort and entreat her on account of her sins; and surely *she knew* and *all* her children knew that there was none who would do or suffer more for her than my precious sister Sarah."

Anna suggested that Angelina, too, had committed cruelties against enslaved people, insisting that Angelina was no more innocent than anyone described in the book. She, too, had benefited from slavery.

If these could be established, Angelina replied, and if she remembered them, she would be glad to publish them. "I have no wish to cover up my own sins," she wrote, "but will make use of it as an additional evidence of the horrible effects of the system."

Some abolitionists thought the book misguided, saying if Theodore wanted to help the movement, he should be accepting new assignments from the Anti-Slavery Society instead of publishing. If he were unable to speak, they thought, he could travel to recruit new agents, join the board of directors, or go to England to meet with abolitionists there. Declining these suggestions, Theodore offered a new idea: "getting into the lecturing field intelligent colored men [he gave six specific names and suggested finding twenty more] *as lecturers*. . . . They could do more in three months to kill prejudice (and our cause moves only as fast as that dies) than all our operations up to now. Besides a colored man who is eloquent will in all parts of the North draw larger audiences than if white, in most places far larger."

Although the sisters continued to decline speaking invitations, Sarah attended an anti-slavery convention in Philadelphia that September. Angelina wrote to her, describing her happy times alone with her husband but saying she missed her, and Theodore added a postscript saying the same.

In May 1839, both sisters traveled to Philadelphia for the third Anti-Slavery Convention of American Women, but ultimately they did not attend because Angelina fell ill. The sisters stayed three weeks at Jane Smith's home while she recovered.

Meanwhile, Sarah likely met with Sarah Mapps Douglass, as they were working together on a project to document prejudice against people of color by American Quakers. British abolitionist Elizabeth Pease had asked the Grimké sisters for information about discriminatory practices in the United States, hoping that British Friends could use the material to pressure the American organization to reform.

Sarah Mapps Douglass provided material for the forty-page *Letter on the Subject of Prejudice Against Colour Amongst the Society of Friends*

Elizabeth Pease was a British Quaker, abolitionist, and suffragist. Although she corresponded frequently with Sarah and Angelina, she never met them in person.

Crushing the Viper 151

in the United States, sent from Sarah to Pease. Identities were protected, but the letter included this statement about Grace Douglass: "A Female of Colour who has been for years convinced of the principles of Friends,—has adopted their dress and language, and goes to their meetings constantly,—*has been advised not to apply to be received into Membership, as she would be REJECTED.* This advice has been given in tenderness, to spare her feelings, but I regret that she abided by it."

Because Grace Douglass could not become a member, her children, like all Black children, were barred from the Quaker-run schools she wanted them to attend. She bore her troubles quietly, but later her daughter Sarah Mapps Douglass complained directly to American publications about her mother's treatment. When a correspondent to an Orthodox Quaker newspaper claimed that Black people were not discriminated against in seating or membership but preferred "their own" churches, with music and excitement, Sarah Mapps Douglass responded, "I myself know some, whose hearts yearn for the quiet of your worshipping places, and who love the 'still small voice' better than harp or viol." Recalling her own feelings of sitting on "the negro bench," she said, "I remember well, wishing, (with the 'foolishness that is bound in the heart of a child') that the meeting house would fall down, or that Friends would forbid our coming, thinking then that my mother would not persist in going among them."

Sarah and Angelina continued to write for abolitionist publications, and they visited neighbors in New Jersey to obtain signatures on a petition to end slavery in the District of Columbia. The task wasn't easy. "One woman," Sarah said, "told me she had rather see the slaves all shot than liberated, another said she would sooner sign a petition to have them all hung than set free."

But they kept trying. Petitions, which by 1837 had become the major form of abolitionist activity, were still the only group action by which women could communicate with politicians. Petitioners sent so many signatures to Congress that each year from 1836 to 1840 the House of Representatives passed an act to table (postpone discussion on) all petitions about slavery. This "gag law" actually encouraged petitions, from abolitionists and also from citizens who protested losing an important right, the right to free speech.

In the fall of 1839, deciding they needed household help, Angelina and Sarah sent for Betsy Dawson, their former servant and wedding guest. "I cannot tell thee how thankful we are that our heavenly Father has put it in our power to have one who was once a slave in our family to sit at our table and be with us as a sister cherished," Sarah wrote to a friend. "I don't know what M.C. [a friend from New York] thought of our having her at table and in our parlor just like one of ourselves."

Sarah, Angelina, and Betsy knew and cared for one another, and the sisters had realized they would soon need help with a new project. Angelina was pregnant.

CHAPTER 17
The Woman Question

1839–1841

On December 14, 1839, Angelina gave birth to a nine-pound baby boy. A midwife and Betsy Dawson helped with the birth, with Sarah and Theodore, unusual for a husband at this time, present in the room. Charles Stuart Faucheraud Weld was named for a beloved abolitionist friend of Theodore's (Charles Stuart) and for Angelina's father (Faucheraud). The new mother suffered from mastitis, an inflammation of the breast, and could not nurse her child. Disappointed, she fed him formula made of sweetened cow's milk diluted with water.

As the youngest in her family, Angelina had no experience with infants, so she consulted advice books on how to care for one. Dietician Sylvester Graham warned against overfeeding. Andrew Combes, author of *Physiological and Moral Management of Infancy*, advised training infants to a strict, regular schedule for eating, sleeping, and bathing. But baby Charles did not cooperate. He slept when he felt tired and cried constantly after meager portions of formula five times a day. His parents thought he had colic, or stomach pain.

Sarah loved babies. Gladly, she cared for him while Angelina recovered from the birth. Her experience with helping raise six younger siblings, including Angelina, encouraged her to experiment. When Angelina wasn't present, she fed the baby as much as he wanted. Charles grew plump and happy. "Thou wilt not know him," Sarah wrote to a friend, "his wrinkled forehead and pallid face have given place to a smooth brow and a pair of cheeks that sometimes vie with the opening rose; his face is always covered with smiles and he looks as happy as a little angel."

Angelina was amazed by the experience of motherhood. "The idea of a baby," she confessed, "exercising moral influence never came into my mind until I felt its power on my own heart. I used to think that all a parent's reward for early care and anxiety was reaped in after-life, save the enjoyment of an infant as a pretty plaything. But the Lord has taught me differently, and woe be unto me if I do not profit by the instructions of this little teacher sent from God."

In March 1840, the family, including Betsy Dawson, moved to a fifty-acre farm on the Passaic River in Belleville, New Jersey. Sarah called it "a sweet little river, gliding noiselessly by thro[ugh] rich meadow land."

Though they had lost their spectacular view of the Hudson, the new place had its charms. The original two-story, five-room stone farmhouse, formerly owned by Revolutionary War General Nathanael Greene, had a large wooden addition in back. A stone wall around the front yard separated it from the highway below and the river beyond. Two enormous weeping willows stood guard at the gate, and the grounds were shaded by spruces, hemlocks, maples, and walnut trees. The house had a forty-eight-foot piazza (the Charleston term for a covered porch), its pillars wrapped with climbing roses. To the north was a woodlot, on the south a garden, and to the west a grassy lot enclosed by a lilac hedge.

Theodore and the sisters bought the farm for $5,750, all the cash they could scrape together. The house was in good repair, but the barn, fences, and corncrib needed work. Lewis Tappan loaned them money for a cow and chickens, manure, horse feed, and fencing, to be repaid after the sisters received the inheritances expected from their mother's will. Sarah still received a modest income from her father's will, but a banker with whom Angelina had invested had lost all her money and his own in the Panic of 1837. This national economic crisis led to a six-year depression that affected the Anti-Slavery Society too. Donations dropped. The organization still owed Theodore back wages, and in Belleville the family realized that they would have to rely on Sarah's inheritance until Theodore could support the family by farming.

Arthur Tappan and his brother Lewis were silk importers, newspaper owners, and famous abolitionists. After pro-slavery mobs destroyed Arthur's Connecticut summer home and damaged his New York house, he hired armed guards to protect his store.

Plunging into the work full tilt, he spent twelve hours a day plowing; hoeing; felling trees, splitting rails, and digging postholes to build a fence; and unearthing and hauling rocks. By summer he had planted the garden with sweet corn, beans, potatoes, beets, and onions. In the fields he grew oats, corn, potatoes, beans, squash, and pumpkins, enough crops to eat and sell.

Until the harvest, the family was strapped for cash and food. Nevertheless, they took in an ailing nephew, plus two impoverished friends from Charleston, for an entire year. They housed and helped Stephen, a man formerly enslaved by their father, by then physically and mentally disabled due to a life of frequent beatings by their brother Henry. They hosted Jane Smith, Theodore's parents and siblings, various missionaries and college students, and new neighbors who seemed needy. Some guests stayed for months, and there was a constant flow of daily visitors too. "Oh how I long to have our little family alone to sit down without any stranger at our meals," Angelina mused when she felt tired.

All rejoiced when Theodore's best friend, Henry Stanton, brought his bride, Elizabeth Cady Stanton, to meet them. She recalled the visit:

> *In company with my husband and Charles Stuart, a Scotch Abolitionist, we took one of those long closely-covered stages peculiar to New Jersey, for a twelve miles drive to Belleville, where at the door of an old Dutch-built stone house, Theodore Weld and the famous daughters of South Carolina gave us a welcome. There was nothing attractive at first sight in those plain, frail women, except their rich voices, fluent language, and Angelina's fine dark eyes. The house with its wide hall, spacious apartments, deep windows, and small panes of glass was severely destitute of all tasteful, womanly touches, and though neat and orderly, had a cheerless atmosphere.*

She didn't realize that the sisters, who were not particularly interested in food, ate little and were always thin. They did not believe in ornamentation of clothing or houses. Elizabeth, who loved frilly clothes and a good, hot meal, complained of the menus. The "peculiar table arrangements," she said, consisted of

Elizabeth Cady Stanton, shown here in 1854, wanted to be a lawyer, like her father, but women were not allowed in the profession.

"cold dishes without a whiff of heat or steam" and no coffee or tea. "But," she wrote later, "the chilling environments of these noble people were modified by the sincere hospitality with which we were received." After dinner, she said: "the high discourse was slightly interrupted by the appearance of the infant, Charles Stuart Weld, and his formal presentation to the distinguished gentleman after whom he was named. . . . How changed was the atmosphere of that home to me next day. True, there were still no pictures on the walls, but the beautiful boy in his bath, the sunlight on his golden hair, with some new grace or trick each day, surpassed what any [paint]brush could trace."

By the end of her three-day visit, she said, she had learned a great deal about the abolitionist movement. The three women parted on intimate terms.

In that month, May 1840, the American Anti-Slavery Society split in two over "the woman question." When the national organization formed in 1833, the founders, all male, expected women to start their own societies. But in 1839 the Massachusetts Anti-Slavery Society admitted women as members, allowing them to hold office. William Lloyd Garrison, always the most extreme of abolitionists, demanded equal rights for women. Of course, the Grimké sisters agreed with him, as did Lucretia Mott, Lydia Maria Child, and Abby Kelley.

Theodore, who believed in equal rights for women, had nevertheless worked closely with the more conservative New York members of the society, including Arthur and Lewis Tappan, Henry Stanton, James Birney, Elizur Wright, Gerrit Smith, and John Greenleaf Whittier. None of them thought that women should be members, let alone equal members. There was a philosophical difference in the groups' approaches too. In New England, Garrison led a moral crusade against slavery, appealing to the conscience of the nation. In New York, abolitionist leaders wanted a more practical, political kind of movement: building alliances with other groups and putting up anti-slavery candidates for elected office.

For the May 1840 American Anti-Slavery national convention, Garrison chartered a boat to bring 450 of his supporters, both white and Black, from Boston to New York to dominate the meeting. Hearing of this plan, Arthur Tappan, who, as president, was supposed to preside, refused to attend, instead resigning his office. Garrison and his supporters elected a new president from their side: Francis Jackson.

Jackson nominated several men from both sides, including Lewis Tappan, to the business committee, and then he added Abby Kelley to the list. Kelley, who modeled herself on the Grimké sisters, had earned a reputation like theirs. Because she spoke to mixed audiences and supported women's rights, newspapers called her a harlot, an Amazon, a sorcerer, and a temptress. After considerable discussion, she won confirmation to the committee; the vote was 557 to 441.

Lewis Tappan objected to a committee that included women, saying it contradicted the Bible. Kelley responded, "In Congress the masters speak while the slaves are denied a voice. I rise because I am not a slave." At that, the New York delegates walked out.

The Tappans formed a new organization, the American and Foreign Anti-Slavery Society, excluding women. Garrison's supporters retained the name American Anti-Slavery Society and included female members. In Belleville, the sisters and Theodore, with friends on both sides, tried to remain neutral but were dismayed by the split. "We mourn that there are divisions amongst us," Sarah said.

In June 1840, both organizations sent delegates to the World Anti-Slavery Convention in London, England. Garrison and Lucretia Mott, among others, represented the American Anti-Slavery Society while Henry Stanton spoke for the New York–based organization. Elizabeth Cady Stanton accompanied her husband as a guest to the convention, where she met Mott. The two women took an instant liking to each other, especially after the convention refused to accept Mott and other American female delegates as members.

"Dear sisters, Sarah & Angelina," Elizabeth Cady Stanton wrote them from London,

> *Yesterday the convention closed, & I hasten to redeem my promise to tell you something about it. We send you papers containing a minute account of all the proceedings, therefore I shall be very general in what I write. . . . The woman's rights question besides monopolizing one whole day by being often referred to, created some little discord. . . . Garrison arrived on the fourth day of the meeting, but as the female delegates were not received and were not permitted to take their seat as delegates, he refused to take his, consequently his voice was not heard throughout the meeting.*

Garrison chose to sit in solidarity with the rejected women delegates and guests, including Stanton, in the visitors' section.

Americans Lucretia Mott and Elizabeth Cady Stanton met the British activist Elizabeth Pease at the 1840 World Anti-Slavery Convention in London. Painting by Benjamin Robert Haydon.

The convention is still remembered chiefly for the way in which it mistreated women.

"Lucretia Mott has just [been] giving me a long message for you," Stanton wrote, "which condensed is that she thinks you have both been in a state of retiracy long enough, & that it is not right for you to be still, longer, that you should either write for the public or speak out for *oppressed woman*. Sarah in particular she thinks should appear in public again as she has no duties to prevent her. She says a great struggle is at hand & that all the friends of freedom for woman must rally round the *Garrison standard*."

While the sisters understood why Mott wanted them to return to public speaking, their home lives were about to get busier. On January 3, 1841, Angelina gave birth to a second son, Theodore Grimké Weld.

CHAPTER 18
The Whole Truth

1841-1844

"I cannot tell thee what a comfort it is to me to nurse him," Angelina wrote to Jane Smith about baby Theodore. Angelina had a young English nurse to help with his birth and her recovery; nevertheless, her health deteriorated. Sarah wrote to a friend that her sister had a prolapsed uterus and a hernia; either these or some other condition caused intermittent pain and weakness for the rest of her life. Such conditions are treatable today but were not then, and they were also not discussed in polite company.

Still, Angelina did her best. With Sarah she cared for the children, cooked, and cleaned, helped by Betsy Dawson and sometimes other servants. Guests made more work, but the family never turned anyone away. They took in an ailing missionary, back from Jamaica, nursing him until his death. Relatives visited, along with famous abolitionists and Theodore's college friends. The house was always full, and the conversation interesting. Many noticed that Theodore's voice was improving, so much that he was able to give a speech at an abolition meeting on July 4.

Angelina, too, thought of returning to public speaking. "My restless, ambitious temper," she wrote, "so different from dear Sister's, craves high duties and high attainments." But when she discussed her desires with Theodore and Sarah (all three having agreed to tell the whole truth, even if it might "grieve and mortify and disappoint and even afflict each other"), they said she craved acclaim, a sinful desire. Now she pondered: should she heed her own feelings or believe the two people she loved most?

Angelina felt another conflict too. She loved Charles, her first son, so dearly that when baby Theodore was born, she feared she would not be able to love him as much. Then she surprised herself by doing so. But loving them and caring for them were two different things. It was "an inexpressibly great trial to take care of my children," she told Theodore, ". . . a continual weariness to me, I had no pleasure in it. . . . I longed to sit down at my ease, read & enjoy the luxury of cultivating my mind."

Luckily, Sarah did enjoy caring for the boys. Both parents were grateful to her (their father did not particularly relish spending time with babies either), especially when Theodore accepted a temporary job offer in Washington, DC.

In 1840 the House of Representatives passed a permanent gag law that prevented petitions against slavery from being introduced on the House floor. This rule was supposedly to save time, since all petitions demanded the same thing—an end to slavery—but really it was passed by the proslavery majority to prevent any discussion of the matter. Ten congressional representatives, all members of the minority abolitionist Whig Party, decided to fight back. They set up an anti-slavery research bureau and invited Theodore to take charge.

The committee covered Theodore's travel, room, and

board but could not pay a salary. Angelina, who thought farming a waste of Theodore's talents, encouraged him to go, even though she feared he might be assassinated in a city where slavery was legal. She took over management of the farm.

Arriving in Washington on December 30, 1841, Theodore lived in a boardinghouse across the street from the Capitol. His landlady employed eight servants: five free Black people and three enslaved servants who worked on hire. Since the boarders were all abolitionists, Theodore wondered if their talk might incite the enslaved servants to run away. On weekdays he did research at the Library of Congress. "In each of the alcoves," he wrote to Angelina, "are tables with pens, ink and paper for copying, which are at the service of any person introduced by a member of Congress."

"Beloved," Angelina wrote to him, "I miss you more than I can express. I can't think of you or talk of you without my heart and eye filling." She wrote of her worry, that it would soon be time for her to start teaching their children and that she lacked the proper education to do so. Theodore responded with specific advice (he always had plenty) and promises to bring home the educational toys, books, and counting slates Angelina had asked for.

Sarah wrote to Theodore, too, usually cheerfully, but in one letter she told him the "whole truth" about himself, that he was "selfish, inconsiderate, slovenly of dress, unneat in appearance, and of careless table manners; in general, he disregarded the amenities." He left clothes and papers strewn about for the sisters to pick up. He was kind to poor strangers, Sarah said, but not equally considerate to his own family. She ended her letter with words of love, as he had ended his "whole truth" letter to her, five years earlier, when he told her that her public speaking was "monotonous and heavy."

It's not known how Theodore felt about Sarah's critique. Free from family responsibilities, he enjoyed life in Washington. In the evenings he met with congressional representatives, including a former president, now a representative, John Quincy Adams of Massachusetts. Adams had presented thousands of petitions against slavery in the House, upsetting the pro-slavery congressional representatives, who formed the majority. Adams realized that the gag law created a conflict between two rights in the United States Constitution.

William Lloyd Garrison took the Grimké sisters to meet Representative John Quincy Adams (*above*) at the start of their New England speaking tour. Five years later, Theodore worked with the former president in Washington.

The First Amendment says: "Congress shall make no law . . . abridging the freedom of speech . . . or the right of the people . . . to petition the Government for a redress of grievances." But the Constitution also grants each part of the legislature the ability to manage its proceedings.

Adams managed to get around the gag law by introducing petitions from women, who were not bound by the law because they could not vote. Similarly, he introduced petitions signed by enslaved people, who were not even considered citizens. Then he started introducing "prayers" instead of petitions, that all would enjoy their God-given rights. He waged a relentless campaign for free speech and the right to petition, always speaking also against slavery with facts and figures provided by Theodore. In the end he transformed the fight from a battle over slavery petitions, and whether slavery was right or wrong, to a debate over petitions as freedom of speech.

Southern congressional representatives, claiming Adams had dishonored them by saying slavery was wrong, moved to censure him. Demanding the right to defend himself, he spoke for almost two weeks until the weary Southerners withdrew their complaint.

"The triumph of Mr. A[dams] is complete," Theodore wrote to Angelina. "This is the first victory over the slaveholders *in a* [legislative] *body* ever yet achieved since the foundation of the government, and from this time, their downfall *takes its date*." It would take two more years to eliminate the gag law entirely.

By April 1842, Theodore was back on the farm, giving weekly anti-slavery lectures in New Jersey. Lewis Tappan tried to convince him to accept the ministry of a church, but Theodore declined. Increasingly, the Grimké-Weld family believed that organized religion stood between God and believers. At home they continued private prayers, services, and lessons, each leading in turn.

Invitations to speak continued to arrive. Some friends tried to pressure them back into the movement. "Where are Theodore Weld and his wife and Sarah M. Grimké?" William Lloyd Garrison demanded in *The Liberator* in August 1842. "Once the land was shaken by their free spirits but now they are neither seen nor felt." After that, Angelina stopped reading his newspaper.

In December 1842, Theodore returned to his job in Washington, living in the same boardinghouse. "*All* the table waiters from last year [inspired by talk of abolition] have *run away*,"

By 1800, most Black American sailors were free. Some carried "Seamen's Protection Passes," issued by the US Customs Service, giving detailed physical descriptions to identify them. Still, they were unsafe in Southern ports.

he wrote to Angelina. "Mrs. Sprigg [the landlady] thinks it quite unsafe to have slaves in such close contact with Abolitionists, so she has taken care to get *free* colored servants in their places!"

In 1843 Theodore's work would vary. He fought reimbursement claims from enslavers whose workers were killed in government service. He also asked Congress to protect free Black sailors in the ports of states where slavery was legal. These sailors were in danger of being kidnapped and enslaved when they docked in slave states. And Theodore tried to convince the government to repeal a Florida law that barred freed Black people from immigrating to the territory. (Florida was not yet a state.) These were important causes, Angelina thought, and although she was pregnant again, she had urged him to go back to Washington.

In January she wrote she would buy a sleigh for eight dollars, since their four-wheeled surrey was useless in the snow.

"Dearest," Theodore replied, "suppose we let that be till my return. A sleigh is an article that may look very well when it is good for nothing. I should wish to examine it very closely."

Five days later, he wrote, "I am *not* sorry to hear that you have purchased the sleigh, but think you had better *defer* getting the bells [to warn of the sleigh's approach] in the present state of our funds. As you will ride only in the day time, Benjamin [the horse] can easily see persons in the road, and with a little care will put no one in peril."

Most letters from this time concerned their sons. As soon as the boys learned to walk, both turned to "Aunt Sai" instead of their mother. Worried that Sarah was coming between her and her children, Angelina suggested dividing their care, one sister taking mornings and the other, afternoons. But this plan failed as Angelina's pregnancy progressed. Exhausted and struggling to run the farm, she could not maintain her half of the schedule.

Sarah adored her nephews, and Angelina's poor health and the boys' needs gave her good reasons not to return to public speaking. With Angelina, she adopted an air of self-sacrifice, but to Theodore she was upbeat. "I'm sure if you looked in upon the boys and myself," she wrote to him, "when we are having a game of romps, you would not think there was much to call forth sympathy."

But three-year-old Charles worried them all. He had temper tantrums, often taking his rage out on his baby brother. As punishment, Angelina locked him in a closet. When that method of reforming him failed, she switched to lecturing and emphasizing his good qualities. From Washington, Theodore offered advice: Encourage him to share and teach him about religion and the plight of enslaved people.

Angelina despaired. "My soul is weary," she wrote, feeling guilty for her impatience in dealing with "our precious little ones." Feeling depressed and worthless, she sought relief in the new, popular teachings of William Miller, a Baptist minister. Millerism taught that the second coming of Jesus Christ (when some Christians believed that he would return to Earth and judge humans there) would occur in 1843 or 1844. Believing that doomsday (the day of final judgment) was near helped Angelina to think less about the present. Theodore thought Millerism was upsetting his wife; he and Sarah both worried about her mental state.

In February Angelina suffered a difficult miscarriage. Theodore rushed home from Washington and declined further requests to work there, wishing to stay closer to his family. When Miller's doomsday dates passed without disasters, Angelina concluded that the second coming would have to be in people's hearts.

Meanwhile, the Belleville household expanded despite the miscarriage. Anna Grimké Frost and her daughter Mary Anna Frost Haskell (now married) spent the winter there. A nephew and elderly aunt and uncle came to stay too. Sometimes the household included lecturers who came to train under Theodore. "We know not whom else the Lord may send us," Angelina wrote to Jane Smith, "and only pray Him to help us fulfil his will towards all whose lot may be cast among us."

Throughout the spring, Theodore planted a hundred peach trees and a similar number of apples, pears, plums, and cherries. By the summer of 1841 Angelina was pregnant again, trying to rest while Sarah ran the household. In August Theodore moved his parents, brother, and sister to a small house nearby. All were dependent on him. They had enough to eat, but with so many mouths to feed, Theodore did not have much harvest left over to sell.

On March 22, 1844, Angelina gave birth to a daughter, Sarah Grimké Weld. Sarah was her only attendant. Angelina calmly gave instructions, telling her sister how to tie the umbilical cord. The birth was an easy one, Sarah said, "Not half as bad as the extraction of a tooth."

CHAPTER 19
The Belleville School

1844-1853

Once Theodore felt sure that Angelina and their new daughter were safe and healthy, he accepted an invitation to speak in Brooklyn, New York. There he reinjured his throat so badly that he again gave up public speaking and returned home. While he devoted himself to the farm, Angelina nursed the baby, and Sarah managed the household. Still, the anti-slavery crusade was never far from their minds.

The movement was again dividing. Some abolitionists, preaching hostility and violence toward enslavers, wanted civil war. Others thought war would be worse than slavery. As longtime pacifists, Sarah, Angelina, and Theodore believed that hating enslavers, and fighting them, would solve nothing. Slaveholders were Americans, too, they insisted.

In 1847 Sarah and Angelina's brother Frederick visited from Ohio. A judge and a staunch opponent of abolition, Frederick believed that the United States offered equal opportunity to enlightened citizens. But he thought Black people were an inferior race, incapable of civilized self-government. Angelina tried to convince him that African Americans simply needed more education.

The three siblings discussed their brother Henry. After his wife died in 1843, Henry bought a large rice plantation twenty-five miles from Charleston. Rice was by far the hardest crop to grow, and it had a high death rate for field hands. They tended the rice while standing in water, sometimes up to their chests, and they were also charged with ridding the area of alligators and water moccasins.

Henry moved there with his children and twenty enslaved servants, including Nancy Weston, the mixed-race nurse who had cared for his dying wife. Nancy became Henry's enslaved mistress. Living in a separate house, she managed his household and many aspects of work on the plantation. Henry's Charleston-based siblings, who disapproved of the relationship, wanted him to return to the city to practice law.

Despite disagreements over slavery, the Grimké brothers and sisters, North and South, maintained family ties, mostly through letters. In 1847 the family learned that Theodore had become superintendent of schools in Belleville. And he began to think of opening his own school in their large farmhouse.

Meanwhile, the flow of guests continued, at times exhausting their hosts. "I hope on," Sarah wrote, "year after year, that there will be less occasion to overexert our physical powers.... [T]his afternoon [a Sunday] we shall probably have twenty to supper." Since most of their visitors were abolitionists, Angelina and Theodore believed that by welcoming them, they were contributing to the cause.

The Grimké-Welds were pleased to see new leaders rising in the movement: Lucy Stone, the first Massachusetts woman to earn a college degree, followed in Angelina and Sarah's footsteps by becoming a professional orator. After escaping slavery

Unusually for the time, Lucy Stone declined to take her husband's name after marrying. "My name is my identity and must not be lost," she said. Other women who followed suit were known as Lucy Stoners.

in 1838, Frederick Douglass founded an abolitionist newspaper, *The North Star*, in Rochester, New York. He became an orator, too, quoting from *American Slavery as It Is* in some of his speeches.

Elizabeth Cady Stanton began taking a more active role. Like Angelina, she loved her children but did not enjoy staying home with them, especially after moving from Boston, with its active social life, to the small town of Seneca Falls in central New York. Her husband, Henry Stanton, traveled frequently on legal or abolitionist business, leaving her with their children, "unreliable" servants, and a longing for intellectual conversation.

Since 1840, when Stanton had met Lucretia Mott in London, the two women had dreamed of organizing a women's rights convention. In July 1848, Mott visited her sister, Martha Coffin Wright, who lived near Stanton. They spent a day with Stanton and two other Quaker women, discussing the idea of a meeting. The five of them planned a convention in Seneca Falls, to be held before Mott had to return to Philadelphia. Stanton wrote to Lydia Maria Child, Maria Weston Chapman, and Sarah to request letters to share at the convention.

The Seneca Falls meeting was held July 19 to 20, 1848, at the Wesleyan Chapel and attracted a crowd of three hundred. The first day was supposed to be for women only; the forty men who were admitted were asked to remain silent. On the second day, when men were allowed to speak, Lucretia Mott's husband, James, presided, as the idea of women chairing a meeting of men and women together was still considered scandalous.

The convention passed a Declaration of Sentiments. "We hold these truths to be self-evident," it said, echoing the Declaration of Independence, "that all men and women are created equal; that they are endowed by their Creator with certain inalienable rights; that among these are life, liberty, and the pursuit of happiness; that to secure these rights governments are instituted, deriving their just powers from the consent of the governed."

Eleven resolutions were offered, one adapted from a resolution Angelina had proposed in 1837 at the first Anti-Slavery Convention of American Woman. "Resolved," the new version said, "That woman has too long rested satisfied in the circumscribed limits which corrupt customs and a perverted application of the Scriptures have marked out for her, and that it is time she should move in the enlarged sphere which her great Creator has assigned her."

All the resolutions, including the new version of Angelina's, passed unanimously, except for one, offered by

After escaping enslavement in Maryland in 1838, Frederick Douglass became the editor of the *North Star* newspaper in Rochester, New York, and a famous advocate for abolition and women's rights.

Elizabeth Cady Stanton. Stanton's proposal called for women to seek the right to vote, an idea considered too radical by many. It passed by a narrow margin after Frederick Douglass, the only Black person present, spoke in its favor. He reiterated Stanton's claim that the power to choose rulers and make laws was the right by which all other rights could be secured.

Mainstream newspapers ridiculed the convention and the women behind it. "Was there ever such a dreadful revolt?" asked the *Oneida Whig* (Utica, NY), calling the convention "the most shocking and unnatural incident ever recorded in the history of womanity.... If our ladies will insist on voting and legislating, where, gentlemen, will be our dinners ... and the holes in our stockings?"

Similarly, the *Lowell (MA) Courier* reported:

The women folks have just held a Convention up in New York State, and passed a sort of "bill of rights".... They should have resolved at the same time, that it was obligatory ... upon the "lords" ... to wash dishes, scour up, be put to the tub, handle the broom, darn stockings, patch breeches, scold the servants, dress in the latest fashion, wear trinkets, look beautiful, and be as fascinating as those blessed morsels of humanity whom God gave to preserve that rough animal man, in something like a reasonable civilization.

Ignoring criticism, the planners scheduled future meetings to promote women's rights.

Three months later, in October 1848, Theodore opened a school in the Belleville house to students from several states. Starting with two boarders, then four, eventually, he enrolled twenty children, including his own. Angelina taught history and writing; her sister, drawing and French. Sarah did so reluctantly, as she did not like teaching and felt her own French was lacking. Theodore handled administration and taught all the other courses, including composition and mathematics. He still did farmwork, too, expecting students to learn specific outdoor jobs. Sarah and Angelina cooked (some students complained about the food), cleaned, washed, and mended. They also mothered the children, many of whom had never before been away from home.

A school for boys and girls together was radical for the time. Many upper-level schools limited attendance to boys, and most boys would not have wanted to attend a girls' school, which offered a watered-down education considered appropriate for females. Theodore encouraged his students to think for themselves, which was also unusual; memorization was more common. Pupils had the run of the house and the surrounding woods, where they collected insects and small animals. Some classes met on the piazza or on the flat roof of the house.

Many famous abolitionists enrolled their children, including Henry and Elizabeth Stanton (who, in 1851, would name their fourth son Theodore Weld Stanton), Martha Coffin Wright, Robert and Harriet Forten Purvis, Gerrit Smith, James Birney, and Elizur Wright. From South Carolina, Sarah and Angelina's brother Henry sent his seventeen-year-old son, Thomas. Many abolitionists began coming to Belleville not just to see the Grimké-Welds but also to visit their own children.

The students loved the school and their teachers, but Angelina, especially, was worn down by the work. In September 1849 she went to a sanitarium, a place for medical treatment, in South Orange, New Jersey. She was given a "water cure," used at that time to treat many health problems, including injuries, pain, stiffness, bruising, and various mental conditions. Patients bathed or showered in mineral water or were wrapped in wet compresses or sheets, and they drank large amounts of the local water. The family hoped this cure would improve Angelina's energy and her apparent depression.

The sanitarium, the Mountain House Spa, was like a luxurious hotel. It had private instead of shared bathrooms, which was unusual for the time. In addition to their treatments, visitors could attend concerts and participate in pseudoscientific activities. For instance, patients could consult phrenologists, who claimed to be able to analyze a person's character and ability by "reading" (feeling) the bumps and depressions on the head. Phrenologists claimed that people could improve themselves by understanding these readings. So, for example, if the "kindness area" of the skull was perceived to be smaller than average, the person could make a special effort to be kinder.

At the spa, Angelina met Andrew Jackson Davis, a self-proclaimed medium (someone who claimed he could speak with the dead) and prophet. Angelina liked his ideas: that all humans had the potential to grow and develop and that heaven was for all people, whatever their race or religion. His belief in cycles of bad times followed by good gave her hope that her unhappy life would improve.

Still she worried. "The fear often comes over me," she wrote to Theodore, "like a dark cloud, that we are not doing the will of God. We are not fulfilling our destiny and yet I cannot see anything definite—don't see any particular thing, to do."

After several months at the sanatorium, Angelina began to feel more self-confident. Now convinced that Theodore and Sarah were mistaken—that she had not sinned by seeking acclaim—she renewed her interest in the women's movement. Reading reports of the Seneca Falls Convention, she recognized some of her own ideas and wished that her name could have been attached to the Declaration of Sentiments.

As the women's movement grew, it followed patterns established by abolitionists and also by leaders in the temperance movement, which was trying to ban consumption of alcohol. In the early 1850s, all three groups joined many Northerners in horrified opposition to a package of federal laws known as the Compromise of 1850. These laws opened new Western territories to slavery if their citizens voted in favor of it. But the most shocking part of the Compromise of 1850 was the Fugitive Slave Act.

Until this time, enslaved people who escaped to free states were considered free. Then the Fugitive Slave Act required that escapees be returned, even from free states, to their enslavers. Northern officials who refused to help catch runaways could

In 1850 Theodore's brother took this picture of a meeting in Cazenovia, New York, to protest the Fugitive Slave Act. Mixed-race gatherings were still unusual and controversial at this time. Theodore sits in front of Frederick Douglass.

be fined $1,000. Anyone who provided food or shelter to a freedom seeker faced a similar fine and six months in prison. Any African American, even a free Black person, could be sent to the South on the word of someone claiming to be his or her enslaver. And if accused of the crime of escaping, they could not testify in their own defense or be tried by a jury, like other Americans, as enslaved people were not considered citizens.

Northerners, including those who previously had not cared about slavery, felt the new law compelled them to become slave catchers. After it passed, citizens in free states insisted that no more slave states be added to the Union. The Fugitive Slave Act was so extreme that it attracted new supporters to the anti-slavery movement, despite the fact that abolitionists would face arrest for helping escapees. Opposition to the law also strengthened the Underground Railroad. "It is clear to my mind," Angelina wrote to a friend, "that the Fugitive Slave Act *ought* to be, *must* be resisted even unto blood."

One author's response to the new law had a huge impact on the nation. Harriet Beecher Stowe, whom Angelina had met at Catharine Beecher's school in 1831, said she slept with a copy of *American Slavery as It Is* under her pillow while writing her best-selling novel *Uncle Tom's Cabin*. Published in 1852, the book depicted the horrors of slavery and depravity of enslavers. Banned in the South, it sold more than three hundred thousand copies in the first year. Theatrical adaptations of the book further popularized the story, which sold well in England too.

In 1853, after proslavery critics accused Stowe of inventing incidents for the novel, she published another book, *A Key to Uncle Tom's Cabin*, explaining that she had borrowed incidents from *American Slavery as It Is* and its source materials. She quoted testimony from Sarah Grimké, whom she called "an unimpeachable witness" and "a personal friend of the author."

She also noted how Theodore, Angelina, and Sarah had saved the papers they used for *American Slavery as It Is* and made them available for the public to see, to set to rest any doubts.

As the abolitionist movement grew, so did the push for women's rights. In 1851 Angelina joined Lucy Stone and Abby Kelley Foster (her married name), giving a speech at the second national women's rights convention in Worcester, Massachusetts.

In early 1852, the *Christian Inquirer* (NY) published a letter from Sarah saying that women had to agree to marriage and dependence on their husbands to ensure their survival. "Those who have long held the reins of power," she said, "and the rank of superiority, naturally look with distrust on a movement which threatens to overturn long established customs and transform the baby and the toy [the woman] into an intellectual being, desiring equal rights with themselves [men] and asserting her claim to all the immunities [protections] they enjoy."

Both sisters sent letters of support to the 1852 national women's rights convention in Syracuse, New York, and both began wearing a new style of clothing seen there. Stone, her hair bobbed short, addressed the convention wearing "reform dress," a short skirt over trousers. The shocking new fashion, which showed that women did indeed have "limbs" (*legs* was a controversial term when applied to women), was nicknamed the bloomer costume after Amelia Bloomer, a newspaper editor who helped popularize it.

In 1853 abolitionists Henry Blackwell and Samuel Dorrance visited the farm in Belleville. Blackwell, whose father was a friend of Theodore's, had fallen in love with Lucy Stone. But although the popular young orator returned his feelings, she feared marriage would require her to sacrifice her independence and her career. Blackwell wanted to ask the Welds for advice about how a marriage could work between equal partners without ending their careers.

"We first met the two ladies," Blackwell wrote to Stone of Sarah and Angelina, "draped in the Bloomer costume which I have learned to like [since Stone had started wearing it]. They were surrounded by a dozen children, three of them their own, comfortably seated on the piazza reading & enjoying themselves."

After dinner, Blackwell asked why the Grimké-Welds had withdrawn from active advocacy. His throat was the immediate cause, Theodore answered for himself, but there was more to it than that. "There is a fighting era in every one's life," he explained. "While you feel so, fight on, it is your duty & the best thing you can possibly do. But when your work in that line is done, you will reach another and a higher view." For him—and perhaps he meant the same for the sisters—the higher view meant teaching young people.

When Henry Browne Blackwell finally convinced Lucy Stone to marry him, they removed the word "obey" from the ceremony and published a pamphlet arguing for equality in marriage.

"I don't think it was *marriage*," Blackwell wrote to Stone, "which is to blame for their withdrawal from public life as so many suppose, but that it arose from a combination of physical, intellectual & moral causes quite independent of it. . . . If there ever was a true marriage it is their's. Both preserve their separate individuality perfectly & on many points differ heartily with the utmost good will."

CHAPTER 20

Splitting in Two

1853–1858

In 1852 Marcus Spring, a New York merchant and philanthropist, with his wife, Rebecca, had founded the Raritan Bay Union to build a new community. He bought 270 acres of land near Perth Amboy, New Jersey, twenty-five miles south of New York. Rebecca Spring named the estate Eagleswood.

Marcus Spring had made his fortune dealing in cotton grown by enslaved workers, but by this time, he considered himself an abolitionist and wanted to create a space where like-minded people could live together. By 1853 he had recruited thirty or forty abolitionist families, including the Grimké-Welds, to join the commune. He asked Theodore to become the director of a school for the children of residents and others. Theodore invited the sisters to teach.

The community promised less physical work for all three. Sarah was resigned to teaching although not happy about it, and she disliked the idea of communal living—sharing meals and other activities. But she agreed to move with the family once facilities were built.

Joining the association cost each adult $1,000; Angelina and Theodore had to borrow from Sarah to pay their fees. Angelina had lost her money long before, Theodore no longer had an income from the American Anti-Slavery Society, and the family had never managed to turn a profit from the Belleville school or farm.

Borrowing from Sarah opened a rift that had been developing for years between the sisters. Angelina resented Sarah's status as primary caregiver, more beloved by the children than their own mother. She felt ashamed that she had to ask for loans from Sarah's small income or accept gifts from her sister to keep the family afloat. She hoped that selling the Belleville farm would allow her and Theodore to repay Sarah. "We have too long been the sole recipient of her bounty," Angelina wrote to their sister Mary in Charleston, "—this obligation has long been *painfully heavy on my heart*—and [Sarah] knows it full well."

Angelina thought Sarah exaggerated the family's money problems to friends and family. She discussed these private matters, Angelina believed, to make herself seem generous by helping and, perhaps, to account for her continued refusal to engage in public life. Angelina insisted that the Belleville school had provided a good living, but no savings, as they had to keep investing in farm improvements. The sisters' unspoken conflict over money, Angelina wrote to a friend, had caused her "14 years of intensive suffering." She thought "decisive action on this point was imperative," and she was surprised that Sarah wanted to continue "a relation which has produced and ever must produce so much friction between us."

When Sarah understood Angelina's bitter feelings, she packed her bags and left Belleville. While traveling and visiting friends, she considered plans for her future. Should she update her *Letters on the Equality of the Sexes*, now considered the basis of the new women's movement? Should she write additional articles about women's history?

"I have for so long been cooking," she wrote to a friend: "sweeping and teaching the abc of French and the angles and curves of drawing that I seem to have lost the mental activity I once had. Besides the powers of my mind have never been allowed expansion; in childhood they were repressed by the false idea that a girl need not have the education I coveted. In early youth, by wrong views of God and religion, then I was fairly ground to powder in the Quaker Society.... Now, after all, what can I expect in old age?"

A few weeks later, sad, homesick, and missing the children dreadfully, she wrote to Angelina, asking to come back. She phrased the request as a proposal, suggesting that her return would give her sister a chance to rest. Angelina said no.

During the winter of 1853–1854, Sarah lived on her own in Washington, DC, perhaps in a boardinghouse, as Theodore had, or with friends. She wrote to the Weld children about Christmas presents she received from the rest of the household there. Missing her niece and nephews, and wanting to help children, she read books about child development. She considered becoming a physician, as a few medical schools had started admitting women. Her friend Sarah Mapps Douglass had begun to study medicine and encouraged her to attend medical lectures. But beginning such difficult studies seemed impossible to sixty-one-year-old Sarah.

She still wanted to study law, but that profession remained closed to women. She could, however, write about the unfair laws pertaining to women and children. In a new essay she said, "Every injustice is a form of falsehood, every falsehood accepted and legalized, works in the social system like poison in the physical frame."

Meanwhile, she wrote to the Weld children, "Dearly beloved Sissy [Sarah], Sody [Theodore], & Charley, I have just been enjoying the delight of looking at your [photographs], poor likenesses it is true of the living countenances of my darlings, but greatly better than nothing." The pictures were likely sent by Angelina, their "Dear Mother," as Sarah called her sister when writing to the children. In one letter to them Sarah described her tour of the House, Senate, and Supreme Court chambers, which at that time were all housed in the Capitol Building in Washington. "I went into the Supreme Court," she wrote, "(not in session) was invited to take my seat in the chair occupied by the Chief Justice—when there I involuntarily exclaimed 'Who knows but a woman may one day preside here.' [M]y companions were much amused."

In nearby Philadelphia, she visited Sarah Mapps Douglass, who, despite an unhappy marriage to a widower with many children, had managed to maintain her career and her independence. A respected teacher, Douglass headed a school for Black girls. She had been appointed to the Philadelphia public school system as one of just a few Black teachers. In the early 1850s she was expanding her career, teaching health and hygiene to Black women and lecturing to mixed audiences of men and woman on anatomy and physiology.

Susan B. Anthony, age twenty-eight. She began her activism in the temperance movement, but when she went to a temperance convention where women were not allowed to speak, she switched her interest and considerable talent to women's rights.

Splitting in Two

Sarah spent another day in Philadelphia sightseeing with Susan B. Anthony, a new young leader in the women's movement. Invited to dine at the home of Lucretia and James Mott, they found themselves on the same side in a genial argument with another guest. Thomas Curtis did not believe in "god" or "immortality," but Sarah and Anthony both had faith that the mind or soul or spirit would continue beyond death.

After some months, Angelina wrote to her sister. "Often, very often," she said, "when I look at all the sorrows and disappointments you have met with in life and all that you have

Angelina, Theodore, and their children Sarah, Theodore, and Charles Stuart, circa 1846. People look serious in early photos because the long exposure times made it impossible to hold smiles still.

done for me, I feel ashamed and confounded at my ingratitude and selfishness. Then again it seems unnatural that a wife and Mother should ever thus be willing equally to share of the affections of her dearest ones with any human being—and my heart refuses its assent."

"You never meant to do me any wrong," Angelina acknowledged. "I would not on any account have you decide *not* to live with us. We *all* feel this to be *your right place*, the home of your heart—We all want you with us and would feel a great blank if you were not with us at the Bay."

The Weld family moved to the Raritan commune in the fall of 1854; Sarah joined them soon afterward. The community had several hundred residents, all of them white. Wealthy members, including the founders, had private homes on the grounds, but the Grimké-Welds lived in a shared stone building overlooking Raritan Bay and the Atlantic Ocean. One end was divided into flats for families—including the Grimké-Welds' six-room apartment—and private rooms for single people. The other side held classrooms, dormitories, and parlors. A communal dining room stood at the center. To eat there, the family modified their Graham diet, taking meat once a day.

Angelina, who enjoyed teaching, taught history and arithmetic and handled medical care and correspondence for the school. Sarah taught French, mothered the children, and served as the school's bookkeeper. Theodore hired additional teachers for the fifty-four boarding pupils. He had hoped to keep fees low to attract middle-class children but could not afford to do so.

The first winter proved difficult as the building was barely heated; everyone got sick. When Theodore felt too ill to shave, he grew a white beard, which Angelina and Sarah persuaded him to keep, "to wear his snowy honors." By the second year, better heat, gaslights, and a newly built gymnasium made the facilities more comfortable. But by then, many adults in the community were embroiled in disagreements over competition, jealousy, selfishness, lack of privacy, and laziness. Sarah said the place was filled with "innumerable sponges who suck up every spare moment."

The community failed in 1856. "Dead and buried," Sarah wrote to a friend, "to my infinite satisfaction." But the school endured. The Grimké-Welds stayed on, renting part of the stone building, sharing with a landlady, who ran the rest as a boardinghouse. Eagleswood School became famous for its forward-thinking curriculum, tailored individually to each student, boy or girl. It offered lessons in vocal and instrumental music, woodworking, household arts, bookkeeping, gymnastics, swimming, and boating. Theodore taught the works of William Shakespeare, not commonly studied in American schools, and students performed plays for the public. They also enjoyed picnics, games, and steamboat trips to New York.

The pupils followed politics too. Led by twelve-year-old Sarah Weld, they campaigned for Kansas to enter the Union as a free state. In that territory, the debate over slavery had turned to guerrilla warfare (small battles fought by private groups, not soldiers) between the two sides. Between 1855 and 1859, fifty-five people died in Kansas in violence over whether the territory should enter the Union as a free or a slave state. At Raritan, students raised money to support the Free-Soilers—who opposed the expansion of slavery—by making and selling knitting, sewing, and craft projects.

When Abby Kelley Foster visited in July 1857, she was surprised to find Sarah and Angelina, both gray-haired, still wearing the bloomer costume. Other women's rights leaders had abandoned the style, worried that the ridicule it attracted interfered with the message they were trying to convey. Their decision came after an incident on a city street in New York:

Lucy Stone and Susan B. Anthony, wearing short skirts over trousers, had to be rescued by a police officer from a crowd of jeering men.

But at Eagleswood, the sisters continued to wear reform dress for freedom of movement, especially on long "rambles." Neither sister admired the style, only the convenience. Sarah found trousers unattractive and more difficult to make than skirts.

Angelina and Sarah liked the way Theodore looked in his beard.

By 1857 fashionable women were wearing ever more extreme dresses, with huge, bell-shaped skirts layered over up to seven petticoats and—growing in popularity—a cage underskirt made of steel hoops. The outfits, which weighed up to fifteen pounds, made movement difficult, especially in tight spaces, such as carriages.

Angelina wrote a letter to a Syracuse Dress Reform Convention, not to promote the bloomer costume but to advocate for some comfortable style to fit new habits of exercise and independence. When women had freedom, education, and the right to work as they pleased, she said, they could spend their own money on clothes that suited them. "Such women will have an indefeasible right to dress elegantly if they wish," she said, "but they will discard cumbersomeness and [skirts of] a useless and absurd circumference and length." Eventually, the sisters also gave up the bloomer style, reverting to their plain, Quaker-like way of dressing.

As time passed, new families in Eagleswood replaced those who had been unhappy, creating what Sarah called "a charming circle of friends." The family and school followed comfortable patterns. On Sunday afternoons they hosted neighbors. Sarah enjoyed the activity, though she noted that "in all free meetings there will be those who love to hear themselves talk, and who are not specially improving or attractive." Still, she appreciated the variety of topics discussed, and she especially enjoyed Theodore's contributions. On special days they hosted famous guest speakers, including the pioneering educator Bronson Alcott; essayist and philosopher Ralph Waldo Emerson; novelist Nathaniel Hawthorne; the formerly enslaved Sojourner Truth, who had become an abolitionist and women's rights advocate; and Harriet Tubman, who, after escaping enslavement herself, made thirteen trips back to the South to rescue dozens of other enslaved people.

The school also hosted weekly dances on Saturday nights. Even important guests such as writer and naturalist Henry David Thoreau joined in. It was thought strange, he wrote to his sister, if one did not participate. Children, teachers, and guests took the floor together. Sarah and Angelina taught the Virginia reel and other steps they remembered from Charleston balls, and Theodore followed along, his long beard flapping.

But while the school whirled in happy unison, the nation was splitting in two.

Harriet Tubman, shown here in 1890, escaped enslavement in Maryland in 1849, then returned many times to guide at least seventy family members and others to safety in the North.

CHAPTER 21
Loyal Women

1859-1863

In October 1859 an abolitionist, John Brown, gathered a troop of eighteen men, five of them African American. They planned to capture a federal arsenal (where firearms were manufactured and stored) in Harper's Ferry, Virginia (present-day West Virginia). In 1856 Brown had been part of the violence in "Bleeding Kansas," where he and his sons had killed five supporters of slavery. Now, in Virginia, believing himself to be an "instrument of God," he planned to arm enslaved people and start a revolution.

In a nighttime attack, his men stopped a train, killing a free Black man—a railroad employee who thought they were robbers. Then the men took about fifty local prisoners: the arsenal guard, two nearby enslavers, townspeople and, as morning broke, arsenal employees arriving for work. Townspeople fired on the raiders, who shot back, killing a grocer.

On the second day of Brown's raid, US Marines, led by Robert E. Lee, stormed the arsenal. Sixteen people were killed, including a marine and six of Brown's men, two of them his

The caption on this illustration, which appeared in *Harper's Weekly* in November 1859, reads: "The Harper's Ferry Insurrection. The U.S. Marines storming the Engine House, Insurgents firing through holes in the wall."

sons. Brown, who was injured, and six supporters who survived the shoot-out were imprisoned in nearby Charles Town. There Brown was tried for treason, found guilty, and sentenced to be hanged on December 2.

News of the attack and trial spread quickly with the help of new technology: the telegraph. In the North, many regarded Brown as a hero and a martyr. "O Sarah!" Sarah Grimké wrote to Sarah Mapps Douglass, "what a glorious spectacle is now before us." She compared Brown to Christians who were burned at the stake in the early 1400s for trying to reform the Catholic Church: "The Jerome of Prague of our country, the John Huss of the United States, now stands ready, as they were, to seal his testimony with his life's blood."

The Grimké-Welds' neighbor, Raritan cofounder Rebecca Spring, had corresponded with Brown. She went to Virginia to nurse his wounds in jail. While there, she learned that two of his men, also condemned to death, had no families to bury them, so she volunteered to give them honorable internment in New Jersey. After returning home, Spring invited Brown's wife, Mary, to Eagleswood. People there grieved for her when she visited her husband the day before he died.

The two men Spring had offered to bury were hanged in March. As the boat carrying their pine coffins approached the port of Perth Amboy, New Jersey, a pro-slavery mob gathered, threatening to throw the caskets overboard. Eventually, abolitionists got the bodies to the nearby Eagleswood Cemetery. Bells tolled as Sarah and Angelina joined a large crowd for the burial. Men and boys, including pupils from Eagleswood, stood guard with dogs over the graves to prevent the pro-slavery supporters from digging them up.

After his death, Brown's status rose in the North as famous writers and abolitionists—including Frederick Douglass, Ralph Waldo Emerson, and Harriet Tubman—praised him. Violence, they now believed, was the only way to end slavery. Southerners, meanwhile, feared additional rebellions modeled on Brown's actions. Brown's raid and its consequences helped to convince the Grimké-Welds that war was inevitable. "O, yes," Angelina wrote to a friend. "—war is better than slavery."

In November 1860, Abraham Lincoln was elected president. As a Republican, he opposed the expansion of slavery into new states, and white people in Southern states believed he would try to end slavery completely. On December 20, South Carolina seceded (withdrew) from the nation, followed quickly by Mississippi, Florida, Alabama, Georgia, Louisiana, and Texas; they formed the Confederate States of America. The states that did not secede from the United States remained known as the Union.

Lincoln was inaugurated on March 4, 1861. On April 12, the South Carolina militia (there was as yet no Confederate army) bombarded Fort Sumter, a Union fort at the entrance to Charleston Harbor. Charleston residents, perhaps including members of the Grimké family, watched the two-day battle, some climbing to rooftops for a better view. Surrounded, outgunned, and short on food and ammunition, the Union commander surrendered in what would become known as the first battle of the Civil War. Northerners called it "the War of the Rebellion" or "the Slaveholders' Rebellion," while Southerners called it "the War for Southern Independence."

Lincoln's appeal for seventy-five thousand volunteers to suppress the rebellion inspired four more states—Virginia, Arkansas, North Carolina, and Tennessee—to join the Confederacy. In the North, as the sons and grandsons of their friends enlisted, Angelina, Theodore, and Sarah felt sad and embarrassed when the Weld boys did not.

The elder son, Charles Stuart, who now went by his middle name, was a twenty-one-year-old student at Harvard when the war began. Labeling himself a conscientious objector, opposed to serving in the armed forces or bearing arms, Stuart refused to enlist. He also would not allow Theodore to pay for a substitute, which people in the North could do. Stuart's elders could understand pacifism, which had long been their belief as well, but they were surprised to learn that he did not object to all wars, only this one, which he thought unjust. Instead of enlisting, he remained at Harvard.

Theodore, nicknamed Sody, was too ill to go, suffering from a condition that no one understood. In his teens, he developed a stutter. At nineteen he sat quietly, lacking energy, interest, or the will to do anything. His worried family sought advice from a variety of experts: doctors, faith healers, and even a medium, but no one could tell what was wrong. Some diagnoses focused on the possibility of masturbation, which, in those days, many believed would lead to madness. The "experts" consulted recommended a variety of treatments for this problem: early marriage, gymnastics, outdoor farmwork, and other "manly" pursuits.

As the search for a treatment continued, Sarah longed to move away from Eagleswood. She wrote to a friend, "Oh I do so long for a little private home, bread and water with quiet and love would be infinitely better than the penitentiary life I have had here for seven weary years." In 1862 she got her wish as the family left the Eagleswood School, which was closing. Hoping that a quieter setting would benefit Sody, they moved to a rented house in Perth Amboy.

But nothing helped. Heartbroken, Sarah, Angelina, and Angelina's daughter, Sissy (Sarah), nursed the young man as he sat unmoving in a wheelchair, barely able to speak above a whisper. That year he went to live on a farm in upstate New York, in the care of one of Theodore's former students. When he was there, the family wrote to him, visited him, and took him on outings.

By then, the North and South were battling on land and sea, mostly in the South. Southerners claimed to be fighting against oppression and for states' rights—that is, the rights of individual states to fight the encroaching power of the federal government. But the war was really about slavery. As the Confederacy was forming, its vice president, Alexander H. Stephens, gave a "Cornerstone Speech," describing the South's ideology as based "upon the great truth that the negro is not equal to the white man; that slavery, subordination to the superior race, is his natural and normal condition."

Angelina wrote to Sody that the nation stood "on the brink of a terrible Revolution," as the South made one last effort "to reopen the Slave Trade and establish Slavery on a wide and permanent basis."

Abolitionists had little faith in the new president. "I see disaster and defeat in Lincoln," Sarah wrote, referring to the president's efforts to preserve the Union without ending slavery.

By the summer of 1862, thousands of enslaved people had escaped to the North. Returning them would have been logistically impossible, though the Fugitive Slave Act required that this be done. In September, citing military necessity, Lincoln released a draft of his Emancipation Proclamation, which would free enslaved people in the rebelling states, effective January 1, 1863. But the proclamation, which assumed a Union victory, did not ban slavery in the loyal border states, where

President Abraham Lincoln, flanked by his Secret Service Chief Allan Pinkerton (*left*) and General John A. McClernand at the Union camp in Antietam, Maryland, in 1862.

slavery was still legal: Delaware, Maryland, Kentucky, Missouri and, after 1863, the new state of West Virginia. (West Virginia separated from Virginia to remain in the Union.) Lincoln believed that outlawing slavery in these states would push them to join the Confederacy.

"Whatever Lincoln and his Cabinet are carrying on the war to accomplish," Sarah said, "God's design is to deliver from bondage his innocent people." Like other abolitionists, the Grimké-Welds were not satisfied with the proclamation, instead demanding a constitutional amendment outlawing slavery.

The family did all they could to support the Northern side of the conflict. Theodore, fifty-nine and newly jobless, applied for a position with the Sanitary Commission, a relief agency for injured and ailing soldiers; but he was turned down due to his lack of medical experience. In November 1862, he accepted an invitation from William Lloyd Garrison to speak in Boston. The two men had been at odds for years but found common ground in supporting the Union. This time, Theodore's voice held, and he launched a speaking tour to increase support for the war across New England, New York, Pennsylvania, and Ohio. Some of his lectures were funded by the federal government.

Angelina felt proud of her husband. "He is doing the very thing my heart wants him to," she wrote to a friend. She, too, had reentered public life. The women's movement had suspended meetings to work for Union causes during the war. In the spring of 1863, Elizabeth Cady Stanton published "An Appeal to the Women of the Republic" in the *New York Tribune*:

> *If it be true that at this hour, the women of the South are more devoted to their cause than we to ours, the fact lies here. They see and feel the horrors of war; the foe is at their*

firesides; while we, in peace and plenty, live and move as heretofore. There is an inspiration, too, in a definite purpose, be it good or bad. The women of the South know what their sons are fighting for. The women of the North do not. They [Southern women] appreciate the blessings of Slavery; we do not the blessings of Liberty.

Stanton followed her appeal with an invitation, cosigned by Susan B. Anthony, to women to come to a national convention to discuss how they could best support the Union's war efforts.

Sarah wrote about this gathering to Sody: "The 14th (of May 1863) was your mother's silver wedding day[,] 25 years since she was married. Your father and I were at Amboy so we celebrated it with a kiss, and by your mother attending the meeting of 'Loyal Women' and opening her mouth once more for the oppressed."

Angelina met that day with a thousand other women at the Church of the Puritans in New York's Union Square. Susan B. Anthony nominated Lucy Stone for president of the convention, and Angelina was named one of several vice presidents. By this time Stone had married Henry Blackwell, keeping her own name, and the two were close friends with the Grimké-Welds.

Angelina had been out of the public eye for so long (twenty-five years) that Stone had to explain to the crowd who she was. "This lady," she said, "once a South Carolina slaveholder, not only gave freedom to her own slaves twenty years ago, but has spent the strength of her younger years in going up and down among the people, urging the Northern States to make their soil sacred to freedom, to so amend their laws and constitutions that slavery can find no protection within their borders."

"My heart is full," Angelina said in her speech, "my country is bleeding, my people are perishing around me. But I feel as a South Carolinian, I am bound to tell the North, go on! go on! Never falter, never abandon the principles which you have adopted."

> "Never falter, never abandon the principles which you have adopted."
> —ANGELINA GRIMKÉ

One resolution introduced at the convention caused considerable debate: "There can never be a true peace in this Republic until the civil and political rights of all citizens of African descent and all women are practically established." Some women objected to connecting the two issues.

A Mrs. Hoyt of Wisconsin said, "We all know that [the idea of woman's rights] has not been received with entire favor by the women of the country, and I know that there are thousands of earnest, loyal, and able women who will not go into any movement of this kind, if this idea is made prominent."

Angelina disagreed. "I rejoice exceedingly that that resolution should combine us with the negro," she said. "I feel that we have not been with him; that the iron has entered into our souls. True, we have not felt the slave-holder's lash; true, we have not had our hands manacled; but our *hearts* have been crushed.... I want to be identified with the negro; until he gets his rights, we shall never have ours."

The resolution passed, followed by another that changed the women's rights movement: "Resolved. That we, loyal women of the nation . . . do hereby pledge ourselves one to another in a Loyal League, to give support to the Government in so far as it makes the war a war for freedom." Previously, the women's movement had been loosely organized, but the Loyal League, with Elizabeth Cady Stanton as its president, became the first national women's political organization.

On the second day of the convention, Angelina presented a message to send to Union soldiers. Asking them to welcome Black men as fellow soldiers, and to reenlist if they could, she said,

> *This war is . . . a war of PRINCIPLES. . . . While the South has waged this war against human rights, the North has stood by holding the garments of those who were stoning liberty to death. . . . The nation is in a death-struggle. It must either become one vast slaveocracy of petty tyrants, or wholly the land of the free. . . . Soldiers of this revolution, to your hands is committed the sacred duty of carrying out . . . the ideal of our fathers, which was to secure to ALL "life, liberty, and the pursuit of happiness."*

The convention wrote Lincoln to thank him for his Emancipation Proclamation, urging him to go further: "The Union as it was—a compromise between barbarism and civilization—can never be restored, for the opposing principles of freedom and slavery can not exist together."

Then, because petitions were still the only way that women could participate in the political process, the league set out to collect a million signatures urging Congress to pass a constitutional amendment abolishing slavery.

Angelina and Sarah gathered signatures in Perth Amboy as the war moved north. The Battle of Gettysburg, in Pennsylvania, which raged from July 1 through 3, 1863, was the bloodiest of the war, leaving more than fifty-one thousand men dead, wounded, captured, or missing. Both sides paid a terrible price, but the hard-fought Union victory marked the beginning of the end for the Confederacy.

CHAPTER 22
Powerfully Impressive

1863-1868

In late 1863, the Grimké-Welds bought a house in Fairmount, Massachusetts, seven miles south of Boston on the Neponset River. They likely chose that location because Boston was an anti-slavery stronghold and because Theodore had made friends with many of the city's Unitarians. Members of the Unitarian denomination stressed individual freedom of belief, the free use of reason in religion, a united world community, and the improvement of life through education. The Grimké-Welds' religious beliefs, which had departed from strict Protestant or Quaker rules, matched Unitarian ideas more closely than the conservative religious views of their friends in New York.

The house at 211 Fairmount Avenue was three stories tall, with a large porch and garden. It soon became a gathering place for abolitionists, women's rights advocates, and temperance campaigners. Some neighbors were shocked by the mingling of Black and white guests; others saw it as a sign of sophistication and progressiveness.

That December marked the thirtieth anniversary of the American Anti-Slavery Society. William Lloyd Garrison, its president, made a special point of inviting Theodore, Angelina, and Sarah to the celebration in Philadelphia. Having just moved into their new home, they could not attend, but they sent a long, heartfelt letter written by Angelina.

Theodore kept lecturing from their new Boston base. The sisters met many neighbors while gathering signatures on petitions, which they sent to the Loyal League in New York. By February 1864, the league had collected six thousand petitions containing one hundred thousand names. The organizers glued these together, end to end. Then they rolled them up to mail in a trunk to Senator Charles Sumner of Massachusetts, the league's closest ally in Congress. Known for his sense of drama, Sumner had the massive scroll, which was too heavy for one person to carry, delivered to his desk in the Senate chamber by two tall Black men. Then he proudly presented the petitions to his fellow senators, delivering a speech which became known as "The Prayer of One Hundred Thousand."

In addition to collecting signatures, Sarah and Angelina kept writing, though some of their work from this time has been lost. For example, Angelina's *A Declaration of War on Slavery*, considered one of her most powerful works, has not survived. Sarah wrote articles for the *New York Tribune*, *The Independent*, and later the *Woman's Journal*. Both wrote letters to their siblings, too, though the task grew more difficult as the war continued. Their brothers Henry and Charles had died before it started, but John, whose poor health had forced him to give up his medical practice, still lived in the family home with sisters Mary and Eliza. In the early days of the war, ships called blockade runners often delivered food, supplies, and mail to lightly guarded Southern ports. When they could get mail out, Mary and Eliza wrote back insisting that slavery was God's will.

Praying for the safety of her relatives while hoping for a Union victory, Angelina dreamed of returning to her hometown. "If it is ever under Federal control," she wrote, "I hope the way may open for me once more to see my aged brother and sisters and breathe her balmy air once more."

As the war continued, the Union blockaded Charleston completely. No food, supplies, or mail could get through. Confederate troops fought back with floating mines, ironclad rams protruding underwater from warships, torpedo boats, and even a submarine, but the blockade held. As food grew scarce in Charleston, hoarding began. Houses and streets fell into disrepair, and enslaved servants escaped.

In April 1864, the US Senate passed the Thirteenth Amendment to the Constitution, outlawing slavery. But the House of Representatives refused to ratify it, so it did not become law. In response, Lincoln made passage of the amendment part of the Republican campaign platform for the upcoming 1864 presidential election.

By August the Loyal League had sent Sumner more than two hundred thousand petition signatures from twenty-three states. Although this number was only a fifth of what it hoped to obtain, the league felt so confident that the amendment would pass that the organization closed its New York office.

About that time, Theodore got a job offer from a well-respected physician whom he'd met when seeking help for Sody. Diocletian (Dio) Lewis was opening a seminary for young women in Lexington, ten miles north of Boston, and he asked Theodore to teach there.

Angelina and Sarah decided to work at the school too. Because the Young Ladies' Seminary was twenty miles away, they lived there during the week, leaving home early Monday morning and returning Friday for the weekend.

Lexington, according to the school's promotional materials, was "a quiet farm village, famous for healthfulness, in a picturesque region, threaded by delightful rides and walks." Built on the site of the Revolutionary War's first battle, the school building was a former hotel called Lexington House, which accommodated two hundred people. Attendance grew from 30 the first year, to 100 the second, to 144 in the third. Students came from across the country as well as from Central America and the West Indies.

Diocletian Lewis was a temperance leader and physical culture advocate. He practiced homeopathic medicine, which believed the body could cure itself using natural substances to aid in healing.

The first students were all white. When a young Black girl applied to enter, Lewis wanted to admit her. He asked his pupils if they would mind, and they said no, but the parents of a dozen girls from Connecticut objected, saying they would remove their daughters if the girl were enrolled. And so she was denied admission.

Later, Lewis hired a young woman of mixed race (her Black mother had been enslaved by her white father) as a servant but assigned her solitary duties, apart from the thirty white servants. Two years later, the girl died of tuberculosis. Lewis and his wife invited her older sister to live in their home. This time, when he asked his pupils whether they would welcome a Black girl as a schoolmate, no one objected, and the girl attended classes for a year, becoming the seminary's first Black pupil.

The curriculum emphasized moral, intellectual, and—unusually for girls at the time—physical education. The third idea was "certainly needed at this particular time," an educational journal wrote, "since a glance at the fashion magazines will show a return to the barbarities in lacing [tying a corset to make the waist look smaller], so prevalent in the time of our grandmothers. Probably no one man has had more to do with eradicating this and other similar fashions than Dr. Dio Lewis."

Some girls, Lewis claimed, arrived at the school nervous and weak, barely able to climb a flight of stairs. A few months later, he said, they could walk five or ten miles "without inconvenience."

Theodore taught Shakespeare and offered moral training. Angelina taught modern history, with a particular emphasis on slavery and abolition. "I am not satisfied," she wrote to a friend, "to teach only what is in the text books. I read a great deal in larger works, so as to be a *live* teacher and lift the pupils' minds above the glitter and pomp of war and conquest." Sarah taught French, according to some sources; others said she worked as an administrator and a housekeeper.

Their hometown of Charleston remained under Confederate control during the war, although it was blockaded by Union warships. On February 17, 1865, General P. G. T. Beauregard ordered Confederate troops to retreat in defeat as Union soldiers, led by General William Tecumseh Sherman, began burning their way across South Carolina.

The remaining Black Charlestonians celebrated the South's defeat, though the city lay in ruins. A visitor to the

Grimkés' neighborhood wrote, "The streets were overgrown with grass, and formerly well-kept gardens were obliterated. . . . [T]he houses were indescribable—all of their windows were broken, many chimneys had fallen . . . piazzas were half gone, and the street looked like it was scattered with diamonds from the broken glass."

On April 9, 1865, the two highest-ranking generals in the Confederate and Union armies met at Appomattox Court House in Virginia. There, Robert E. Lee, the commander of the Confederate army, formally surrendered for the South to Ulysses S. Grant, who headed the Union army. Recent estimates say that 750,000 men died in what is still the United States' deadliest war. More than half the deaths resulted from disease, infected wounds, and poor sanitary conditions.

Five days after the surrender, on April 14, President Abraham Lincoln was gunned down by an assassin in a Washington theater. He died the next morning. Though the sisters had not always agreed with him, they had celebrated his reelection in 1864. After his death, they mourned with the rest of the nation.

On December 6, 1865, the Thirteenth Amendment to the Constitution was ratified, formally abolishing slavery across the country. By then the Grimké-Welds were already working in the movement to help "freedmen," raising money, collecting clothing, and advocating for laws to guarantee equal rights for Black people, including citizenship. Black people, though at last freed from slavery, were still not citizens and therefore had no right to vote.

With communications to Charleston reestablished, Sarah and Angelina sent their sisters Mary and Eliza $200 worth of necessities. Their brother John had died during the war at the age of sixty-nine. Sarah and Angelina invited Mary and

Eliza to live in Fairmount, and they accepted. But as they made arrangements to travel, Mary, who was seventy-six, died.

Eliza, sixty-eight, came by herself. Bitter over the outcome of the war, and still convinced that slavery was what God wanted, she nevertheless enjoyed Fairmount, keeping house for the others when they were in Lexington. Despite their differences in opinion, Sarah called her "a sunbeam in the family." Eliza told the Grimké-Welds how the Union had confiscated their family lands and how most of the enslaved servants had run away. In 1866 Eliza returned to Charleston, where she died in 1867.

On September 7, 1867, the Young Ladies' Seminary burned down. The school carried on for a time in a nearby summer hotel but closed at the end of the school year. Finally, the Grimké-Welds retired with enough money from Grimké and new Weld family inheritances to live comfortably in Fairmount. Stuart, their older son, had become a writer after graduating from Harvard and lived with them while their daughter, Sissy, pursued her studies. Sody, still in poor health, lived with others and sometimes at home. The family read and wrote constantly, discussing issues of the day. Sarah amused herself by translating French articles and stories about social reforms. At the age of seventy-five, she published an abridged English translation of Alphonse de Lamartine's biography *Jeanne d'Arc* (Joan of Arc), which was well received.

Theodore stayed active in the Fairmount community, opening a public library and fighting to include controversial materials in the collection. "Any book," he told his library colleagues, "in regard to God or Man, so long as it is worded in decent language, cannot be corrupting in its influence if read in the right spirit. We should be pleased to see even the strongest and most radical works on Atheism placed on the library shelves, so that all may have an opportunity of reading them if they chose to do so." His argument convinced his fellow trustees not to ban books, even on unpopular subjects.

Theodore also helped to organize a new Unitarian church and served on a school committee. With Sarah and Angelina, he campaigned for the rights of freedmen but also found time to enjoy a close circle of friends—abolitionists William Lloyd Garrison and Elizur Wright and poets John Greenleaf Whittier and Henry Wadsworth Longfellow and their families. Former students called too. Lucy Stone, now a leader in the revived women's movement, and her husband brought their young daughter, Alice Stone Blackwell, to visit.

One evening in February 1868, Angelina read an article, "Negroes and the Higher Studies," in the *National Anti-Slavery Standard*. It said that Black scholarship was not inferior to the academic work of white people. The article quoted a professor at Lincoln University, a Presbyterian institution for African Americans in Pennsylvania. He told of a student "by the name of Grimkie who came here, two years ago, just out of slavery." When the young man spoke, the professor said, he "was thrillingly, powerfully impressive."

The article sparked an interest in Angelina, who,

Lucy Stone with her daughter, Alice Stone Blackwell, who grew up to be a prominent advocate for women's suffrage.

after conferring with Sarah and Theodore, wrote the young man named in the article a letter:

> Mr Grimké
>
> Sir
>
> In a recent number of the Anti-Slavery Standard I saw a notice of a meeting at Lincoln University of a Literary Society at which a young gentleman of the name of Grimké deliver'd an address. My maiden name was Grimké. I am the youngest sister of Dr. John Grimké of So Carolina, & as this name is a very uncommon one it occurred to me that you had probably been the slave of one of my brothers & I feel a great desire to know all about you. My Sister Sarah & myself have long been interested in the Anti-slavery Cause, & left Charleston nearly 40 years ago, because we could not endure to live in the midst of the oppressions of Slavery. Will you therefore be so kind as to tell us who you are whether you have any brothers & sisters—who your parents were etc. etc.
>
> We rejoice to find you are enjoying the advantages of such an institution & should be glad to know how you came introduc'd into it, & whatever you are willing to tell me about yourself.
>
> My husband Theodore D. Weld was one of the earliest Anti Slavery lecturers at the West.
>
> Hoping soon to hear from you
>
> I remain, Sir
> Respectfully,
>
> Angelina Grimké Weld
> Fairmount
> Massachusetts

Francis (*left*) and Archibald Grimké, probably in their late teens, when they attended Lincoln University.

CHAPTER 23
The Grimké Brothers

1868-1869

The reply came in just a week.

> Dear Madam,
>
> I am very happy to hear from Miss Angelina Grimké of Anti-Slavery celebrity. I am the son of Henry Grimké, your brother. Of course you know more about my father than I do, suffice it to say he was a lawyer and was married to a Miss Simons. She died, leaving three children . . . Henrietta, Montague, and Thomas. After her death he took my mother, who was his slave and his children's nurse, her name is Nancy Weston. I don't think you know her. By my mother he had three children Also. Archibald, which is my name, and Francis and John. He died about fifteen years ago, leaving my mother, with two children and in a pregnant state, for John was born two mos. after he died, in the care of his son, Mr. E. M. [Montague] Grimké in his own words, as I heard, "I leave Nancy and her two children to be treated as members of the family."

> I am the eldest of the bros., was born 17th Aug. 1849. Therefore, my poor mother a defenceless woman, crippled in one arm, with no one to care for her in the world, for Mr. G. did not do as his father commanded, and three small children to provide for, was thrown upon the uncharitable world. . . .
>
> [Montague Grimké] informed my mother [in 1860] that he wanted me [as an enslaved servant] and that she should send me to his house. His mandate was irresistible; it was a severe shock to my mother. But this was only the beginning of her sorrows, thus he kept on until she was rendered childless. . . .
>
> I hope dear Madam you will excuse this badly written epistle [letter]. . . . Perhaps you would like to see our pictures, they are enclosed. I shall hope to hear from you soon. Most respectfully yours,
>
> Archibald Henry Grimké

Three nephews, new to them! John, the youngest, remained in Charleston, but Archibald (Archie), eighteen, and Francis (Frank), seventeen, were second-year students at Lincoln University, near Philadelphia. Angelina wanted to go meet them; Sarah and Theodore agreed she should. Angelina's friend and later biographer Catherine Birney summed up the family discussion at this time: "Her brother had wronged these children; his sisters must right them."

"Dear young friends," Angelina replied to Archibald, "I cannot express the mingled emotions with which I perused your deeply interesting and touching letter. The facts disclosed were *no* surprise to me. Indeed had I not suspected that you might be my nephews, I should probably not have addressed you. . . . I will not dwell on the past . . . it cannot be altered. . . . Our work is in the present. I am glad you have taken the name of Grimké."

In June, Angelina's older son, Stuart, escorted her to Lincoln University. They stayed a week, getting to know their new relatives, who, Angelina said, looked like Grimkés and acted like Grimkés—polite, articulate, and kind.

Several months later, the young men visited the Grimké-Weld home in Fairmount, which had been combined with several other towns and given a new name, Hyde Park. Years later, Archibald's daughter wrote about what happened when they arrived:

> *They [her father and uncle] often laugh, now over the picture they must have presented to the astonished eyes of the Weld family that was the simplest of the simple in manner, dress and living. To the boys this was a great occasion, the greatest in all their lives and, cost what it might, they were determined to live up to it. They were virtually penniless, but each carried a cane, wore a high silk hat which had been made to order, and boots that were custom-made.*
>
> *Whatever the aunts and the Welds thought of the young men's attire, the nephews were welcomed with wide open arms and hearts and made to feel at home.*

The elders were thrilled to have a chance to practice in their own family the equality principles they had advocated. "They are very promising young men," Sarah wrote to Sarah Mapps Douglass. "We all feel deeply interested in them, and I hope to be able to get together money enough to pay the college expenses of the younger."

Through frequent correspondence and visits, Archibald and Francis told their newfound relatives the story of their lives. Their mother, Nancy Weston, was the enslaved nursemaid to Henry's three white children. She nursed his wife, too, as she lay dying in 1843 and then consoled Henry's teenaged daughter and two young sons on the loss of their mother. Although Nancy could not read or write, after the boys went away to school, she sent them messages and sometimes gifts in their father's letters.

In 1847 Henry bought a rice plantation, Cane Acre, twenty-five miles from Charleston, taking with him about twenty enslaved workers, including Nancy. He had her live in a cottage with a yard, where she raised ducks, chickens, and pigs for her own income. Archibald was born a year after the move and Francis a year later.

According to their sons, Henry and Nancy cared for each other. To pro-slavery Southerners, this idea was more shocking than thinking that Henry had forced Nancy to have sex against her will. It implied that she could be an equal. Henry took care of her when she was ill. At Cane Acre, all enslaved boys were called James, but Henry made a point of naming Nancy's older sons distinctively. She named her third son John after Henry's brother.

In South Carolina, it was against the law to free enslaved people privately; at that time, it required an act of the state legislature. Before his death, Henry told the mother of his Black sons: "[I will] leave you better than free, because I leave you to be taken care of." In his will, he gave the "mulatto Servant girl named Nancy, with her present and future issue [children]" to his son Montague and his descendants.

Montague was only nineteen when his father died in 1852 from typhoid fever. Henry had designated his sister Eliza to handle his will. She auctioned the plantation, the house, and the enslaved workers, except for Nancy and her sons, whom she brought to Charleston. Eliza gave Nancy money from the sale of her livestock, which allowed her to buy a small cottage on Cummings Street, in the part of town where many free Black people lived. (About three thousand free African Americans lived in Charleston; Nancy herself came from a distinguished Black family.) Eliza helped her to find jobs sewing, washing, and ironing for homes and hotels. The boys handled some of the tasks and made deliveries. All worked hard, but they were poor and often hungry. Sometimes Nancy's brothers, who were butchers, gave them meat customers would not buy.

Although it was still illegal to teach enslaved people to read or write, there were schools for free Black children near their house. Nancy paid a dollar a month for her sons to attend. For eight years, they lived peacefully. Then Montague, who had recently married, took twelve-year-old Archibald, a wiry boy with auburn curls, to be a servant in his house.

Soon he took eleven-year-old Francis too. Both were outfitted in black uniforms with brass buttons. Montague loosened some servant rules for his half brothers, allowing them to attend school part-time and to spend nights at home with their mother. In protest of their forced servitude, the boys pretended to be stupid. Archibald set the table incorrectly over and over so that his aunt Eliza would have to redo his work.

One day, when Montague thought Archibald had done a poor job building a fire, he beat the boy until his wife stopped him. She told her husband to send him to the workhouse, as she didn't want people to hear the beating and think the Grimkés were cruel. At thirteen, Archibald had his feet locked in stocks and his hands tied to a pulley as he received thirty lashes with a leather strap, which drew blood on his bare back.

Swearing he would never return to Montague, Archibald hid for a time with free Black friends, moving from house to house at night, dressed as a girl. Eventually, he settled with the Cole family, who hid him for two years. He studied and read books, including *Uncle Tom's Cabin*.

Later, Francis ran away. Presenting himself as a free Black person to a Confederate soldier, he found work as a valet to an officer. When the regiment was posted near Charleston, Francis occasionally slipped away to visit his mother. At some point, Montague placed a notice in the *Charleston Mercury*:

FIFTY DOLLARS REWARD
FRANCIS (a brown boy) about 15
years old, 4 feet 9 inches high;
He ran away from the Charleston
Hotel in July

Two months later, Francis was recognized, captured, and locked into the workhouse. "There I remained for several months," he wrote later, "and there I was taken dangerously ill from exposure and bad treatment, and came very near losing my life. It was only by being finally removed to my mother's house, and by the most skillful treatment that I recovered."

Before Francis had fully regained his health, and before he could run away again, Montague sold him to the same Confederate officer Francis had previously served as a valet.

Then Montague took John, the youngest son. When Nancy protested, Archibald said, "she was thrown into a loathsome cell, and kept there for six days, eating nothing . . . until at last sickness prostrated [weakened] her." The workhouse doctor insisted that she be released. Even Montague's white relatives were shocked by his cruel treatment of Nancy.

Distress over these stories impacted Angelina's already fragile health. "Nina has been sick all summer," Sarah wrote to Sarah Mapps Douglass, "is a mere skeleton and looks ten or fifteen years older than she did before that fatal visit to Lincoln University."

Angelina anguished, trying to understand her white relatives' actions. "I feel more & more," she said, "that slaveholders are by nature no worse than nonslaveholders & are the *victims* of the very system they have clung to with a death-grasp." The exercise of unchecked power, she thought, corrupted enslavers such as Eliza, who did nothing to protect her Black nephews from her white nephew.

After the war, Nancy's family reunited. She sent her sons to a new freedmen's school established by Northerners. Teacher Frances Pillsbury, a friend of Theodore's, found jobs in Massachusetts for the two older boys, assuring their mother that they could continue their educations there. Since Nancy could not read, her youngest son John read her the letters that Archibald and Francis sent from the North. When she learned that their employers were working them hard, paying them little, and denying them their promised education, Nancy sought out Pillsbury to ask for better conditions. Pillsbury arranged for them to attend the Ashmun Institute in Pennsylvania.

The Presbyterian Church had founded the college in 1853 "for the scientific, classical, and theological education of colored youth of the male sex." Renamed in 1866 after Abraham Lincoln, by then the college admitted white students too. Archibald's fees were supported by a Presbyterian minister from New York, and Francis was backed by one from Connecticut. The boys studied Greek and other difficult subjects, and both joined clubs for debate and composition.

The sisters and Theodore brought John, the youngest brother, to Lincoln too. But eventually he returned to Charleston and lost contact with his Northern family.

The Grimké-Welds gave Archibald and Francis what money they could spare and considerable advice. All three emphasized the need for financial and moral independence. Sarah urged them to answer letters promptly. Angelina thought that after graduating from Lincoln they should continue their educations at Oberlin, "where scores of color'd young men & women," she wrote to Archibald, "have been educated in the *same* classes with white men & women—*no* distinction of color or race has been recognized there." She also recommended Cornell, which emphasized physical culture to develop the body as well as the mind. Howard, a Black university, was another possibility. Theodore believed their education should include physical work in addition to studies. He was pleased when they took summer jobs as waiters.

All three elders took pride in their nephews' accomplishments, writing about them to friends and introducing them to important abolitionists, including William Lloyd Garrison, Lucy Stone and Henry Blackwell; Charles Sumner; and Black leaders Frederick Douglass and Lewis Hayden. In Hyde Park the expanded family's broad discussions encompassed many contemporary issues, including women's rights, racial prejudice, and citizenship for Black Americans. Sarah, Angelina, and Theodore learned from their young relatives too. Archibald's daughter said later that this new family and friends made him "a liberal in religion, a radical in the woman suffrage movement, in politics and on the race question."

Archibald and Francis listened respectfully to all recommendations and often followed them, but they made their own plans for the future. The Grimké-Welds backed the young men's decisions. As the five grew closer, Angelina, Sarah, and Theodore celebrated the idea that these intelligent, hardworking nephews would likely continue their work.

CHAPTER 24
One Grand Idea

1869–1873

The whole country needed help to heal and to reunite in the post–Civil War period known as Reconstruction. Although the Thirteenth Amendment had freed enslaved people, racial prejudice ran rampant throughout the United States. Sarah, Angelina, Theodore, Archibald, and Francis, with their abolitionist friends, campaigned for additional laws to protect the rights of African Americans. Archibald and Francis offered practical help, teaching summer school in Maryland as part of a Lincoln University program to send educated freedmen back to help rebuild the South.

In response to a growing national movement, Congress passed the Fourteenth Amendment, making anyone born in the United States a citizen, and the Fifteenth, guaranteeing voting rights to all male citizens. It was the first use of the word "male" in the Constitution to define voters in the United States. Together, these amendments granted Black men the right to vote in America, but there was more work to do. States still needed to ratify the amendments, and not everyone was satisfied with how the documents were written.

When the new laws were being considered, Elizabeth Cady Stanton warned, "If the word 'male' be inserted, it will take us a century at least to get it out." But the word stayed in, so she and Susan B. Anthony called a national women's rights convention to consider how to proceed. Other speakers at the New York gathering—the first women's rights meeting since the war—included Lucretia Mott, who was elected president; Lucy Stone; Henry Blackwell; Frederick Douglass; and Abby Kelley Foster. Sarah and Angelina followed the proceedings by newspaper and letters.

Elizabeth Cady Stanton (*left*) and Susan B. Anthony, shown about 1871, were close friends and leaders for decades in the women's rights movement.

The convention audience cheered when Mott introduced eighty-year-old Sojourner Truth. "There is a great stir about colored men getting their rights," said the famous former slave turned political activist, "but not a word about the colored women; and if colored men get their rights, you see the colored men will be masters over the women, and it will be just as bad as it was before."

The convention formed the American Equal Rights Association, which instead of campaigning for the voting rights of Black people and women separately, would promote "one grand, distinctive national idea—universal suffrage."

But in 1869, the new association, and with it, the women's movement, split in two. One group, led by Mott, Stanton, Anthony, and Matilda Joslyn Gage, formed the National Woman Suffrage Association in New York. The National, as it was known, opposed the Fifteenth Amendment because it limited voting to men. National members wanted a Sixteenth Amendment, applying to women, to guarantee universal suffrage.

The second group thought that obtaining voting rights for Black men before votes for women was a practical step in the right direction. They formed the American Woman Suffrage Association (the American), led by Lucy Stone and Julia Ward Howe, an author most famous for writing the words to "The Battle Hymn of the Republic," the Union's unofficial song.

Although Sarah and Angelina favored immediate equal rights for all, they knew and admired Stone, whose organization was based in Boston. Angelina's daughter Sissy even worked for a time at the American's newspaper, the *Woman's Journal*, and Sarah wrote for it. So, when Stone founded the Massachusetts Woman Suffrage Association as a branch of the American, Sarah and Angelina agreed to serve as vice presidents of the state organization.

In February 1870, Stone gave a lecture to a group of abolitionists and temperance advocates at the Grimké-Weld home in Hyde Park. In the discussion that followed, women in the audience decided that they needed to organize, speak out for women's suffrage, and vote in the annual town meeting.

Soon a placard went up, inviting the women of Hyde Park and men who supported women's suffrage to a March 4 caucus. Its purpose was to nominate candidates for town offices.

The meeting was well attended by women and men in equal numbers. "Stirring addresses [including one by Theodore] were made," said a newspaper account, "inciting the auditors to stand by the position they had taken in the front rank of the woman-suffrage movement, to make up their ticket and back it at the polls."

Late in the afternoon of election day, March 7, in a blinding snowstorm, the Grimké sisters and forty-five other women gathered in the parlors of a hotel, the Everett House. Their husbands, fathers, and sons came, too, presenting flowers to the women to show their support. The group set off down River Street toward the town hall.

A crowd of men milled inside. "The anti female suffrage masculines were in high glee," a local newspaper reported. But the elected official in charge, a novelist named Sylvanus Cobb Jr., quieted them, saying the women's votes "of course would not be counted and would have no influence, for or against the election." The newspaper continued, "He . . . expressed the hope that the ladies would be treated with civility and respect, at which there were affirmative responses and cheers mingled with a few hisses. When Mr Cobb had finished his few remarks the eyes of all were turned towards the door to witness the grand entree of the coming women."

"They came in a body to the polling place," said the *New York Herald*, "with bouquets and cotton umbrellas in their hands and a modest determination in their countenances, some of them old and gray headed, and many of them young and pretty." Sarah, seventy-seven, and Angelina, sixty-five, escorted by Theodore, led the procession.

"[The women's] presence," the *New York Herald* said, "which should have cast a benign influence over the unhallowed [wicked] precincts which heretofore had been accessible to men and the vile odors of rum and tobacco, was the occasion of hisses on the part of some of the disorderly men in the crowd."

As the women filed in, jeers grew so loud that Cobb threatened to have certain men arrested. "Base ruffians!" he boomed, pointing a finger at them. "Ain't you ashamed of yourselves. Do you think you are acting like men?"

In the uproar that ensued, some insisted that Cobb had no right to criticize the action of those who opposed women's suffrage. Others demanded that he resign, but he maintained that he had a right to his opinion and a duty to preserve order.

Gradually, "his attitude . . . produced a calm on the floor, and the ladies, without further molestation, advanced and deposited their ballots in a separate box, and at once left the room. The deed was done! The women had voted." When the results were announced, they were glad to learn their ticket had been elected, even though their votes were symbolic and did not count. All agreed that newspaper coverage helped to promote their cause.

At home, the Grimké-Welds were happy too. The Welds' younger son, Sody, still considered ill, visited them sometimes. Stuart, the eldest child, was living at home, writing and teaching. In 1870 Sissy married a Unitarian minister, and Archibald and Francis graduated from Lincoln. The nephews decided to stay another year to attend law school there. As usual, the aunts respected their nephews' choices. Sarah wrote to William Lloyd Garrison, "Is it not remarkable that those young men should far exceed in talents any of my other Grimké nephews, even their half-brothers bear no comparison with them and my brother Thomas' sons, distinguished as he was, are far inferior to them in intellectual power."

Angelina's health had declined, but Sarah maintained

strength and energy for physical campaigning. In May 1871 she wrote, "I have been travelling all through our town and vicinity on foot, to get signers to a petition to Congress for woman suffrage. It is not a pleasant work, often subjecting me to rudeness and coolness; but we are so frequently taunted with: 'Women don't want the ballot,' that we are trying to get one hundred thousand names of women who do want it, to reply to this taunt."

That summer she walked for miles selling copies of John Stuart Mills's essay "The Subjection of Women." A member of the British Parliament, Mills shocked British society by comparing married women to enslaved people and demanding that women should have the right to vote. His ideas echoed Sarah's in her *Letters on the Equality of the Sexes and the Condition of Women*. She sold 150 copies of his work.

Sarah Grimké in her seventies.

Sometimes she carried heavy bundles of old clothing she collected to send to freedmen. "I have been so happy this winter," she wrote to Sarah Mapps Douglass, "going about to beg old clothing for the unfortunate freedmen in Florida. I have sent off several barrels of clothes already.... I think of these destitute ones night and day, and feel so glad to help them even a little."

Happiest whenever she could help, Sarah longed to pay Archibald's expenses when, in 1872, he enrolled in Harvard Law School as one of its first Black students. Sending what little she could, she celebrated with the family when he won a scholarship to help cover his tuition.

As her eyesight and hearing began to fail, Sarah stayed active, knitting and visiting the sick for as long as she could and likely attending her nephew Stuart Weld's wedding. But in the winter of 1872–1873, she suffered several fainting spells. "My days of active usefulness are over," she wrote to a friend, "but there is a passive work to be done, far harder than actual work—namely, to exercise patience and study humble resignation to the will of God, whatever that may be. Thanks to Him, I have not yet felt like complaining; nay, verily, the song of my heart is, Who so blest as I?"

Angelina was by Sarah's side when she died at eighty-one from complications of a cold, on December 23, 1873. Angelina wrote to a friend, "You know what I have lost, not a *sister only*, but a mother, friend, counsellor,—everything I could lose in a woman."

> *"My days of active usefulness are over, but there is a passive work to be done, far harder than actual work."*
> —SARAH GRIMKÉ

Sarah's funeral was conducted by a Unitarian minister at the Weld home. The coffin, at Sarah's request, was plain pine; her family and friends covered it with flowers. Angelina's daughter, Sissy, attended with her husband and toddler daughter. Archibald came from Harvard; newspaper obituaries noted the presence of "Miss Grimké's colored nephew."

William Lloyd Garrison and Lucy Stone offered tributes,

and Theodore wept as he said, "Her heart embraced all good. She knew no creed, but loved all and identified herself with all." Led by Angelina, Black and white mourners walked together as Sarah was laid to rest at Mount Hope Cemetery, three miles from the house.

On her death certificate, in the space left for occupation, Theodore wrote, "Doing good."

CHAPTER 25
A Great Life Purpose

1874-1895

One morning after Sarah's funeral, sixty-nine-year-old Angelina awoke Theodore, saying quietly, "I've something to tell you.... Don't be alarmed.... I'm not.... Something ails my right side, I can't move hand or foot. It must be paralysis.... I wonder if a hard rubbing of your strong hands might n't throw it off." Eventually, they realized she had suffered a stroke.

Remaining cheerful, thanking God for giving her a chance to learn patience, Angelina set about rehabilitating herself. After three months, she could again write, sew, knit, and sweep, doing almost everything she had before. But as time passed, she weakened.

Still, she rejoiced in 1874 when Archibald got his law degree from Harvard, graduating first in his class, and in 1875 when Francis entered Princeton Theological Seminary, a Presbyterian institution in New Jersey. Angelina hoped the brothers would someday return to Charleston. She wanted them to redeem the Grimké name there by being upstanding citizens, not slaveholders. Instead, Archibald found a job with a Boston law firm, fighting for pensions for Black Civil War veterans, which were supposed to be the same as for white veterans but were routinely denied. Later, Archibald opened his own office and brought his mother, Nancy Weston, to live with him in Hyde Park. Their rented rooms were close to the Weld house, where they visited frequently.

After Francis graduated in 1877, he began a forty-year career as minister at the Fifteenth Street Presbyterian Church in Washington, DC. That year marked the end of Reconstruction. As President Rutherford B. Hayes withdrew federal troops from the South, white supremacists took control of state governments, denying Black citizens their constitutional rights, including the right to vote. Violence against African Americans—including race riots and lynching, with no punishment for the white perpetrators—increased. New "Jim Crow" laws mandated segregation in various states. Public transportation, parks, restaurants, hotels, theaters, and cemeteries established separate sections for Blacks or barred them completely.

A 1903 photo of Francis James Grimké.

Meanwhile, Archibald began courting Sarah Stanley, a white student at Boston University. Her father, an Episcopal priest in Michigan, had worked in the abolitionist movement. But when Archibald wrote asking permission to marry Sarah, her father answered that he and his wife had "misgivings" over the problems a mixed-race marriage would cause, especially for their daughter. In a letter to his daughter, Moses Stanley complained that she had betrayed the family, falling under the influence of Unitarians. "We look upon it as a sad day," he wrote, "when you went to Boston and especially when you associated yourself with the deniers of Christ and the insane theorizers of that infidel city."

Archibald Henry Grimké, after 1897

But Sarah Stanley did not agree with her father. In April 1879, Archibald and Sarah were married in a quiet ceremony by a Unitarian minister the groom met through the Welds. *The New York Times* republished an article about the wedding from the *Boston Journal*, "Marriage of a Colored Lawyer":

> *"An interesting event took place last Saturday," it began, "when A. H. Grimke, Esq., a well-known colored lawyer of this city was united in marriage to Miss Sarah E. Stanley, the daughter of an Episcopal clergyman of Wisconsin, and a lady of Caucasian blood."*

After extolling Archibald's advanced education and professional accomplishments, the article continued, "Mr. and Mrs. Grimké have the warm friendship of a circle of friends moving in the best ranks of Boston Society. It is rare that we chronicle the intermarriage of the races . . . and we do not remember the parallel of the above record, so far as the social circumstances attending it are concerned."

Angelina probably did not attend the ceremony. She had suffered a second stroke, and later that autumn, a third paralyzed her completely, leaving her unable to speak. Her family knew she welcomed the idea of death, which she viewed as "light and peace," but her last days brought physical pain or mental anguish—they could not tell which.

To Theodore and all who loved her, her passing, on October 26, 1879, at seventy-four, seemed a blessing. "I *cannot* mourn," Theodore wrote to a friend. "Indeed I have *no sorrow*. It is all swallowed up in a great abounding joy—in *her deliverance* [from pain and suffering]."

Angelina left a note for the family: "I have purposely selected my oldest clothes to be buried in," she wrote, "that my good ones may be given to the poor, that they may do good after I am gone."

Her funeral was held at the Weld house. "The women of to-day," Lucy Stone said there, "owe more than they will ever know to the high courage, the rare insight, and fidelity to principle of

Angelina Grimké Weld in her sixties

this woman, by whose suffering easy paths have been made for them. Her example was a bugle-call to all other women. Who can tell how many have been quickened in a great life purpose by the heroism and self-forgetting devotion of her whose voice we shall never hear again, but who, 'being dead, yet speaketh.'"

> *"The women of to-day owe more than they will ever know to the high courage, the rare insight, and fidelity to principle of this woman."*
> —LUCY STONE

Angelina was buried in Mount Hope Cemetery, side by side with her sister Sarah.

Two months after Angelina's death, her nephew Francis married Charlotte Forten, an African American woman thirteen years his senior (he was twenty-eight; she was forty-one). The two had met at the Massachusetts Freemen's Aid Society when Francis first came north, but they grew close after she applied to join his church in Washington, DC. Frederick Douglass attended their wedding.

Charlotte, an educator, poet, and essayist, published articles in the *Atlantic Monthly* (she was the first Black woman to be published there) about her experiences during the Civil War. She had taught free Black students in a school on the Sea Islands of South Carolina, which were held by the North. Later, she applied to teach at Dio Lewis's school in Lexington, but he feared that hiring a woman of color would upset white parents.

Charlotte's marriage to Francis united the Grimkés with two other famous anti-slavery families, the Fortens and the Purvises of Philadelphia (Charlotte's paternal aunts had married brothers, Joseph and William Purvis). As founding members of the Female Anti-Slavery Society, Charlotte's paternal aunts were friends with Angelina and Sarah for decades. Sarah Grimké and Sarah Forten Purvis were especially close.

After Francis and Charlotte married, his mother, Nancy, moved from Archibald's apartment in Hyde Park to the newlyweds' house in Washington. There Nancy helped Charlotte to prepare for the birth of her daughter, who was named Theodora. The doting grandmother and parents grieved when the baby died six months later.

Archibald and Sarah Stanley Grimké had a daughter of their own in 1880; they named her Angelina Weld Grimké. For reasons unknown to historians, in 1883 Sarah asked Archibald for a divorce and custody of their daughter. He agreed, hoping they would someday reconcile. Sarah and little Angelina lived for a time in Michigan with Sarah's parents, who had come to accept Archibald and a mixed-race granddaughter. They, too, hoped the family would reunite. But it was not to be. In 1887 Sarah sent the seven-year-old girl to Archibald on the train, all by herself. Then Sarah took to the lecture circuit, speaking on popular subjects, including astrology, the occult, and spiritual healing. She traveled the world, writing and speaking. Although she wrote to her daughter, she never saw her again; Sarah died by suicide in 1898.

Theodore Weld loved the little girl, who attended Fairmount Elementary School in Hyde Park. Outliving his wife by fifteen years, Theodore enjoyed life as a beloved elder. He taught about Shakespeare, abolition, and religion, and helped found the Hyde Park Historical Society. He lived at home with

Stuart and Stuart's wife, Anna, who steadied him on walks and sometimes helped with his writing. Theodore doted on their son, Louis Weld, and, at eighty-eight, was hardy enough to play blind man's bluff at the boy's birthday party.

On Theodore's ninetieth birthday, thirteen-year-old Angelina read him a birthday poem she had written. He died in his sleep, aged ninety-one, on February 3, 1895. In his will he left money to "my nephew, Archibald Grimké" for the education of his daughter.

CHAPTER 26
Answering the Bugle Call

1895-1958

As Sarah, Angelina, and Theodore had hoped, the nephews continued their work. Both assumed national leadership roles in the Black intellectual community and in the growing Civil Rights Movement. Francis, pastor of one of the largest and most important Black churches in Washington, DC, was a fiery orator who campaigned against discrimination, lynchings and, much later, the racist domestic policies of President Woodrow Wilson. When Wilson took office in 1913, the federal workforce was 10 percent Black. In his first year, Wilson, a Southerner, gave his cabinet members permission to segregate their departments.

Francis, who had formerly supported Wilson, turned against him when the president halted Black advancement possibilities for Washington, DC's thriving Black middle class, some of whom were Francis's parishioners. Francis knew and influenced many political leaders, including Frederick Douglass, whose second marriage (to a white woman) Francis performed. He served as a trustee for District of Columbia public schools and Howard University, and helped found the American Negro Academy in 1897.

Meanwhile, Archibald gave up practicing law to become the editor of a Boston newspaper, *The Hub*, which championed the rights of both African Americans and women. A talented speaker, he enhanced his public presence by publishing biographies of William Lloyd Garrison and Charles Sumner. He served for years as a trustee of a hospital for mentally ill people. After Theodore died, his children Stuart and Sarah arranged for their brother, Sody, to live there.

When Archibald traveled out of town on business, his daughter Angelina stayed at the Weld house, playing with Stuart's son, Louis, who was two years younger.

In 1894 President Grover Cleveland appointed Archibald consul to Santo Domingo, in the Dominican Republic. A consul's job was to live in a foreign country, while promoting the interests of the United States government and of American citizens living in the country. Anxious to do his best for his fifteen-year-old daughter, Archibald left Angelina in Washington with Francis, Charlotte, and Nancy.

In Santo Domingo, Archibald lived with a white American sugar baron. He

Charlotte Forten in a photo from the 1870s

socialized with consuls from other countries, members of the American community, and with Dominican government officials, and he met often with the country's dictator president, Ulises Heureaux, a Black man who had risen from poverty to power, and then sank to great cruelty and corruption. Archibald negotiated business deals over land and construction that benefited wealthy Americans and Dominicans but displaced poor workers as the nation changed from small-scale tobacco farming to massive sugar operations.

Archibald saw Heureaux's faults but admired him for leading a country where Black and white people lived together in peace. After attending a state ball, he wrote to his brother, "There is not the slightest hint on such an occasion of the existence of such a thing as prejudice against color, not even among the Americans. You will hardly credit it that after they live here a while they (the Americans) seem to lose their diabolic ability of detecting the presence of a drop of black blood in one of us. The gift seems to be reversed for they seem to have a marvelous faculty for finding in one of us a drop of white blood. And a few drops of this blood have a wonderfully whitening effect." After years of coping with the opposite attitude, that one drop of Black blood made an American Black, this reversal interested him.

At the end of the school year, Charlotte wrote that she and Francis could no longer handle their unruly niece, Angelina, who argued with them and made little effort at her studies. She remained close to her grandmother Nancy, sitting with her and holding her hand through her final illness. Angelina was romantically attracted to other girls, writing and receiving love letters that probably distressed her aunt and uncle. Chastising his daughter in letters for upsetting them and squandering her opportunities, Archibald, with Francis and Charlotte, arranged for the fifteen-year-old to attend the Northfield Academy in Minnesota. She stayed a year and then returned to Boston, where she attended Cushing Academy and then the Boston Normal School of Gymnastics, which later became Wellesley College.

In 1897 Archibald returned from the Dominican Republic to the United States. In 1902 Angelina graduated from college and came to live with him in Washington, DC. She had begun publishing poetry about nature, life, and race in newspapers while also writing—but not publishing—poems about her love for women. She never lived openly as a lesbian, perhaps out of respect for her father or to protect her job as a high school English teacher or just to maintain her privacy. Instead, she devoted her life to Archibald and to writing fiction, nonfiction, and plays that focused on issues near to his heart: racial prejudice and lynching.

In the first two decades of the twentieth century, the African American community was divided over which leaders and strategies to follow. For a time, Archibald and Francis supported Booker T. Washington, founder of the Tuskegee Institute in Alabama. Washington's theory of providing practical education to Black students, and his best-selling 1901 autobiography, *Up from Slavery*, won support from Black and white people alike. Washington believed in accommodation: that Black people would accept an inferior role in society, supporting segregation, if white people would just stop murdering them. "In all things that are purely social," he said, "we can be as separate fingers, yet one as the hand in all things essential to mutual progress."

Later, however, Francis urged a more militant approach to civil rights, protesting groups that practiced racism including the Presbyterian Church and the Young Men's Christian

Association. He urged African Americans to stop acting against their own best interests by doing what white people demanded and advised them to choose self-defense instead. "A race that permits itself to be trampled upon will be trampled upon," he said.

In 1903 W. E. B. Du Bois, a Black sociologist, published *The Souls of Black Folk*. The book, which included an attack on Booker T. Washington, made Du Bois the leader of a more radical group of reformers. In 1909 Archibald and Francis joined Du Bois, Ida Wells-Barnett, Mary Church Terrell, and other, mostly white leaders in founding the organization later named the National Association for the Advancement of Colored People, or NAACP. Four years later, Archibald was elected president of the largest NAACP chapter, in Washington, DC, and he became a member of the national organization's board of directors.

After Francis's wife, Charlotte, died in 1914, Archibald and Angelina continued to live with him in a beautiful row house in northwest Washington. There, for several years, Angelina worked on a play, *Rachel*, which was first produced in 1916. The main character, Rachel Loving, is a young woman of color, living in a Northern city during the first decade of the twentieth century. A student who longs someday to have babies, she befriends the children in her apartment building. Rachel's mother reveals to Rachel and her brother Tom that when they were very young, she escaped with them from the South after her husband and older son were lynched.

The second act of the play takes place four years later. The family has adopted an orphan named Jimmy. Rachel has graduated, and Tom is an electrical engineer, but they cannot find suitable jobs because of their color. After white boys stone Jimmy and call him by the worst possible racial slur, Rachel

Angelina Weld Grimké about 1923

decides not to marry the man she loves because she cannot bear to bring any more Black or brown babies into the world for white people to hate and kill. "Why—it would be more merciful," she says, "—to strangle the little things at birth. And this nation—this white Christian nation—has deliberately set its curse upon the most beautiful—the most holy thing in life—motherhood! Why—it—makes—you doubt—God!"

Rachel, Angelina's most enduring creation, linked the violence of the past to the contemporary horror of lynchings that occurred frequently in her lifetime. The NAACP contrasted the play with the 1915 silent movie *The Birth of a Nation*. This movie, proudly shown by President Wilson at the White House, portrayed the hate group, the Ku Klux Klan, as heroes saving the South from Black rule after the Civil War.

Archibald died in 1930, and Francis died seven years later. After her father died, Angelina retired from writing and moved to New York, where she lived a quiet life. She died in 1958. Although she did not write in New York, she is remembered as one of the earliest and most distinguished writers of the Harlem Renaissance, a cultural movement of the 1920s that was centered in Harlem. It is considered the first time when Black artists celebrated their own culture in literature, arts, music, and theater. Angelina Weld Grimké's poetry, which is still being discovered and published, continues to gain in popularity and critical acclaim, and *Rachel* is still performed.

Sarah and Angelina hoped their nephews and their descendants would carry on their revolutionary beliefs. And indeed, the two young men from humble beginnings and the talented playwright and poet fulfilled their aunts' wishes in ways the sisters could not have imagined. Archibald, Francis, and young Angelina created tactics for a new century, based on methods they learned in years spent with their elders: speaking the truth, standing up to established power if it was wrong, and advocating for equal rights for all people.

As young women, the Grimké sisters were expected to lead predictable, comfortable lives, ordinary for their time and class. Their early desire to make a difference seemed limited by their being just two individuals, females lacking in education and power. But the injustices they saw and experienced made them decide to defy family, custom, religion, and even laws. In doing so, they created their own kind of power, one that changed American society. Their standing as women, and as Southerners who had lived with, benefited from, and then rejected slavery made them unique among abolitionists, and so did their certainty that the struggles for racial equality and gender equality were inseparable.

The discovery of their mixed-race nephews gave the sisters another way to demonstrate their convictions. Slavery, they insisted, destroyed families, Black and white. They took personal responsibility for the horrors their Black relatives had faced, remaking their own formerly white family in the process. The amends they offered and the love they shared had an impact that eventually reached far beyond their home circle.

Working side by side, Sarah and Angelina turned a part of the world upside down, and their efforts continue to inspire people to this day.

AFTERWORD
A History of the History of the Grimké Sisters

In 2019 the city of Boston renamed a newly reconstructed bridge in Hyde Park the Grimké Sisters Bridge. The Hyde Park Historical Association said, "Their places in both the abolition and women's suffrage movements are long overdue for recognition and restoration to prominence. It is impossible to overemphasize the role they both played in the struggle for justice in both these fields. A bridge, as a symbol of movement and connection, is a fitting way to honor all they worked for."

Recognition of the sisters' work has waxed and waned. At Angelina's funeral in 1879, Lucy Stone said, "Outside of her home circle, the generation that is alive today did not know her." Subsequent generations did not know her either, or her sister Sarah, who had died six years earlier. Nor did they remember her husband, Theodore, who survived her. Yet in the 1830s, all three were nationally recognized figures.

The first person to document the sisters' lives was Theodore, who compiled personal memories, along with addresses from their funerals, in a short book, *In Memory, Angelina Grimké Weld* (1880).

Elizabeth Cady Stanton, Matilda Joslyn Gage, and Susan B. Anthony wrote about the sisters in the first volume of their *History of Woman Suffrage* in 1881. The book was dedicated to the memory of Sarah and Angelina and fifteen other early women's rights leaders who had died. Twenty-two pages about the sisters include a biographical sketch of Angelina, written by Stanton. It ends with these words: "All through the years that Angelina was illustrating woman's capacity on the platform by holding her audiences spell-bound, Sarah was defending woman's right to be there with her pen."

Theodore worked with a family friend, Catherine Birney, on the earliest full-length biography of the sisters, published in 1885, *The Grimké Sisters: Sarah and Angelina Grimké: The First American Women Advocates of Abolition and Woman's Rights*. Birney, who lived for two years in the Raritan Bay apartment building with the Grimké-Welds, had grown close to the sisters, especially Sarah. In her book, she recounts stories they told her and quotes their diaries and letters.

In 1919 Congress passed the Nineteenth Amendment to the Constitution: "The right of citizens of the United States to vote shall not be denied or abridged by the United States or by any State on account of sex." The amendment was ratified the following year. Eighty years after the sisters had first fought for women's rights, a part of their vision had been realized while their names had been forgotten, along with those of other early leaders, including Sarah Mapps Douglass, Matilda Joslyn Gage, Abby Kelley Foster, Lucretia Mott, Elizabeth Cady Stanton, Lucy Stone, and Sojourner Truth. (In recent years, many books about these women have been published.) Although Stanton drafted it, the Nineteenth Amendment was called the Anthony Amendment, after Susan B. Anthony, and hers was the name most associated with women's rights as time passed.

In 1934 many of the sisters' letters were published in *Letters of Theodore Dwight Weld, Angelina Grimké Weld and Sarah Grimké, 1822–1844*, but Theodore was the main focus of this book. And in the years that followed, male historians and publishers, who controlled the study of history, lost interest in women's rights as the country moved through the Great Depression, World War II, and the postwar boom of economic growth.

Not until the 1960s, during the renewed American Civil Rights Movement, did a second-wave women's rights movement surface. Women still faced inequality in many areas, some of which prevails to this day. Job discrimination was blatant. Women were excluded from leadership positions in government, business, and even the Civil Rights Movement. Working women faced prejudices based on their ages, looks, and marital and pregnancy status. Abortion was illegal in the United States, denying women control over their own bodies. (In 1973 the Supreme Court established the legal right to abortion nationwide in the *Roe v. Wade* case. In 2022 the court overturned that decision and upheld *Dobbs v. Jackson Women's Health Organization*, and since then, access to abortions has been banned or tightly restricted in a number of states.)

In 1964, outraged that women's rights were routinely withheld, activists led the battle to pass a new Civil Rights Act. The act barred employment discrimination based on race, national origin, skin color, religion, and sex. After that, women could sue employers who discriminated against them. And sue they did, winning many cases, sometimes taking them all the way to the Supreme Court.

In 1966 women's rights activists founded the National Organization for Women. They wrote books to show that women's experiences had been buried and never studied by historians. They pushed for an Equal Rights Amendment to the Constitution (which we still don't have). Female scholars founded women's studies departments at universities to document current happenings, to look to the past for lessons, and to equip leaders for the future.

One of those scholars, Gerda Lerner, had fled as a young woman from the Nazi regime in her native Austria. Immigrating to the United States, she earned a PhD in history at Columbia University and helped establish pioneering graduate programs in women's studies at several universities. She wrote her PhD dissertation about the Grimké sisters, who were then virtually unknown by the American public. Lerner submitted her manuscript to multiple publishers; twenty-four refused it on the grounds that it would not sell. "The rejection letters were, on the whole, very flattering," Lerner said. "They praised the writing . . . and in several cases openly stated that it was the topic they were rejecting. Books on women do not sell, was the common wisdom. And books on nineteenth-century women were even less likely to sell."

Finally, in 1964, Houghton Mifflin agreed to publish the book, but only if Lerner would drop the last five words of her proposed title: *The Grimké Sisters from South Carolina: Rebels Against Slavery and Pioneers for Woman's Rights.* (Lerner used the term "woman's rights," which is how the earliest women's rights advocates named the movement.) Women's rights, her editor insisted, would not sell books. Lerner gave in, the title was shortened, the book was published, and it remains the definitive biography of Sarah and Angelina. By the time Schocken Books offered to print the book in paperback in

1970, the second phase of the women's rights movement had kicked in, and Lerner was able to insist on using her original title (later editions changed the word "woman's" in the title to "women's.")

Katharine Du Pre Lumpkin spent twenty years researching and writing a book about Angelina. This research included a 1955 interview with her grandniece Angelina Weld Grimké, who added fresh family stories and new documentation to the published record. Lumpkin's *The Emancipation of Angelina Grimké* was published in 1974.

Mark Perry's *Lift Up Thy Voice: The Grimké Family's Journey from Slaveholders to Civil Rights Leaders*, released in 2001, extended the family history from the sisters to their famous nephews and grandniece. All these books portrayed the sisters as heroes of the anti-slavery and women's rights movements.

Kerri K. Greenidge offered a different view of Sarah and Angelina in her 2022 collective biography *The Grimkes: The Legacy of Slavery in an American Family*. While acknowledging the sisters as important abolitionists, she also criticized them for living on family inheritances gained from slave labor. Greenidge said the sisters wanted to end slavery for their own salvation and that they saw Black people, even their nephews, as less than equal human beings.

The sisters' own writings, first appearing in pamphlets, newspapers, and books, were republished in new, stand-alone books beginning in the 1980s. Three biographies of the sisters written for young people were published from 1972 to 1999, and in recent years, articles about them have begun to appear in collective biographies for young readers.

The most famous recent book about Sarah and Angelina is a best-selling historical novel *The Invention of Wings* (2014) by

Sue Monk Kidd. Talk show host Oprah Winfrey chose it for her Oprah's Book Club and bought the rights to turn it into a film. The novel boosted Charleston tourism, making sites connected with the sisters, including two family homes, more popular. In 2023 Charleston launched a new International African American Museum at Gadsden's Wharf, where enslaved Africans were first brought to the United States and which the Grimkés could see from their house.

Supreme Court Justice Ruth Bader Ginsburg, who began her career during the second phase of the women's movement, admired the sisters. In two 2018 movies about herself—a drama titled *On the Basis of Sex* and a documentary, *RBG*—the real Ginsburg speaks on camera, quoting Sarah Grimké as she did in her first oral arguments before the Supreme Court in 1973: "I ask no favor for my sex. All I ask of our brethren is that they take their feet off our necks."

> *"I ask no favor for my sex. All I ask of our brethren is that they take their feet off our necks."*
> —SARAH GRIMKÉ

Over the years, people have held varying views of the Grimké sisters. Sarah's parents considered her a rebellious child. The whole family thought both sisters were deluded in their opinions about slavery but admired their courage and devotion. Orthodox Quakers called them disobedient and self-centered. When they began speaking and writing, some abolitionists admired them, but many more Americans judged them to be evil and unwomanly. After they retired from public life, some former colleagues thought they were shirkers, abandoning the abolitionist cause. In the twentieth century, historians and publishers considered them insignificant, boring, and unmarketable as biographical subjects because they were women. In recent years, as historians have begun to compile information about culturally diverse leaders in the women's rights and Civil Rights Movement, publishers again labeled the sisters unmarketable, calling them "white saviors." And Greenidge's book portrayed them as often self-centered and cruel.

> *"I recognize no rights but human rights."*
> —ANGELINA GRIMKÉ

No matter how people saw them, the sisters remained true to what they thought was right. Sarah and Angelina made a difference in the United States. And the issues they fought—racial prejudice and injustice toward women—still impact our lives. Angelina's ideal still serves as the perfect guide for future change: "I recognize no rights but human rights."

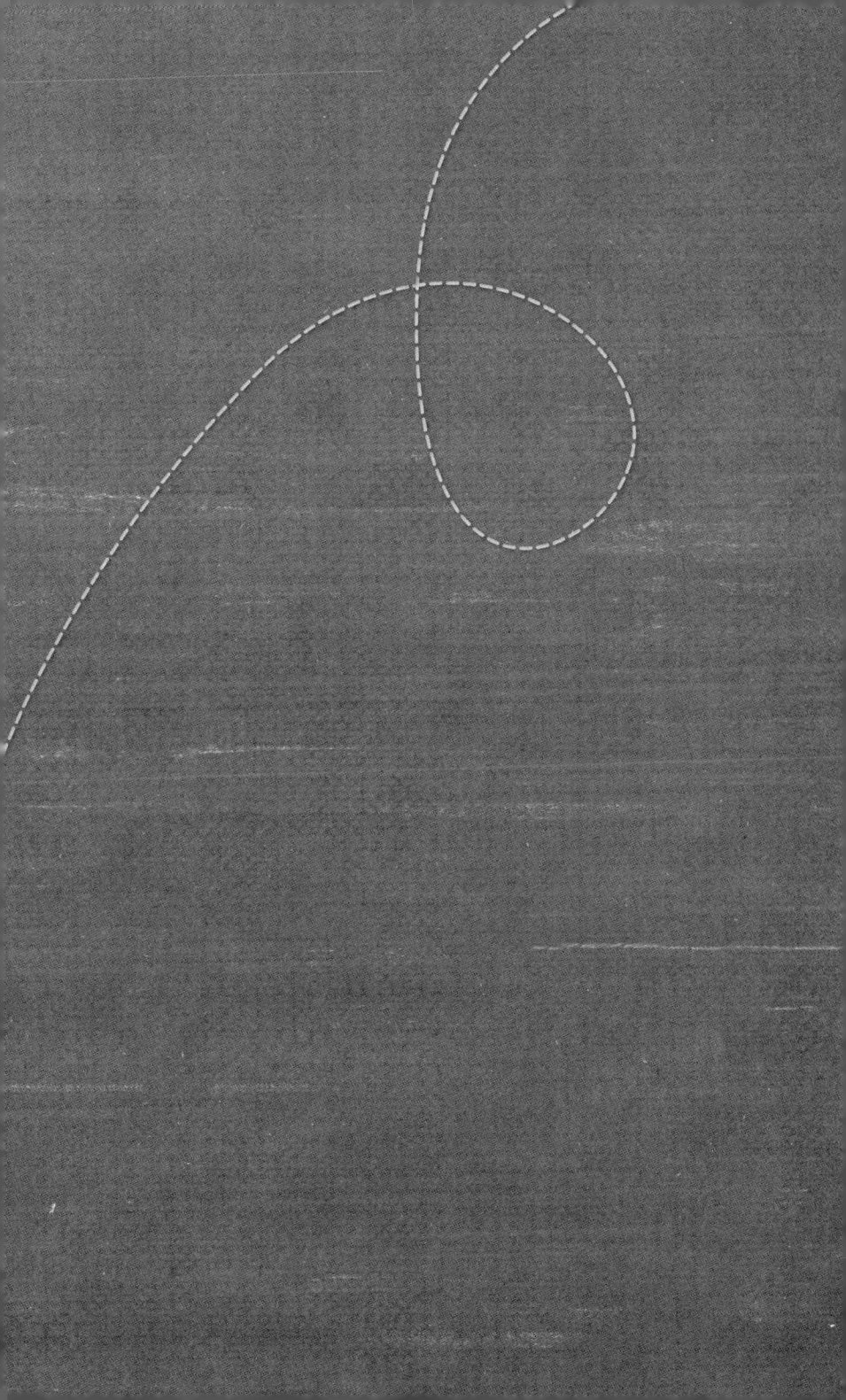

Author's Note

"How do you choose your subjects?" people ask. It may sound strange, but many of my ideas begin with Oz. My mother was a childhood Oz fan who inherited her uncle's Oz books. Then I came along, the family's third-generation fan, but the first Oz nut. Those books have shaped my life's work.

My mother, Jean Shirley, was always a writer. When I was a teenager, she published a series of biographies for children. After I became a librarian, we started writing together. In 1990 we published a middle-grade biography for Lerner, *L. Frank Baum, Royal Historian of Oz*. While writing that book, we learned about Baum's mother-in-law, Matilda Joslyn Gage, a leader for almost fifty years in the women's rights movement.

Gage, born in 1826, worked closely for decades with Elizabeth Cady Stanton and Susan B. Anthony, but they had a falling-out late in life. Gage died first, and after she did, her so-called friends wrote her out of history. I decided to write her back in. My biography *Born Criminal: Matilda Joslyn Gage, Radical Suffragist* came out in 2018, and it was Gage who led me to two women she particularly admired: Sarah and Angelina Grimké.

When I began my research, the sisters were known primarily from Sue Monk Kidd's 2015 novel *The Invention of Wings*. "Wait a minute," people stopped me, when I said the unusual name *Grimké*, "I read a book about them." I read it, too, and enjoyed it, but I knew it was fiction. When I started learning about, and then talking about, the real sisters—rejecting slavery, leaving a life of luxury in Charleston, going North to live simply as Quakers, becoming abolitionists and women's rights advocates—people seemed interested and I was hooked.

Writing a biography feels like putting together a jigsaw puzzle. Sometimes I have too many pieces—too much information about one particular event, like the burning of Pennsylvania Hall. Sometimes I don't have enough. Readers ask if Sarah received marriage proposals when she was young and they want to know how she met Susan B. Anthony. I wonder, too. If I knew, I would have told those stories in the book.

Authors make the best biography subjects, I think, since they write about themselves. As I worked, I learned that I share many beliefs with the sisters, especially the necessity for equal rights for all and the value of education. Their continued love for their hometown and family of origin reinforced my belief that we can love a place or person while acknowledging deep flaws; that we can press people to be better *because* we love them; that we can maintain contact even with people with whom we have fundamental disagreements.

Doing research about the past is a kind of time travel. But the twenty-first century seems to be repeating happenings from the sisters' lifetime. Racism continues. Sarah Grimké's plea for men to take their feet off women's necks acquired new resonance after the murder of George Floyd. The Black Lives Matter movement upset modern white supremacists in the same way that abolitionists upset pro-slavery advocates.

To the sisters, the two issues—Black rights and women's rights—were inevitably linked. In the 1830s, Southern senators and representatives who favored enslavement controlled the United States Congress. Today Congress is controlled by a political party with a newly diminished interest in equality for all. The current administration is dismantling diversity, equality, and inclusion programs in the public and private sectors.

The country's new "patriotic" education policy says that our schools should teach only history that makes children feel proud, with no mention of past injustices. Book banning, which Theodore fought in 1875, is making headlines now as states pass laws to prohibit teachers and librarians from teaching, and students from reading, about the real history of our country.

Women's rights can be won and then lost. After two hundred years of struggle, we still don't have an equal rights amendment, or equal pay for equal work. As I wrote this book, the Supreme Court reversed the 1973 *Roe v. Wade* decision, which gave an individual, not the government, the right to decide about terminating a pregnancy. Now abortion is illegal in many places and access to birth control is under attack.

Technology changes. The Grimké sisters used their pens and their voices, with newspapers and pamphlets, to spread their opinions; today we have social media. Microphones, videos, and podcasts let modern speakers reach large audiences, but we have no better messages or techniques than Sarah and Angelina did: standing up and speaking out, insisting on the truth. Studying the past provides ammunition—motivation and methods—that can help us in the future, to make a better world for all.

Grimké Family Tree

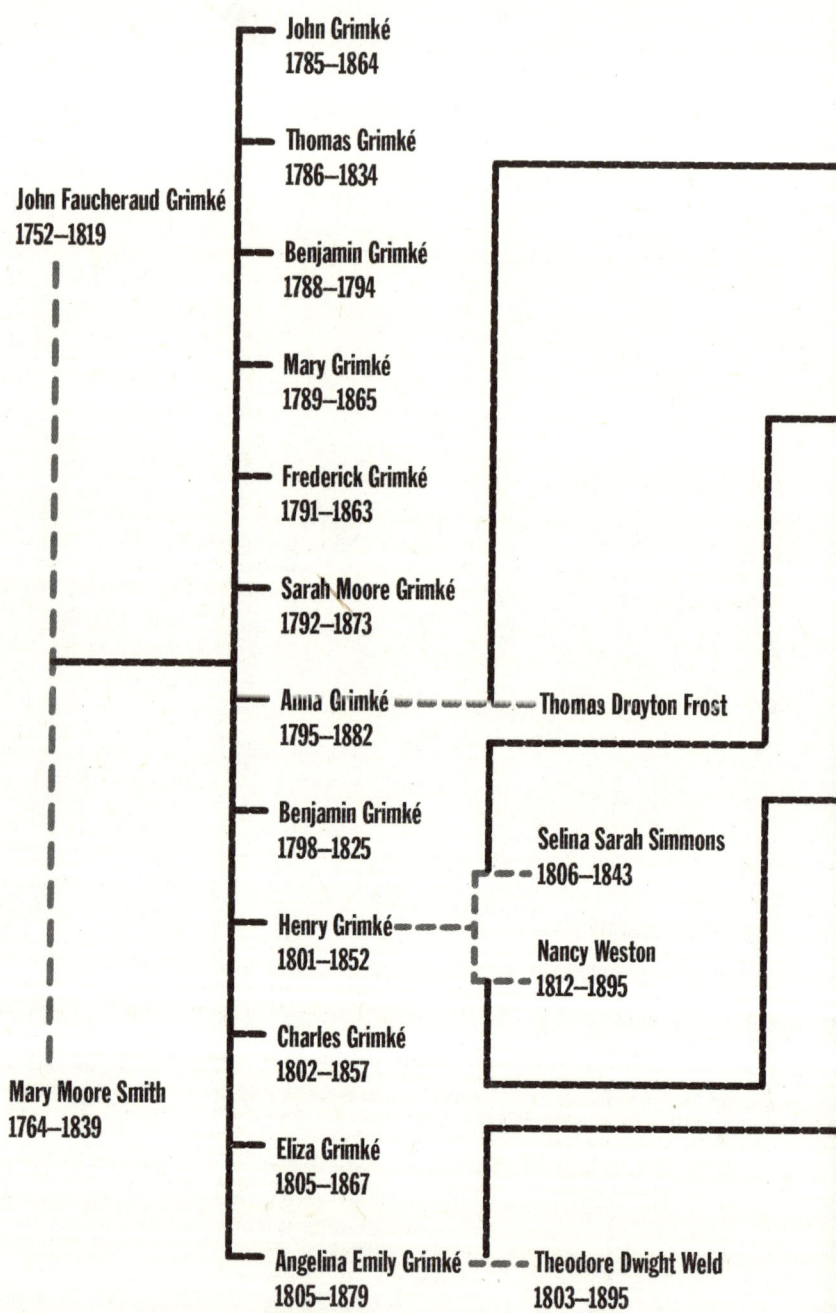

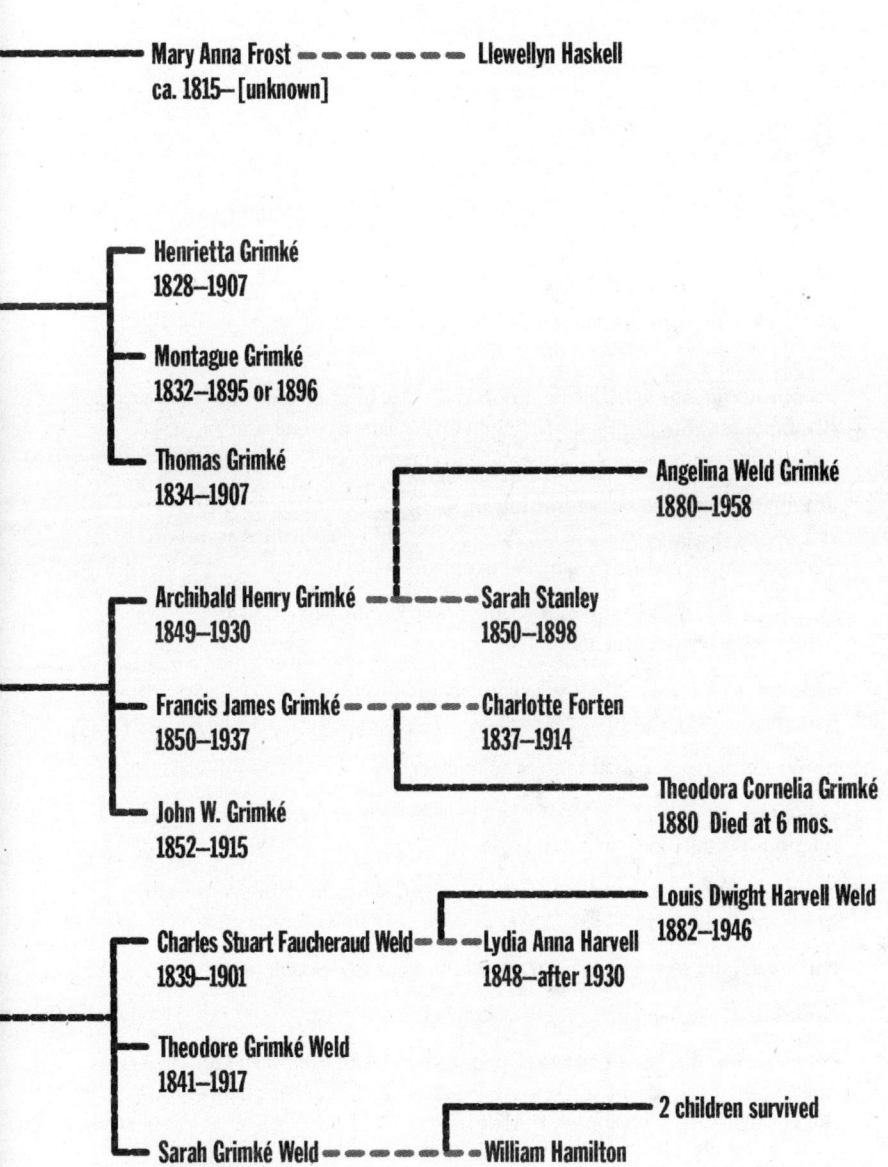

Glossary

Note: This glossary includes words that are likely unfamiliar to young readers today. Many words in this book, used in the 1800s, are considered offensive today.

abolition: the act of stopping something; in the United States, especially, the act of ending enslavement

accommodation: a belief by Booker T. Washington and others that Black people should pursue the right to be left separate and in peace, rather than demanding equality and full integration

amalgamation: the act of uniting or merging two different things. In the 1800s, the term was used to describe sexual relationships and reproduction between white people and people of color

amanuensis: an assistant who writes down words spoken by another or makes copies of documents

arsenal: a place, usually a government establishment, where arms are manufactured or stored

body servant: a personal servant to one person

celibacy: the state of not having sex, especially because you have made a religious promise not to

censure: express strong disapproval of someone or something, especially in a formal statement

chaise: a light, horse-drawn carriage for one or two people

colonialist: one who believed in colonization

colonization: to send settlers to live elsewhere. The American Colonization Society desired to send formerly enslaved and free Black people from the United States to colonies in Africa.

colored: a dark-skinned person. Considered polite in the 1800s, the term is still used in some names, such as the National Association for the Advancement of Colored People, but in the 1960s, it was replaced by *black* (capitalized since the early 2020s) and African American.

commune: a group of people living together and sharing possessions and responsibilities

conscientious objector: one who refuses to bear arms or serve in the armed forces for moral or religious reasons

distaff: a stick or a spindle on which wool is wound for spinning

driver: an overseer of enslaved laborers or prisoners

emancipation: setting people free from enslavement

enslave: to make a person or people subordinate to another; to deprive of freedom, especially political or religious freedom; to make a person work without pay

enslaver: one who enslaves. In the 1800s, an enslaver was called an "owner," "master," or "mistress."

envenomed: made poisonous

expatriation: banishing a person from his or her country

fallen woman: one who has had sex outside of marriage, often a prostitute

fetter: to restrain or chain; a chain or shackle, often on the feet

flogging: a beating, for punishment or torture, with a whip

freedmen: people who had been emancipated from enslavement

free produce: produce or products grown, processed, or manufactured, or all of these without the use of enslaved labor

Free-Soiler: a person who wanted Kansas to enter the nation as a free state, where enslavement would be illegal

Hicksites: Quakers who followed the teachings of Elias Hicks (1748–1830) and were more liberal than Orthodox Quakers

Jim Crow laws: laws restricting the rights of Black people, probably named for a Black character in a derogatory song

jurist: lawyer or judge

laudanum: a pain-killing tincture of opium dissolved in alcohol

lyceum: a hall for public lectures

lynch: to kill someone without legal authority, often by hanging, for an alleged offense

manacle: shackles or handcuffs for the hands or wrists

medium: a person believed to be able to contact spirits of the dead and to enable communication between the living and the dead. Mediums were part of the popular trend of spiritualism that began in the 1840s.

miscegenation: a derogatory term referring to mixing of or reproduction between those considered to be of different races, especially sexual relationships and reproduction between white and nonwhite people

mulatto: a person with one Black parent and one white parent

Negro: a member of a dark-skinned group of people having sub-Saharan African ancestry. Considered polite in the 1800s, the term began to be phased out in the 1960s and by the 1980s had been replaced by *black* (capitalized starting in the 2020s) or African American.

nursemaid: a woman other than the biological mother who took care of a baby or young child

Orthodox: holding strict or extreme religious beliefs

overseer: a person in charge of a job or workforce

pacifism: belief in peaceful methods of settling disagreements as opposed to war or violence

phrenologist: one who practices the pseudoscientific belief that bumps and depressions on people's heads reflected their characters

plantation: a large estate cultivated by laborers to grow cash crops

poke bonnet: a woman's hat with a small crown and a wide and rounded front brim that extends beyond the face

promiscuous: including both men and women, as in a mixed audience of men and women

Reconstruction: the period from 1865 to 1877 in which the Southern states that had seceded during the American Civil War rejoined the United States

salvation: deliverance from sin and its consequences, believed by Christians to be the result of faith in Jesus Christ

sanatorium: a place that treated patients with long-term illnesses or those recovering from illness

scourging: a whipping

seminary: an institution of learning or a place where students train for a particular profession

slavery: the state of being the legal property of another person, having no freedom or rights, and used for enforced labor

suffrage: the right to vote in political elections

tar and feather: a form of torture that involved stripping a person to the waist, pouring hot pine tar on the skin, and then adding feathers; victims usually survived

temperance: a movement seeking to eliminate or limit consumption of alcoholic beverages

Underground Railroad: a network of people, shelters, and escape plans to aid runaways from enslavement in the United States in the early and mid-nineteenth century

wench: a term which once meant a young girl, but at this time, it was used to mean a prostitute

workhouse: in Charleston, a punishment prison for enslaved people

Source Notes

11 Whipping of enslaved woman: Sarah Grimké left no description of the whipping she saw. This description is taken from Frederick Douglass's account of how he, as a child, saw his teenaged aunt being whipped. Frederick Douglass, *The Narrative of the Life of Frederick Douglass, an American Slave* (Floating Press, 2008), 31–32.

17 "The warmth of . . . from *ennui* [boredom].": John Benwell, *Englishman's Travels in America* (Carlisle, MA, 1857), 204–205.

17 "the females [in . . . females amoung them.": Benwell, 205.

19–20 "My great desire . . . of South Carolina.": Sarah Grimké, quoted in Catherine H. Birney, *The Grimké Sisters: Sarah and Angelina Grimké, the First American Women Advocates of Abolition and Women's Rights* (Haskell House, 1970), 12.

20 "Woe betide anything . . . of neat housekeeping,": Grimké, quoted in Birney, 8.

20 "I had to . . . these unpaid toilers.": Grimké, quoted in Birney, 9.

21 "Slavery was a . . . enjoyed him thoroughly.": Grimké, quoted in Birney, 10–11.

21 "Never lose an . . . thankful to have it.": John Grimké, quoted in Birney, 9.

21 "polite education for ladies,": Gerda Lerner, *The Grimké Sisters from South Carolina: Rebels Against Slavery* (Houghton Mifflin, 1967), 13–14.

21 "the greatest jurist . . . in the land.": John Grimké, quoted in Birney, *Grimké Sisters*, 8.

22 "You are a . . . never use them.": Grimké, quoted in Birney, 18.

22 "unwomanly.": Grimké, quoted in Birney, 18.

23 "Oh, how good . . . blessed to her!": Grimké, quoted in Birney, 13.

24 "Only two meals . . . way of punishment.": Angelina Grimké, quoted in Theodore Dwight Weld, *American Slavery as It Is: Testimony of a Thousand Witnesses*, originally published in 1839 (Arno / New York Times, 1969), 56. The original title capitalized "As," but we have lower cased the title to conform with modern standards.

25 "Mother is perfectly . . . brought us up,": Angelina Grimké, quoted in Birney, *Grimké Sisters*, 72.

25 "She rules slaves . . . rod of fear!": Angelina Grimké, quoted in Katharine Du Pre Lumpkin, *The Emancipation of Angelina Grimké* (University of North Carolina Press, 1974), 3.

25 "I tried to . . . continually before them.": Angelina Grimké, quoted in Birney, *Grimké Sisters*, 15.

26 "I saw *nothing* . . . out for show.": Angelina Grimké, quoted in Weld, *American Slavery as It Is*, 53.

26 "I remember very . . . excitement or enquiry.": Grimké, quoted in Weld, 54.

26 "I saw [slavery] . . . out for show.": Grimké, quoted in Weld, 53.

26 "sweetened up.": John Davis, "The Woods of South Carolina," in Jennie Holton Fant, ed., *The Travelers' Charleston: Accounts of Charleston and Lowcountry, South Carolina, 1666–1861* (University of South Carolina Press, 2016), 82–83.

27–28 "That house of . . . under their torture.": Angelina Grimké, quoted in Weld, *American Slavery as It Is*, 54–55.

28 "When I was . . . *I fainted away*.": Grimké, quoted in Weld, 54–55.

29 "I used to . . . outrages and pollutions.": Grimké, quoted in Weld, 52.

29 "an active, efficient, *devoted* officer": Barbara L. Bellows, *Benevolence Among Slaveholders: Assisting the Poor in Charleston* (Louisiana State University Press, 1993), 49.

29 "fallen": Bellows, 47.

29 "certificates signed by . . . character and necessities.": Cynthia Kennedy, *Braided Relations, Entwined Lives: The Women of Charleston's Urban Slave Society* (Indiana University Press, 2005), 210.

30 "Few have exceeded . . . pride and vanity.": Sarah Grimké, quoted in Birney, *Grimké Sisters*, 18.

32 "As I was . . . from running away.": Sarah Grimké, quoted in Weld, *American Slavery as It Is*, 23.

32 "men and women . . . standing in society.": Grimké, quoted in Weld, 22.

32–33 "A heavy iron . . . from personal inspection.": Grimké, quoted in Weld, 22.

33 "Their cruelties did . . . standing in society.": Grimké, quoted in Weld, 22.

33 "with her lacerated . . . heavy iron collar,": Grimké, quoted in Weld, 22.

33 "Often during this . . . its gilded toys.": Sarah Grimké, quoted in Birney, *Grimké Sisters*, 18.

33 "*amanuensis*": Birney, 11.

34 "a course of . . . to everlasting punishment,": Birney, 20.

34 "butterfly life,": Birney, 19.

35 "Your father's life . . . the Lord's hands": Specialist, quoted in Lerner, *Grimké Sisters*, 31.

35 "Do not indulge . . . I desire it.": John Grimké, quoted in Lerner, 33.

37 "burst on my mind with renewed horror.": Sarah Grimké, quoted in Lerner, 37.

37 "any five of . . . belonging to me.": John Faucheraud Grimké, Will of John Facheraud Grimke', signed 1818, proved October 28, 1818, held in the South Carolina Room, Charleston County Public Library, 1.

39 "until they becames . . . incessantly gnawing.": Birney, *Grimké Sisters*, 25–26.

39 "I was as . . . on their sufferings.": Sarah Grimké, quoted in Lerner, *Grimké Sisters*, 37.

39 "How dreadful did . . . despair of salvation.": Sarah Grimké, quoted in Birney, *Grimké Sisters*, 28.

39 "Thee had better . . . their sober dress.": Thomas Grimké, quoted in Birney, 30.

40 "Go North,": Sarah Grimké, quoted in Mark Perry, *Lift Up Thy Voice: The Grimké Family's Journey from Slaveholders to Civil Rights Leaders* (Viking, 2001), 54.

43–44 "Oh! had I . . . poor and unfortunate.": Sarah Grimké, quoted in Birney, *Grimké Sisters*, 38.

44–45 "Can it be . . . to do it.": Grimké, quoted in Birney, 36.

45 "I struggle against . . . to think of,": Sarah Grimké, quoted in Perry, *Lift Up Thy Voice*, 68–69.
45 "the snare of Satan,": Grimké, quoted in Perry, 68–69.
45 "That was a . . . and my God.": Sarah Grimké, quoted in Mary Townsend McChesney Bushkovitch, *The Grimkés of Charleston* (Southern Historical, 1992), 504.
46 "starving on the cold water of Episcopacy.": Angelina Grimké, quoted in Bushkovitch, 500–501.
46 "quite beyond the pale.": Grimké, quoted in Bushkovitch, 502.
46 "My attention has . . . dressing quite plain.": Angelina Emily Grimké, *Walking by Faith: The Diary of Angelina Grimké, 1828–1835* (University of South Carolina Press, 2003), 7.
46 "My hat I . . . look like one.": Grimké, 2.
47 "The subject of . . . in humble faith.": Sarah Grimké, quoted in Bushkovitch, *Grimkés*, 513.
47 "Go, and I will be with thee.": Grimké, quoted in Bushkovitch, 513.
48 "The Spirit whispers . . . from among them,": Angelina Grimké, quoted in Birney, *Grimké Sisters*, 60.
48 "My mind is . . . the fountain itself.": Grimké, quoted in Birney, 59–60.
48 "I feel that . . . in this city.": Grimké, quoted in Birney, 60.
49 "several of whom . . . and paying nothing.": Birney, 68.
49 "It is true . . . is in Christ.": Sarah Grimké, quoted in Birney, 67.
49–50 "*[Mother] said it . . . change my sentiments?*": Angelina Grimké, quoted in Birney, 71.
50 "very painful conversation,": Grimké, *Walking by Faith*, 88.
50–51 "No wonder poor . . . daggers to my heart.": Angelina Grimké, quoted in Birney, *Grimké Sisters*, 76.
51 "said rather than . . . leave mother's house.": Grimké, quoted in Birney, 77.
51 "excessive ornamentation.": editor of Grimké, *Walking by Faith*, 90.
51 "Though we considered . . . a feeling of awe.": unnamed Grimké sister, quoted in Birney, *Grimké Sisters*, 82.
52 "a colored woman . . . side of her.": Birney, 73.
52 "As I approached . . . of the Slave?": Angelina Grimké, quoted in Birney, 73–74.

52 "Night & day ... chains of iron.": Grimké, quoted in Birney, 74.
52 "When shall I ... be quite willing": Grimké, quoted in Birney, 66.
52 "O Lord, how ... of the slave.": Grimké, quoted in Birney, 73–74.
53 "My soul sometimes ... the Captain's care,": Grimké, *Walking by Faith*, 128.
53–54 "I had a ... I had supposed.": Grimké, 130.
54 "I have parted ... see you again.": Grimké, 134.
55 "Very often do ... was taken from.": Angelina Grimké, quoted in Birney, *Grimké Sisters*, 104.
56 "feeling as if ... whenever I arise.": Sarah Grimké, quoted in Birney, 96.
57 "I sobbed aloud ... in Slave country.": Grimké, *Walking by Faith*, 139.
58 "O Lord, be ... to be *still*.": Sarah Grimké, quoted in Birney, *Grimké Sisters*, 98.
59 "far inferior to those of Phila[delphia]": Grimké, *Walking by Faith*, 148.
60 "a moving mass of gayity & fashion": Grimké, 148.
60 "A lady should ... but to *act*.": Catharine Beecher, quoted in Kathryn Kish Sklar, *Catharine Beecher: A Study in American Domesticity* (Yale University Press, 1973), 221.
62 "We had many ... full five minutes.": Grimké, *Walking by Faith*, 171.
62 "When I told ... receive his visits." Grimké, 181.
62 "How humbling to ...her any attention.": Grimké, 181.
62 "This was my ... her own house.": Grimké, 192.
63 "My heart is ... attached to E,": Grimké, 197.
63 "I cannot but ... he really is.": Grimké, 198.
63 "I was most ... Sisters & niece,": Grimké, 202.
63 "I am grieved ... be most welcome.": Mary Grimké, quoted in Bushkovitch, *Grimkés*.
63 "Last week Charles ... mother, Mary Grimké.": Grimké, quoted in Bushkovitch.
64 "Five months have ... will be destroyed.": Angelina Grimké, quoted in Birney, *Grimké Sisters*, 123.

65 "[Angelina] found to . . . for the slave.": Sarah Grimké, quoted in Lerner, *Grimké Sisters*, 82.

66 "matters entirely outside of the Society.": Catherine Morris, quoted in Birney, *Grimké Sisters*, 114.

66 "a heinous crime . . . sight of God.": Garrison, William Lloyd, "Letter from William Lloyd Garrison to the Public," Teaching American History website, accessed April 16, 2025, https://teachingamericanhistory.org/document/to-the-public/.

66 "its immediate abandonment, without expatriation.": William Lloyd Garrison, *The Letters of William Lloyd Garrison*, vol. 2 (Belknap of Harvard University Press, 1971), 597.

67 "so thoroughly imbued . . . an early day.": Lucretia Mott, quoted in Otelia Cromwell, *Lucretia Mott* (Harvard University Press, 1958), 125.

68 "sphere": Perry, *Lift Up Thy Voice*, 125.

68 "Is it right . . . of the day?": Grimké, *Walking by Faith*, 210.

69 "is my own, my native land": Sarah Mapps Douglass, quoted in Marie Lindhorst, "Politics in a Box: Sarah Mapps Douglass and the Female Literary Association, 1831–1833," in *Pennsylvania History: A Journal of Mid-Atlantic Studies* (Penn State University Press), 274.

69 "unkindly strives to . . . from her bosom.": Sarah Mapps Douglass, writing as Zillah, "Extract from a Letter Written to a Friend, Feb. 23d, 1832," *Liberator* 2, no. 29 (July 21, 1832): 115.

69 "the negro seat,": Birney, *Grimké Sisters*, 122.

70 "If Friends take . . . to [leave] them?": Angelina Grimké, *Walking by Faith*, 210.

70 "Satan is tempting . . . my own Society.": Sarah Grimké, quoted in Birney, *Grimké Sisters*, 114.

71 "a tremendously forceful . . . just race prejudice.": Frederick Grimké, quoted in Bushkovitch, *Grimkés*, 565.

71 "[He] stands with . . . most remarkable man.": Grimké, quoted in Bushkovitch, 565.

72 "We often conversed . . . approval of it.": Sarah Grimké, quoted in Birney, *Grimké Sisters*, 118.

72 "He had never . . . works worth studying.": Grimké, quoted in Birney, 118.

74 "What to do? What to do?": Angelina Grimké, quoted in Perry, 113.

74 *"Abolitionists have never, . . . YIELD AN INCH."*: William Lloyd Garrison, "Appeal to Our Fellow Citizens," *Liberator* 5, no. 34 (1835): 134.

75–76 "Respected Friend, I . . . worth dying for." Angelina Emily Grimké, "Angelina E. Grimke," *Liberator* 8, no. 9 (March 2, 1838): 35.

76 "The following epistle . . . danger and distress.": William Lloyd Garrison, "Christian Heroism," *Liberator* 5, no. 38, (September 19, 1835): 150.

76 "I see God-given . . . or the complexion.": Garrison, Wendell Phillips and Francis Jackson Garrison. *William Lloyd Garrison, 1805–1879: The Story of his Life Told by his Children, Vol. 3, 1841–1860.* New York: Century Co., 1889. Accessed April 16, 2025, https://archives.byui.edu/s/public/page/william-lloyd-garrison.

76–77 "I had some . . . not myself alone.": Grimké, *Walking by Faith*, 211–212.

77 "The suffering which . . . that she suffers.": Sarah Grimké, "Sarah Grimke Diary, 1819–1836," vol. 17-2, Weld-Grimké Family Papers, William L. Clements Library, University of Michigan, 107.

79 "My mind is , , , and anti-slavery causes.": Angelina Grimké, quoted in Birney, *Grimké Sisters*, 137–138.

79 "It has all . . . justice and humanity.": Grimké, quoted in Birney, 138.

79 "I will speak . . . justice and humanity.": Grimké, quoted in Birney, 138.

80 "Sisters in Christ." Angelina Emily Grimké, *Appeal to the Christian Women of the South*, 3rd ed. (Arno, 1969), 16–17.

80 *"I know you . . . them at liberty."*: Grimké, 16–17.

80 "Now dearest, what . . . think of it?": Angelina Grimké, quoted in Birney, 141.

80 "My beloved sister . . . in this world." Sarah Grimké, quoted in Birney, *Grimké Sisters*, 139.

81 "I have just . . . will publish it.": Elizur Wright, quoted in Birney, 147.

81 "As I was . . . power is undisputed." Sarah Grimké, quoted in Theodore Dwight Weld, *Letters of Theodore Dwight Weld, Angelina Grimké and Sarah Grimké, 1822–1844* (P. Smith, 1965), 373.

81 "has proved the . . . destroyed my mind.": Sarah Grimké, quoted in Carol Berkin, *Civil War Wives: The Lives and Times of Angelina Grimké Weld, Varina Howell Davis, and Julia Dent Grant* (Knopf Books, 2009), 33.

82 "Language cannot express . . . set you free." Angelina Grimké, quoted in Larry Ceplair, *The Public Years of Sarah and Angelina Grimké: Selected Writings, 1835–1839* (Columbia University Press, 1989), 80.

83 "startling in color and size.": "1830–1839," Fashion History Timeline, last updated August 18, 2020, https://fashionhistory.fitnyc.edu/1830-1839/.

83 "It was like . . . to do so.": Sarah Grimké, quoted in Lerner, *Grimké Sisters*, 99.

83 "Where thou goest . . . and work together.": Sarah Grimké, quoted in Birney, *Grimké Sisters*, 155.

84 "A *single* female . . . protect each other.": Official, quoted in Weld, *Letters of Theodore Dwight Weld*, 390.

85 "After these things . . . himself would come.": Luke, Chapter 10, verse 1. *The Holy Bible*, New Testament (London and NY: Collins' Clear-Type Press, 1953), 70.

85–86 "for the purpose . . . or steel traps.": Elizur Wright, quoted in Weld, 338.

86 "the thunderer of the West,": Perry, *Lift Up Thy Voice*, 143.

86 "Perhaps now, thou . . . benevolence, and frankness.": Angelina Grimké, quoted in Ellen H. Todras, *Angelina Grimké: Voice of Abolition* (Linnet, 1999), 65, 67.

87 "Slavery is terrible . . . peculiarly their own.": Harriet Jacobs [Linda Brent, pseud.], *Incidents in the Life of a Slave Girl*, ed. L. Maria Child (Boston, 1861), 119.

87 "When woman was . . . then beat them.": Formerly enslaved woman, quoted in *Federal Writers' Project: Slave Narrative Project, Vol. 16, Texas, Part 1, Adams-Duhon*, 1936, Library of Congress, https://www.loc.gov/item/mesn161.

88 "It is so . . . are never tired." Sarah Grimké, quoted in Bushkovitch, *Grimkés*, 589.

88 "we cannot name.": Sarah Grimké, quoted in Perry, *Lift Up Thy Voice*, 136.

89 "Let your women . . . in the church.": 1 Corinthians Chapter 14, Verses 34–35, p. 171 in *The Holy Bible*, New Testament (London and NY: Collins' Clear-Type Press, 1953).

89–90 "How supremely ridiculous . . . a woman speak!": Theodore Weld, quoted in Birney, *Grimké Sisters*, 164.

90 "sins of the north,": Bushkovitch, *Grimké Sisters*, 595.

90 "The Richmond papers . . . two 'fanatical women,'": Sarah Grimké, quoted in Weld, *Letters of Theodore Dwight Weld*, 364.

90 "idle and curious women.": Unnamed writer, quoted in Birney, *Grimké Sisters*, 182.

90 "Why are all . . . [race-mixing] fashionable.": *Boston Morning Post*, quoted in Todras, *Angelina Grimké*, 78.

91 "Ladies, what would you have us do?": Unnamed writer, quoted in Bushkovitch, *Grimkés*, 596.

91 "They think to . . . do unto us.": Sarah Grimké, quoted in Birney, *Grimké Sisters*, 183.

91 "Thou remember the . . . am doing now.": Sarah Grimké, quoted in Bushkovitch, *Grimkés*, 607.

92 "that the object . . . of American slavery.": Sarah Grimké, quoted in Anti-Slavery Convention of American Women, *Proceeding[s] of the Anti-Slavery Convention of American Women, Held in Philadelphia. May 15th, 16th, 17th and 18th, 1838*. Anti-Slavery Convention of American Women—Stone, Lucy—National American Woman Suffrage Association Collection, 3–4, Library of Congress, accessed April 16, 2025, https://tile.loc.gov/storage-services/service/rbc/rbnawsa/n1926/n1926.pdf.

92 "Resolved, That as . . . of American slavery.": Angelina Grimké, quoted in Anti-Slavery Convention of American Women, 9.

93 "the dreadful effects . . . scheme of expatriation": Anti-Slavery Convention of American Women, 13.

93 "It is the . . . of American slavery.": Anti-Slavery Convention of American Women, 9.

93 "because Friends do . . . of thy color.": Margaret Hope Bacon, "New Light on Sarah Mapps Douglass and Her Reconciliation with Friends," *Quaker History* 90, no. 1 (2001): 31.

93 "I believe they . . . for our color": Sarah Mapps Douglass, "Letter to William Basset," Brotherly Love Resource Bank, 1837, accessed January 11, 2024, https://www.pbs.org/wgbh/aia/part3/3h99.html. Credit: Weld-Grimké Collection, Clements Library, University of Michigan, Ann Arbor.

93–94   "Angelina has given . . . to do anything.'": Sarah Grimké, quoted in Weld, *Letters of Theodore Dwight Weld*, 388.

94   "Tell Mr. Weld . . . *without* his directions.": Angelina Grimké, quoted in Weld, 388.

94   "*The female slaves . . . a liberal education.*": Angelina Grimké, quoted in Bushkovitch, *Grimkés*, 602.

94   "farce.": Dorothy Sterling, *Ahead of Her Time: Abby Kelley and the Politics of Antislavery* (W. W. Norton, 1991), 50.

94–95   "*Yes, most unbelieving . . . of international policy.*": "Extract from an Editorial Article in the 'New-York Commercial Advertiser,' of May 17, 1837," *Liberator* 7, no. 27 (June 2, 1837), accessed April 16, 2025, http://fair-use.org/the-liberator/1847/07/02/the-liberator-17-27.pdf

95   "My Dear Friend . . . in the North.": Catharine E. Beecher, *An Essay on Slavery and Abolitionism, with Reference to the Duty of American Females* (Philadelphia, 1837), 5.

95   "in the domestic and social circle,": Beecher, 100.

96   "The great fundamental . . . man as property.": Angelina Emily Grimké, *Letters to Catharine E. Beecher* (Arno / New York Times, 1969), 4.

96   "I have never . . . of our hearts.": Grimké, 36–40.

96   "I recognize no . . . Church or State.": Grimké, 118.

96   "Your letters to . . . they were *better*.": Weld, *Letters of Theodore Dwight Weld*, 413.

97   "I thank thee . . . been done by?": Angelina Grimké, quoted in Weld, 416.

98   "*We invite your . . . degeneracy and ruin.*": Congregational Ministers of Massachusetts, quoted in General Association of Massachusetts, *Minutes of the General Association of Massachusetts at Their Meeting at North Brookfield, June 28, 1837, with the Narrative of the State of Religion, and the Pastoral Letter* (Boston, 1837), 20–21.

99   "*Confusion has seized . . . by the ears!*": Maria Weston Chapman, quoted in Elizabeth Cady Stanton, Susan B. Anthony, and Matilda Joslyn Gage, *History of Woman Suffrage*, (New York, 1881), 1:82.

100   "I am inclined . . . we now have.": Sarah Moore Grimké, *Letters on the Equality of the Sexes and the Condition of Women* (Boston, 1838; repr., Source Book, 1970), 16.

100   "*Even admitting that . . . is his inferior.*": Grimké, 10–11.

101	"Intellect is not . . . of erring mortals.": Grimké, 60.
101	"I ask no . . . us to occupy.": Grimké, 10.
101	"*barn* beautifully fitted . . . with green boughs.": Sarah Grimké, quoted in Weld, *Letters*, 421.
101	"*So this is . . . a 'Pastoral Letter!'*": John Greenleaf Whittier, quoted in Birney, *Grimké Sisters*, 186.
102	"Why is it . . . may ourselves suffer?": Whittier, quoted in Birney, 203–204.
102–103	"I do most . . . babies *into* women.": Weld, *Letters of Theodore Dwight Weld*, 425–427.
103	"What is the . . . suppress my own?": Angelina Grimké, quoted in Birney, *Grimké Sisters*, 214–215.
103	"Why dear child! . . . Patience! Rally yourself.": Weld, *Letters of Theodore Dwight Weld*, 457.
104–105	"The [church] was . . . congregation to remain.": Sarah Grimké, quoted in Weld, *Letters*, 468.
105	"scratchifications": Lerner, *Grimké Sisters*, 151.
105	"theeing and thouing, . . . amalgamation of colors!": Weld, *Letters of Theodore Dwight Weld*, 411.
106	"Would the condition . . . rights and duties?": Perry, *Lift Up Thy Voice*, 162.
106	"was conducted with . . . would be freed.": Angelina Grimké, quoted in Birney, *Grimké Sisters*, 226.
107	"*I know it . . . the* whole truth.": Weld, *Letters of Theodore Dwight Weld*, 533–535.
107	"*Your letter was . . . to each other.*": Angelina Grimké, quoted in Weld, 536–538.
107	"Thy letter to . . . were kindred spirits.": Sarah Grimké, quoted in Weld, 539.
107	"My heart is . . . four days ago!": Weld, 554.
109	"the Lord was . . . like a trumpet.": Angelina Grimké, quoted in Weld, *Letters*, 572.
109	"Mr. Chairman . . . sisters in bonds.": Angelina Emily Grimké, "Angelina E. Grimke," 35.
109–110	"a committee be . . . from Miss Grimké.": Legislature, quoted in Lydia Maria Child, *Letters of Lydia Maria Child* (Negro Universities Press, 1969), 27.

110 "Clothed in a . . . assigned to woman.": Angelina Emily Grimké, "Untitled Entry," *Burlington (VT) Free Press*, March 20, 1838, 1, Library of Congress.

110–111 "She exhibited considerable . . . like all possessed.": Lerner, *Grimké Sisters*, 9.

111 "the sound part . . . in this city.": Child, *Letters*, 27.

111 "The hall was . . . from the doorway.": Angelina Grimké, quoted in Weld, *Letters of Theodore Dwight Weld*, 572–573.

111 "I never felt . . . in my life": Grimké, quoted in Weld, 567.

111 "What the effect . . . world upside down.": Angelina Grimké, quoted in Birney, *Grimké Sisters*, 229.

112 "I will be . . . *alone* with you.": Weld, *Letters of Theodore Dwight Weld*, 602.

113 "keeping an extinguisher": Lerner, *Grimké Sisters*, 163.

113 "I cant see . . . of the work.": Angelina Grimké, quoted in Weld, *Letters of Theodore Dwight Weld*, 627.

113–114 "I could easily . . . one hundred acres.": Weld, 629.

114 "old maids who . . . by decent women.": Bushkovitch, *Grimkés*, 625.

114–115 "My dear sister . . . the whole season.": Weld, *Letters of Theodore Dwight Weld*, 604–605.

115 "I found the . . . monotonous and heavy.": Weld, 604–605.

115 "If you can . . . better do it.": Weld, 606.

115 "She read it . . . words can tell.": Angelina Grimké, quoted in Weld, 611–612.

115–116 "The end crowned . . . never go out.": Sarah Grimké, quoted in Weld, 651.

116 "*1st. Persons who . . . to be regulated.*": Weld, 635–636.

116–117 "I feel assured . . . to your station.": Mary Grimké, quoted in Weld, 617–618.

117 "I . . . go up . . . cant do ourselves.": Weld, 641.

117 "By the way . . . with variegated colors": Weld, 630.

117–118 "*Wilt thou grant . . . Weld May 1st.*": Lumpkin, *Emancipation of Angelina Grimké*, 147.

118 "M[ary] A[nna Frost] . . . grief is assuaged.": Angelina Grimké, quoted in Weld, *Letters of Theodore Dwight Weld*, 653.

118 "I mean to . . . of free sugar.": Grimké, quoted in Weld, 665.

118–119 "Do pray tell . . . *not at all.*": Weld, 655.
119 "Now for thy . . . *nothing* high priced.": Angelina Grimké. quoted in Weld, 661.
119 "*White* vest and . . . to attract attention.": Weld, 668.
119 "*Alack and Alas! . . . the enemy's halter!*": James Greenleaf Whittier poem, "On Leaving Me and Taking a Wife," quoted in Weld, *Letters*, 671.
120 "not of an immoral character.": Pennsylvania Hall Association, *History of Pennsylvania Hall, Which Was Destroyed by a Mob on the 17th of May, 1838* (Negro Universities Press, 1969), 6.
121 "I here promise . . . the marriage ceremony.": Theodore Dwight Weld, quoted in "A Philadelphia Informs Us . . ." *New York Herald* 4, no. 24, 2, accessed January 14, 2024, Gale Primary Sources database.
121 "Angelina's address to . . . by the company.": Sarah Grimké, quoted in Birney, *Grimké Sisters*, 232–233.
121 "A more interesting . . . an abolitionist wedding.": Maria Weston Chapman, quoted in Dorothy Sterling, *Ahead of Her Time: Abby Kelley and the Politics of Antislavery* (W. W. Norton, 1991), 62.
121 "we feel no regret,": Sarah Grimké, in a letter written to a friend in England after Angelina's wedding, quoted in Birney, *Grimké Sisters*, 232.
123 "Whereas a convention . . . heretofore held sacred.": Pennsylvania Hall Association, *History of Pennsylvania Hall*, 136.
124 "We would therefore . . . May 15, 1838.": Pennsylvania Hall Association, 136.
125 "petticoat convention": David Hale, "Philadelphia Abolitionists," *Journal of Commerce*, May 19, 1838, 209, Google Books.
125 "Agitation Hall,": Hale, 209.
125 "incendiary": Unknown speaker, quoted in Pennsylvania Hall Association, *History of Pennsylvania Hall*, 136.
125 "white dandies with . . . and white wenches.": Hale, "Philadelphia Abolitionists," 209.
125 "the hall was . . . to obtain access.": Unknown speaker, quoted in Pennsylvania Hall Association, *History of Pennsylvania Hall*, 117.
125 "Virtue, Liberty, and Independence.": Charlene Mires, *Independence Hall in American Memory* (University of Pennsylvania Press, 2015), 91.

126 "An audience promiscuously . . . with wooly heads.": Unknown speaker, Pennsylvania Hall Association, *History of Pennsylvania Hall*, 167–168.

126 "Frequent vollies of . . . frighten the audience.": Pennsylvania Hall Association, 117.

127 "When he took . . . up the meeting.": Pennsylvania Hall Association, 123.

127 "Men, brethren, and . . . large audience together?": Angelina Grimké, quoted in Pennsylvania Hall Association, 123.

127 *"Those voices without . . . other unpopular subject."*: Grimké, quoted in Pennsylvania Hall Association, 123.

127–128 *"As a Southerner . . . to-morrow we die."*: Grimké, quoted in Pennsylvania Hall Association, 123–124.

128 "Her eloquence kindled . . . her cheeks glowed,": William Lloyd Garrison, quoted in Henry Mayer, *All on Fire: William Lloyd Garrison and the Abolition of Slavery* (St. Martin's, 1998), 245–246.

128 "What is a . . . the slaves endure?": Angelina Grimké, quoted in Pennsylvania Hall Association, *History of Pennsylvania Hall*, 124.

129 "I have *never* seen a happy slave.": Grimké, quoted in Pennsylvania Hall Association, 123–124.

128 "All this disturbance . . . say or do.": Grimké, quoted in Pennsylvania Hall Association, 124.

129 "such false notions . . . this enlightened country.": Lucretia Mott, quoted in Pennsylvania Hall Association, 127.

129 "Abby, if you . . . will smite you!": Theodore Weld, quoted in Sterling, *Ahead of Her Time*, 65.

129 "Pairs and trios . . . daughters of Philadelphia.": Unknown speaker, quoted in Pennsylvania Hall Association, *History of Pennsylvania Hall*, 169.

129 "a number of . . . was severely injured.": Unknown speaker, quoted in Pennsylvania Hall Association, 148.

130 "We call upon . . . of general interest.": Unknown speaker, quoted in Pennsylvania Hall Association, 138.

130 "There are always . . . are against you.": John Swift, quoted in Pennsylvania Hall Association, 138.

130 "Miss Grimké was . . . the free states.": Laura H. Lovell, *Report of a Delegate to the Anti-Slavery Convention of American Women, Held in Philadelphia, May, 1838; Including an Account of Other Meetings Held in Pennsylvania Hall, and of the Riot* (Boston, 1838), 14.

130 "We are told . . . morality, of religion.": Unknown author, quoted in Stanton, Anthony, and Gage, *History of Woman Suffrage*, 1:339.
130–131 "their colored sisters . . . meeting this evening.": Lucretia Mott, quoted in Lovell, *Report of a Delegate*, 16.
131 "Mrs. Weld proposed . . . by the arm.": Lovell, 16–17.
131 "We passed out . . . walk, two abreast.": Lovell, 16.
131 "Fellow Citizens . . . *for the night*.": John Swift, quoted in Pennsylvania Hall Association, *History of Pennsylvania Hall*, 140.
131 "Three cheers for the mayor!": Pennsylvania Hall Association, 149.
132 "ruddy crimson": Pennsylvania Hall Association, 150.
132 "We are decidely . . . and disorderly whites.": *The Philadelphia Ledger*, May 18, 1838, quoted in Celia Cast-Ellenbogen's article "Pennsylvania Hall Association" on the "Quakers and Slavery" website, https://web.tricolib.brynmawr.edu/speccoll/quakersandslavery/commentary/organizations/pennsylvania_hall.php.
133 "a legal lynching.": William Lloyd Garrison, "Legal Lynching," *Liberator* 8, no. 43 (October 26, 1838): 171.
133 "by sitting with . . . white fellow citizens.": Sarah Grimké, quoted in Anti-Slavery Convention of American Women, *Proceeding[s]*, 8.
133 "A white woman . . . the abolitionist lectures.": Unknown speaker, quoted in Pennsylvania Hall Association, *History of Pennsylvania Hall*, 170.
134 "though contrary to . . . destroy the Union!": Unknown speaker, quoted in Pennsylvania Hall Association, 167.
134 "*Least of all* . . . *read at home*.": Unknown speaker, quoted in Cromwell, *Lucretia Mott*, 56–59.
135 "Probably no female . . . a Satanic eagerness.": Weld, *Letters of Theodore Dwight Weld*, 636–638.
137 "It is just . . . and the poor.": Angelina Grimké, quoted in Birney, *Grimké Sisters*, 247–248.
137 "dear little No. 3,": Grimké, quoted in Birney, 245.
137 "years of tossing and buffeting": Sarah Grimké, quoted in Weld, *Letters of Theodore Dwight Weld*, 708.
138 "Oh, Jane, words . . . love public work.": Sarah Grimké, quoted in Lumpkin, *Emancipation of Angelina Grimké*, 166.

138 "Pray, have you . . . other strange notions.": Mary Grimké, quoted in Lerner, *Grimké Sisters*, 179.

139 "It is our . . . or in reason.": Sarah Grimké, quoted in Birney, *Grimké Sisters*, 243.

139 "one heart and mind.": Sarah Grimké, quoted in Lumpkin, *Emancipation of Angelina Grimké*, 167.

140 "We can make . . . our food cool.": Sarah Grimké, quoted in Birney, *Grimké Sisters*, 246.

140 "It so happens . . . fit to eat.": Angelina Grimké, quoted in Birney, 246.

140 "With bread and . . . with tolerable appetite.": Sarah Grimké, quoted in Birney, 246.

141 "It seemed to . . . an acceptable visitor.": Sarah Mapps Douglass, quoted in Birney, 248.

141 "Great disappointment . . . from public work.": Birney, 259.

141–142 "I cannot tell . . . this private life,": Angelina Grimké, quoted in Birney, 252.

142 "My dear Theodore . . . of my lecturing,": Grimké, quoted in Birney, 252.

142 "We keep no . . . to *promiscuous* audiences.": Angelina Grimké, quoted in Ceplair, *Public Years*, 326.

142 "It looks like . . . abolition of slavery.": Sarah Grimké, quoted in Birney, *Grimké Sisters*, 242.

143 "I do not . . . of the nation.": Grimké, quoted in Birney, 258.

143–144 "Reader, you are . . . bad, or indifferent?": Weld, *American Slavery as It Is*, 7.

144 "facts and testimony . . . and *moral* condition.": Weld, iv.

144 "Those dear souls . . . for the book.": Theodore Dwight Weld, quoted in Birney, *Grimké Sisters*, 258.

144 "We will prove . . . with barbarous inhumanity.": Weld, *American Slavery as It Is*, 9.

145 "one of the . . . produced intense agony.": Sarah Grimké, quoted in Weld, 23.

145 "her daughters disputing . . . blood-bought luxuries indeed.": Angelina Grimké, quoted in Weld, 55.

145–146 "used to keep . . . fault at all.": Grimké, quoted in Weld, 53.

146 "Ten dollars reward . . . *ears by whipping*.": Weld, 62.

146 "Was committed to . . . *or cut off.*": Weld, 78.
146–147 "NEGRO HIRINGS. Will . . . George Ash, deceased.": Weld, 137.
147 "NEGROES FOR SALE. . . . *exchanged for* groceries.": Unknown speaker, quoted in Weld, 168.
147 "*120 Negroes for* . . . *in the trade.*": Unknown speaker, quoted in Weld, 167.
148 "After the work . . . let that suffice.'": Theodore Dwight Weld, quoted in Birney, *Grimké Sisters*, 258–259.
148 "Those who think . . . read for themselves.": Weld, *American Slavery as It Is*, iii.
148 "but when the . . . to cry *mew*?": Unknown speaker, "From the New York American," *Emancipator and Free American* 4, no. 33 (December, 1839): 4.
148 "that American slavery . . . its faithful pages.": Theodore Dwight Weld, quoted in "American Slavery As It Is," *Emancipator*, May 30, 1839, 19, Gale Primary Sources database.
149 "Our beloved mother . . . upstaid by Jesus.": Weld, *Letters of Theodore Dwight Weld*, 781.
149 "last infamous publication.": Anna Frost Grimké, quoted in Bushkovitch, *Grimkés*, 651.
149 "We wrote them . . . as the oppressed.": Angelina Grimké, quoted in Bushkovitch, 651.
149–150 "I am indeed . . . as the oppressed.": Angelina Grimké, quoted in Kathryn Cullen-DuPont, *American Women's Activist Writings: 1637–2001* (Cooper Square Press, 2002), 74.
150 "I am very . . . precious sister Sarah.": Angelina Grimké, quoted in Theodore Dwight Weld, *Slavery In America: Theodore Dwight Weld's American Slavery as It Is* (F. E. Peacock, Publishers, 1972), 235.
150 "I have no . . . of the system.": Angelina Grimké, quoted in Lerner, *Grimké Sisters*, 189.
150–151 "getting into the . . . places far larger.": Weld, *Letters of Theodore Dwight Weld*, 811.
152 "A Female of . . . abided by it.": Sarah Mapps Douglass, quoted in William Bassett, *Society of Friends in the United States: The Views of the Anti-Slavery Question, and Treatment of the People of Colour* (Darlington, UK, 1840), 23.

152 "I myself know . . . harp or viol.": Sarah Mapps Douglass, quoted in Margaret Hope Bacon, "New Light on Sarah Mapps Douglass and Her Reconciliation with Friends," *Quaker History* 90, no. 1, 32.

152 "I remember well . . . going among them.": Douglass, quoted in Bacon, 31; Grimké-Weld Papers, Clements Library, University of Michigan.

152 "One woman told . . . than set free.": Sarah Grimké, quoted in Lerner, *Grimké Sisters*, 193.

153 "I cannot tell . . . one of ourselves.": Sarah Grimké, quoted in Birney, *Grimké Sisters*, 251.

155 "Thou wilt not . . . a little angel.": Sarah Grimké, quoted in Weld, *Letters of Theodore Dwight Weld*, 841.

155 "The idea of . . . sent from God.": Angelina Grimké, quoted in Birney, *Grimké Sisters*, 261.

155 "a sweet little . . . rich meadow land.": Sarah Grimké, quoted in Benjamin P. Thomas, *Theodore Weld: Crusader for Freedom* (Rutgers University Press, 1950), 177.

157 "Oh how I . . . at our meals,": Angelina Grimké, quoted in Lerner, *Grimké Sisters*, 199.

157 "*In company with . . . a cheerless atmosphere.*": Elizabeth Cady Stanton, "Angelina Grimké. Reminiscences by E.C.S," in Stanton, Anthony, and Gage, *History of Woman Suffrage*, 1:392, Project Gutenberg, accessed November 21, 2021, https://www.gutenberg.org/cache/epub/28020/pg28020-images.html.

157–158 "peculiar taste arrangments . . . [paint]brush could trace.": Stanton, 392–393.

159 "In Congress the . . . not a slave.": Abby Kelley, quoted in Karen Folkes, "Our Dearest Abby," Worcester Women's History Project, Worcester Historical Museum, October 4, 2010, 20, https://www.wwhp.org/news-events/news-articles/2010/our-dearest-abby.

160 "We mourn that . . . divisions amongst us,": Sarah Grimké, quoted in Lumpkin, 178.

160 "Dear sisters, Sarah . . . throughout the meeting.": Elizabeth Cady Stanton, quoted in Elizabeth Cady Stanton and Susan B. Anthony, *The Selected Papers of Elizabeth Cady Stanton and Susan B. Anthony, Volume 1: In the School of Anti-Slavery, 1840–1866* (Rutgers University Press, 1997), 8–9.

161 "Lucretia Mott has . . . the *Garrison standard*.": Elizabeth Cady Stanton, quoted in Elizabeth Cady Stanton and Susan B. Anthony, *The Selected Papers*, 10.

162 "I cannot tell . . . to nurse him,": Angelina Grimké, quoted in Lerner, *Grimké Sisters*, 202.

163 "My restless, ambitious . . . and high attainments.": Angelina Grimké, quoted in Birney, *Grimké Sisters*, 81.

163 "grieve and mortify . . . afflict each other": Weld, *Letters of Theodore Dwight Weld*, 604.

163 "an inexpressibly great . . . cultivating my mind.": Angelina Grimké, quoted in Lumpkin, *Emancipation of Angelina Grimké*, 186.

164 "In each of . . . member of Congress.": Weld, quoted in Weld, *Letters*, 887.

164 "Beloved, I miss . . . and eye filling.": Angelina Grimké, quoted in Lerner, *Grimké Sisters*, 214.

164 "selfish, inconsiderate, slovenly . . . disregarded the amenities.": Sarah Grimké, quoted in Lumpkin, *Emancipation of Angelina Grimké*, 196–197.

165 "Congress shall make . . . redress of grievances.": First amendment to the Constitution of the United States.

166 "The triumph of . . . takes its date.": Weld, *Letters of Theodore Dwight Weld*, 913.

166 "Where are Theodore . . . seen nor felt.": William Lloyd Garrison, *Liberator* 12, no. 32 (August 12, 1842): 127.

166–167 "*All* the table . . . in their places!": Weld, *Letters of Theodore Dwight Weld*, 948.

168 "Dearest, suppose we . . . it very closely.": Weld, quoted in Weld, *Letters*, 957.

168 "I am *not* . . . one in peril.": Weld, 959.

168 "Aunt Sai": Birney, *Grimké Sisters*, 266.

168 "I'm sure if . . . call forth sympathy.": Sarah Grimké, quoted in Lumpkin, *Emancipation of Angelina Grimké*, 190.

169 "My soul is . . . precious little ones.": Angelina Grimké, quoted in Lumpkin, 195.

169 "We know not . . . cast among us.": Angelina Grimké, quoted in Birney, *Grimké Sisters*, 263.

170 "Not half as ... of a tooth.": Sarah Grimké, quoted in Thomas, *Theodore Weld*, 217.

172 "I hope on ... twenty to supper.": Sarah Grimké, quoted in Lumpkin, *Emancipation of Angelina Grimké*, 193.

173 "My name is ... not be lost,": Brainy Quotes, "Lucy Stone Quotes," accessed April 16, 2025, https://www.brainyquote.com/authors/lucy-stone-quotes.

174 "We hold these ... of the governed.": Women's Rights Convention, *Report of the Woman's Rights Convention, Held at Seneca Falls, New York, July 19th and 20th, 1848. Proceedings and Declaration of Sentiments* (Rochester, NY, 1848), Library of Congress, https://www.loc.gov/resource/rbcmil.scrp4006702/?sp=7&st=image.

174 "Resolved, That woman ... has assigned her." : Anti-Slavery Convention of American Women, *Turning the World Upside Down: The Anti-Slavery Convention of American Women, Held in New York City, May 9–12, 1837*, ed. Dorothy Sterling (Feminist Press at the City University of New York, 1987), 13.

175 "Was there ever ... in our stockings?": "Bolting Among the Ladies," *Oneida Whig* [Utica, NY], August 1, 1848, Newspaper Coverage of the Seneca Falls Convention, October 29, 2022, https://senecafallscoverage.tumblr.com.

175 *"The women folks ... a reasonable civilization."*: Unnamed speaker, *Lowell (Massachusetts) Courier*, no date, "Women and the American Story," website, "Declaration of Rights and Sentiments, Text ... accompanied by reactions to the document in the press," accessed February 25, 2025, https://wams.nyhistory.org/expansions-and-inequalities/politics-and-society/declaration-of-rights-and-sentiments.

177 "The fear often ... thing, to do.": Angelina Grimké, quoted in Robert H. Abzug, *Passionate Liberator: Theodore Dwight Weld and the Dilemma of Reform* (Oxford University Press, 1980), 254.

179 "It is clear ... even unto blood.": Angelina Grimké, quoted in Lumpkin, *Emancipation of Angelina Grimké*, 211.

179 "an unimpeachable witness ... of the author.": Harriet Beecher Stowe, *A Key to Uncle Tom's Cabin: Presenting the Original Facts and Documents upon Which the Story Is Founded. Together with Corroborative Statements Verifying the Truth of the Work* (London, 1853), 198.

180 "Those who have . . . [protections] they enjoy.": Sarah Grimké, quoted in Stanton, Anthony, and Gage, *History of Woman Suffrage*, 1:353–355.

181 "We first met . . . & enjoying themselves.": Henry B. Blackwell, quoted in Lucy Stone and Henry B. Blackwell, *Loving Warriors: Selected Letters of Lucy Stone and Henry B. Blackwell, 1853 to 1893*, ed. Leslie Wheeler (Dial, 1981), 36.

181 "There is a . . . a higher view.": Theodore Dwight Weld, quoted in Stone and Blackwell, 37.

181 "I don't think . . . utmost good will.": Henry B. Blackwell, quoted in Stone and Blackwell, 37.

183 "We have too . . . it full well.": Angelina Grimké, quoted in Lerner, *Grimké Sisters*, 223.

183 "14 years of . . . friction between us.": Grimké, quoted in Lerner, 224.

184 "I have for . . . in old age?": Sarah Grimké, quoted in Lerner, 224.

184 "Every injustice is . . . the physical frame.": Grimké, quoted in Lerner, Gerda, and Sarah M. Grimké, "Sarah M. Grimké's 'Sisters of Charity,'" *Signs* 1, no. 1 (1975): 246–256, http://www.jstor.org/stable/3172981.

185 "Dearly beloved Sissy . . . better than nothing.": Sarah Grimké, Weld-Grimke family papers Clements Library Finding Aid provides link to letter, accessed February 25, 2025, https://spaces.hightail.com/receive/A4a07gRy9N/fi-d5d6c369-382e-498b-b5bc-7f46a7db0049/fv-d263e94b-237c-472e-a239-66cefb4d6d5f/Carpenter_Weld-Grimke%20ltrs.pdf#pageThumbnail-1.

185 "I went into . . . were much amused.": Sarah Grimké, quoted in Weld-Grimké Family Papers, 1740–1930, https://quod.lib.umich.edu/c/clementsead/umich-wcl-M-400wel?view=text.

186–187 "Often, very often . . . refuses its assent.": Angelina Grimké, quoted in Lumpkin, *Emancipation of Angelina Grimké*, 202.

187 "You never meant . . . at the Bay.": Grimké, quoted in Lumpkin, 202.

187 "to wear his snowy honors.": Sarah Grimké, in a letter to Harriot Hunt, December 20, 1854, quoted in Thomas, *Theodore Weld*, 228.

188 "innumerable sponges who . . . every spare moment.": Birney, *Grimké Sisters*, 284.

188 "Dead and buried . . . my infinite satisfaction.": Lerner, *Grimké Sisters*, 238.

189 "Such women will . . . circumference and length.": Angelina Grimké, quoted in Birney, *Grimké Sisters*, 282.

189–190 "a charming circle of friends.": quoted in Lerner, *Grimké Sisters*, 238.

190 "in all free . . . improving or attractive.": Sarah Grimké, quoted in Thomas, *Theodore Weld*, 234.

192 "O Sarah! what . . . his life's blood.": Sarah Grimké, quoted in Birney, *Grimké Sisters*, 282.

193 "O, yes,—war is better than slavery.": Angelina Grimké, quoted in Thomas, *Theodore Weld*, 245.

195 "Oh I do . . . seven weary years.": Sarah Grimké, in a letter to Harriot Hunt, June 19, 1861, quoted in Lumpkin, *Emancipation of Angelina Grimké*, 215.

195 "upon the great . . . and normal condition.": Alexander H. Stephens, "Cornerstone Address, March 21, 1861," Modern History Sourcebook, Fordham University Internet History Sourcebooks Project, ed. Paul Halsall, accessed October 30, 2022, https://sourcebooks.fordham.edu/mod/1861stephens.asp.

195–196 "on the brink . . . and permanent basis.": Angelina Grimké, quoted in Lumpkin, *Emancipation of Angelina Grimké*, 214.

196 "I see disaster . . . defeat in Lincoln,": Sarah Grimké, quoted in Lerner, *Grimké Sisters*, 245.

197 "Whatever Lincoln and . . . his innocent people.": Sarah Grimké, quoted in Birney, *Grimké Sisters*, 285.

197 "He is doing . . . wants him to,": Angelina Grimké, quoted in Thomas, *Theodore Weld*, 277.

197–198 "*If it be* . . . *blessings of Liberty.*": Elizabeth Cady Stanton, quoted in Elizabeth Cady Stanton and Susan B. Anthony, "Appeal by Elizabeth Cady Stanton," *Selected Papers of Stanton and Anthony*, 483.

198 "The 14th (of . . . for the oppressed.": Sarah Grimké, quoted in Lumpkin, *Emancipation of Angelina Grimké*, 218.

198 "This lady, once . . . within their borders.": Lucy Stone, quoted in Stanton, Anthony, and Gage, *History of Woman Suffrage*, 2:54.

198–199 "My heart is . . . you have adopted.": Angelina Grimké, quoted in Stanton, Anthony, and Gage, 2:54.

199 "Never falter, never . . . you have adopted.": Angelina Grimké, quoted in Stanton, Anthony, and Gage, 2:54.

199 "There can never . . . are practically established.": Unknown speaker, quoted in Stanton, Anthony, and Gage, 2:57.

199 "We all know . . . is made prominent.": "Mrs. Hoyt," quoted in Stanton, Anthony, and Gage, 2:59–60.

199 "I rejoice exceedingly . . . never have ours.": Angelina Grimké, quoted in Stanton, Anthony, and Gage, 2:60–61.

199 "Resolved. That we . . . war for freedom.": Unknown speaker, quoted in Stanton, Anthony, and Gage, 2:66.

200 "*This war is . . . pursuit of happiness.*": Angelina Grimké, quoted in Stanton, Anthony, and Gage, 2:68–69.

200 "The Union as . . . not exist together.": Unknown speaker, quoted in Stanton, Anthony, and Gage, 2:68–69.

203 "If it is . . . air once more.": Angelina Grimké, quoted in Lumpkin, *Emancipation of Angelina Grimké*, 217.

204 "a quiet farm . . . rides and walks.": Unknown speaker, quoted in Thomas, *Theodore Weld*, 254.

205 "certainly needed at . . . Dr. Dio Lewis.": Unknown speaker, "Physical Education and One of Its Apostles," *Iowa Normal Monthly* 7 (Cambridge, MA, 1883), 113. Google Books.

205 "without inconvenience.": Dio Lewis, "The Health of American Women," *North American Review* 135, no. 315 (December 1882): 506.

205 "I am not . . . war and conquest.": Angelina Grimké, quoted in Lerner, *Grimké Sisters*, 255.

206 "The streets were . . . the broken glass.": Unknown speaker, quoted in Todras, *Angelina Grimké*, 137.

207 "a sunbeam in the family.": Sarah Grimké, quoted in Birney, *Grimké Sisters*, 287.

207–208 "Any book, in . . . to do so.": Theodore Dwight Weld, quoted in Abzug, *Passionate Liberator*, 291.

208 "by the name . . . thrillingly, powerfully impressive.": Unknown speaker, quoted in Lumpkin, *Emancipation of Angelina Grimké*, 220.

209 "*Mr Grimké Sir . . . Weld Fairmount Massachusetts*": Angelina Grimké, quoted in Lumpkin, 221.

211–212 "*Dear Madam, I . . . Archibald Henry Grimké*": Archibald Grimké, quoted in Lumpkin, 245.

212 "Her brother had . . . must right them.": Birney, *Grimké Sisters*, 292.

212 "Dear young friends . . . name of Grimké.": Angelina Grimké, quoted in Bushkovitch, *Grimkés*, 682–683.

213 *"They [her father . . . feel at home."*: Angelina Weld Grimké, "A Biographical Sketch of Archibald H. Grimke," *Opportunity: A Journal of Negro Life* 3, no. 26 (February 1925): 46.

213 "They are very . . . of the younger.": Sarah Grimké, quoted in Birney, *Grimké Sisters*, 294.

214 "[I will] leave . . . taken care of.": Henry Grimké, quoted in Dickson D. Bruce, *Archibald Grimké: Portrait of a Black Independent* (Louisiana State University Press, 1993), 6.

214 "mulatto Servant girl . . . future issue [children].": Bruce, 6, cites the will of Henry Grimké, Aug. 24, 1848, Codicil, Dec. 15, 1849, Court of Probate, Will Book No. L., 1851-1856, p. 103, Charleston, South Carolina.

216 *"FIFTY DOLLARS REWARD . . . Hotel in July"*: Montague Grimké, quoted in Perry, *Lift Up Thy Voice*, 243.

216 "There I remained . . . that I recovered.": Francis J. Grimké, *The Works of Francis J. Grimke*, vol. 1, ed. Carter G. Woodson (Associated Publishers, 1942), 24.

216 "she was thrown . . . prostrated [weakened] her.": Archibald Grimké, quoted in Lumpkin, *Emancipation of Angelina Grimké*, 223.

216 "Nina has been . . . to Lincoln University.": Sarah Grimké, quoted in Birney, *Grimké Sisters*, 295.

217 "I feel more . . . with a death-grasp.": Angelina Grimké, quoted in Lumpkin, *Emancipation of Angelina Grimké*, 225.

217 "for the scientific . . . the male sex.": "Special Report of the Commissioner of Education on the Condition and Improvement of Public Schools in the District of Columbia," submitted to the Senate June 1868 and to the House, with additions, June 1870. Google Books.

218 "Where scores of . . . been recognized there.": Angelina Grimké Weld, quoted in Bruce, Archibald Grimké, 27, cites Angelina to Archibald, Juy 24, 1842, in Archibald Grimke Papers, Box 1, Folder 27, Feb. 29, 1868. Howard U.

218 "a liberal in . . . the race question.": Grimké, "A Biographical Sketch," 45.

220 "If the word . . . get it out.": Elizabeth Cady Stanton, letter from Stanton to Gerrit Smith, January 1, 1866, quoted in Ellen Carol DuBois, *Feminism and Suffrage: The Emergence of an Independent Women's Movement in America* (Cornell University Press, 1978), 61.

220 "There is a . . . it was before.": Sojourner Truth, quoted in Stanton, Anthony, and Gage, *History of Woman Suffrage*, 2:193.

221 "one grand, distinctive . . . idea—universal suffrage.": Unknown speaker, quoted in Stanton, Anthony, and Gage, 2:172.

222 "Stirring addresses [including . . . at the polls.": Unknown speaker, quoted in "Votes for Women in Hyde Park," Historic Boston Incorporated, March 26, 2012, https://historicboston.org/votes-for-women-in-hyde-park/.

222 "The anti female . . . the coming women.": Unknown speaker, quoted in "1870 Women's March and Vote," *Norfolk County Gazette*, available at Hyde Park Historical Society, accessed February 25, 2025, https://www.hydeparkhistoricalsociety.org/1870-womens-march-and-vote/.

222 "They came in . . . young and pretty.": unknown speaker, *New York Herald*, available at Historic Boston Incorporated, accessed February 25, 2025, https://historicboston.org/womens-sufferage-in-boston-those-hyde-park-women/.

222–223 "[The women's] presence . . . in the crowd.": unknown speaker, *New York Herald*, available at Historic Boston Incorporated, accessed February 25, 2025, https://historicboston.org/womens-sufferage-in-boston-those-hyde-park-women/.

223 "Base ruffians!": Sylvanus Cobb Jr., quoted in the *New York Herald*, no date, on the Hyde Park Website, https://historicboston.org/womens-sufferage-in-boston-those-hyde-park-women/

223 "Ain't you ashamed . . . acting like men?": Unknown speaker, quoted in "1870 Women's March and Vote," *Norfolk County Gazette*.

223 "his attitude . . . women had voted.": "Woman Suffrage in Boston: Those Hyde Park Women!" Blog by Historic Boston, Inc, accessed November 4, 2022, https://historicboston.org/womens-sufferage-in-boston-those-hyde-park-women/.

223 "Is it not . . . in intellectual power.": Sarah Grimké, quoted in Lerner, *Grimké Sisters*, 261.

224 "I have been . . . to this taunt.": Sarah Grimké, quoted in Birney, *Grimké Sisters*, 297.

224 "I have been . . . even a little.": Grimké, quoted in Birney, 298.
225 "My days of . . . blest as I?": Grimké, quoted in Birney, 300.
225 "My days of . . . than actual work.": Grimké, quoted in Birney, 300.
225 "You know what . . . in a woman.": Angelina Grimké, quoted in Birney, 308.
225 "Miss Grimké's colored nephew.": Unknown speaker, Obituary entitled "Sarah Grimke," quoted in the *Cleveland Daily Herald*, January 7, 1874, Vol. 40, Issue 6, no page number, Gale Primary Sources database.
226 "Her heart embraced . . . herself with all.": Theodore Dwight Weld, quoted in Thomas, *Theodore Weld*, 262.
226 "Doing good.": Weld, quoted in Todras, *Angelina Grimké*, 147.
227 "I've something to . . . throw it off.": Angelina Grimké Weld, quoted in Weld, *In Memory, Angelina Grimké Weld*, 57.
229 "misgivings": M.C. Stanley, quoted in Bruce, *Archibald Grimké*, 37.
229 "We look upon . . . that infidel city.": Moses Stanley, quoted in Bruce, *Archibald Grimké*, 38.
229 "*An interesting event . . . of Caucasian blood.*": Unknown speaker, quoted in "From the Boston Journal, April 22," *New York Times*, April 28, 1879, ProQuest Historical Newspapers, 5, https://www.proquest.com/docview/93797470/5FFBAB46B2D746C0PQ/6?accountid=10349.
229–230 "Mr. and Mrs. . . . it are concerned.": Unknown speaker, quoted in "From the Boston Journal, April 22," *New York Times*, April 28, 1879, ProQuest Historical Newspapers, 5, https://www.proquest.com/docview/93797470/5FFBAB46B2D746C0PQ/6?accountid=10349.
230 "light and peace,": Birney, *Grimké Sisters*, 311.
230 "I *cannot* mourn . . . pain and suffering].": Theodore Dwight Weld, quoted in Abzug, *Passionate Liberator*, 296.
230 "I have purposely . . . I am gone.": Thomas, *Theodore Weld*, 262.
230–231 "The women of . . . dead, yet speaketh.'": Lucy Stone, quoted in Birney, *Grimké Sisters*, 316.
231 "The women of . . . of this woman.": Lucy Stone, quoted in Birney, 316.

233 "my nephew, Archibald Grimké": Theodore Weld, quoted in Thomas, *Theodore Weld*, 259.

236 "There is not . . . wonderfully whitening effect.": Archibald Grimké, quoted in Perry, *Lift Up Thy Voice*, 297.

237 "In all things . . . to mutual progress.": Booker T. Washington, "The Atlanta Address," 2.

238 "A race that . . . be trampled upon,": Francis Grimké, *The Works of Francis J. Grimke*, vol. 1, 258.

239 "Why—it would . . . you doubt—God!": Angelina Weld Grimké, *Selected Works of Angelina Weld Grimké*, ed. Carolivia Herron (Oxford University Press, 1991), 149.

242 "Their places in . . . they worked for.": "City Bridge Named in Honor of the Grimké Sisters," City of Boston, November 15, 2019, https://www.boston.gov/news/city-bridge-named-honor-grimke-sisters.

242 "Outside of her . . . not know her.": Lucy Stone, quoted in Weld, *In Memory*, 25.

243 "All through the . . . with her pen.": Elizabeth Cady Stanton, quoted in Stanton, Anthony, and Gage, *History of Woman Suffrage*, 1:406.

243 "The right of . . . account of sex.": Nineteenth amendment to the Constitution of the United States.

245 "The rejection letters . . . likely to sell.": Lerner, *Grimké Sisters*, xvii.

247 "I ask no . . . off our necks.": Sarah Grimké, letter 2, "Women Subject Only to God," *Letters on Equality*.

248 "I recognize no . . . but human rights.": Angelina Grimké, *Letters to Catharine Beecher*, 118.

Selected Bibliography

Abzug, Robert H. *Passionate Liberator: Theodore Dwight Weld and the Dilemma of Reform.* Oxford University Press, 1980.

Birney, Catherine H. *The Grimké Sisters: Sarah and Angelina Grimké, the First American Women Advocates of Abolition and Women's Rights.* Haskell House, 1970. First published 1885.

Bruce, Dickson D. *Archibald Grimké: Portrait of a Black Independent.* Louisiana State University Press, 1993.

Ceplair, Larry, ed. *The Public Years of Sarah and Angelina Grimké: Selected Writings, 1835–1839.* Columbia University Press, 1989.

Durso, Pamela R. *The Power of Woman: The Life and Writings of Sarah Moore Grimké.* Mercer University Press, 2003.

Greenidge, Kerri K. *The Grimkes: The Legacy of Slavery in an American Family.* Liveright, 2023.

Grimké, Angelina Emily. *Walking by Faith: The Diary of Angelina Grimké, 1828–1835.* University of South Carolina Press, 2003.

Grimké, Angelina Weld. *Selected Works of Angelina Weld Grimké.* Edited by Carolivia Herron. Oxford University Press, 1991.

Grimké, Sarah Moore. *Letters on the Equality of the Sexes and Other Essays.* Edited and with an introduction by Elizabeth Anne Bartlett. Yale University Press, 1988.

Lerner, Gerda. *The Grimké Sisters from South Carolina: Pioneers for Women's Rights and Abolition.* University of North Carolina Press, 2004.

Lumpkin, Katharine Du Pre. *The Emancipation of Angelina Grimké.* University of North Carolina Press, 1974.

Perry, Mark. *Lift Up Thy Voice: The Grimké Family's Journey from Slaveholders to Civil Rights Leaders.* Viking, 2001.

Stanton, Elizabeth Cady, Susan B. Anthony, and Matilda Joslyn Gage. *History of Woman Suffrage.* 3 vols. Salem, NH, 1881. Google Books.

Thomas, Benjamin P. *Theodore Weld: Crusader for Freedom.* Rutgers University Press, 1950. Available at https://www.gospel-truth.net/Weld/weldbioindex.htm.

Todras, Ellen H. *Angelina Grimké: Voice of Abolition.* Linnet, 1999.

Weld, Theodore Dwight. *American Slavery as It Is: Testimony of a Thousand Witnesses.* Arno / New York Times, 1969. Originally published in 1839 in New York. Google Books.

Weld, Theodore Dwight. *Letters of Theodore Dwight Weld, Angelina Grimké and Sarah Grimké, 1822–1844.* 2 vols. P. Smith, 1965.

Weld-Grimké Family Papers, 1740–1930. Manuscripts Division, William L. Clements Library, University of Michigan. http://quod.lib.umich.edu/c/clementsmss/umich-wcl-M-400wel.

Further Reading, Websites, Videos for Young Readers

Books

Down, Susan Brophy. *Theodore Weld: Architect of Abolitionism.* Crabtree, 2013. A well-illustrated biography for young readers.

Edinger, Monica, and Lesley Younge. *Nearer My Freedom: The Interesting Life of Equiano Olaudah by Himself.* Zest Books, 2023. The memoir of Equiano Olaudah is retold with added "found poetry."

Kidd, Sue Monk. *The Invention of Wings.* Penguin Books, 2014. This novel imagines that Sarah Grimké and her childhood serving maid grow up together, plotting an escape to the North.

Websites

"Born in Slavery: Slave Narratives from the Federal Writers' Project, 1936–1938." Library of Congress. Accessed February 4, 2023. https://www.loc.gov/collections/slave-narratives-from-the-federal-writers-project-1936-to-1938/about-this-collection/.

"The Grimké Sisters Through the Civil War." Part 1 of a trilogy, *Sisterhood: South Carolina Suffragists*. SCETV Special. Written, directed, narrated, and produced by Beryl Dakers. First aired December 17, 2020. https://www.pbs.org/video/sc-suffragists-the-grimke-sisters-thru-the-civil-war-tiqpth/.

International African American Museum. Accessed February 5, 2023. https://iaamuseum.org/.

Index

Adams, John Quincy, 165–166
Address to Free Colored Americans, An (Sarah Grimké), 94
American Anti-Slavery Society, 84, 88, 97, 113, 116, 138, 148, 150, 156, 183, 202
   division of, 158, 160
   executive committee of, 80–81, 104, 108
   women's membership, 67, 160
American Convention of Anti-Slavery Women, 93
American Slavery as It Is: Testimony of a Thousand Witnesses (Theodore Weld), 143–150, 173, 179–180
Anti-Slavery Convention of American Women, 91, 123–134, 151, 174
Appeal to the Christian Women of the South (Angelina Grimké), 80–82, 88
Appeal to the Women of the Nominally Free States (Angelina Grimké), 94
Arch Street Meeting, 42–44, 56–59, 62, 68–70, 72, 79
   criticism of Grimké sisters, 43, 57
   stance on abolition, 77

Back-to-Africa movement, 70
Beecher, Catharine, 59–61, 95–97, 103, 179
Belleville school, 172–176, 183
Bettle, Edward, 59, 62–64
Bettle, Jane, 57, 59, 62
Bettle, Samuel, 59, 77
Bible Against Slavery, The (Theodore Weld), 141
Birney, Catherine, 212, 243
Birth of a Nation, The, 239
Blackwell, Henry, 180–181, 198, 218, 220
Boston Lyceum, 105–106
Brown, John, 191–193

careers for women, 21, 44, 59, 181–182, 184–185, 247
Chapman, Maria Weston, 92, 99, 108, 120–121, 125–127, 173
Charleston, SC, 12, 34, 36, 59, 72–73, 82, 137, 149, 157, 214–216, 227
   Grimké residency, 15–16, 37–38, 45, 47, 57, 62–63, 172, 183, 206–207, 209, 212, 217, 247, 251
   impacts of Civil War, 194, 203, 205–206
   society, 17, 19–22, 29–31, 40–41, 48–49, 52–53, 145, 147, 190

Child, Lydia Maria, 91, 111, 158, 173
Civil War, 194–200, 202–203, 205–207, 216–217, 219–220, 228, 231, 239
Cobb, Sylvanus, Jr., 222–223

Dawson, Betsy, 120, 153–155, 162
Declaration of Sentiments, 174, 177
Douglass, Frederick, 173, 174–175, 193, 218, 220, 231, 234
Douglass, Grace Bustill, 67–69, 73, 91, 93, 141, 152
Douglass, Sarah Mapps, 67–69, 73, 120, 243
  career, 93, 124, 151–152, 184–185
  correspondence with Grimké sisters, 80, 90–91, 104, 109, 111, 141, 192, 213, 216, 224
Du Bois, W. E. B., 238

Eagleswood, 182–183, 188–189, 193, 195
Emancipator, 68, 97, 148
Episcopalians, 29, 34, 37, 40–41, 46, 62, 228–229
Essay on Slavery and Abolitionism, with Reference to the Duty of American Females (Beecher), 95

Forten, Charlotte Vandine, 67–68, 73
Forten, James, 67–68, 73, 133
Fort Lee, NJ, 117, 136
Foster, Abby Kelley, 121, 126, 129, 158–159, 180, 220, 243
free produce, 68, 113, 118, 124
Frost, Anna Grimké, 41, 59, 62, 113, 117, 119–120, 123, 125, 149–150, 169
Fugitive Slave Act, 178–179, 196

Gage, Matilda Joslyn, 221, 243
Garrison, William Lloyd, 99, 133, 235
  career, 66, 68, 76, 202
  criticism, 73, 77, 84, 108, 122, 126
  relationship with Grimké-Welds, 74–78, 107, 120–121, 128–129, 166, 197, 208, 218, 223, 225
  women's rights, 104, 158–161
Graham, Sylvester, 139–140, 154
Graham diet, 139–140, 187
Green Hill estate, 42–43
Grimké, Angelina Weld, 232–233, 235–240, 246
Grimké, Archibald Henry, 210–211, 216, 232–233, 239–240
  career, 219, 227–230, 235–238
  education, 212–213, 217–218, 223, 225, 227
  enslavement, 214–215
Grimké, Benjamin, 22, 39
Grimké, Charles, 49, 63, 202
Grimké, Eliza, 25, 202–203, 206–207, 214–215, 217
Grimké, Francis John, 210–211, 231–232, 236, 239
  career, 228, 234–235, 237–238, 240
  education, 212–213, 217–219, 223, 227–228
  enslavement, 214–216
Grimké, Frederick, 22, 70–72, 91, 171
Grimké, Henry, 37, 59, 63, 176
  death, 202
  mistress, 172, 211, 213–214
  treatment of enslaved people, 50–51, 157
Grimké, John, 22

Grimké, John Faucheraud
  beliefs on slavery, 20
  death, 34–37
  education, 20–22
  law career, 15–16, 24
Grimké, Mary, 22, 25, 46, 183,
    202–203, 206–207
Grimké, Mary Smith, 15, 46, 54,
    57, 82–83, 116
  charity work, 29
  death, 149
  treatment of enslaved people,
    18–19, 24–26, 50–51, 63
Grimké, Sarah E. Stanley,
    228–229, 232
Grimké, Sarah "Sally" Moore
  abolition, 9, 78, 83–95, 114–117,
    123–126, 129–130, 134,
    141–153, 171–172, 179–181,
    192–194, 200–202, 208, 234,
    240–248
  appearance, 30, 36, 181,
    188–189, 224
  beliefs on marriage, 45, 59
  career, 176–177, 182–184,
    187–188, 205
  childhood, 15–17
  childhood beliefs on slavery,
    11–14, 19–20, 25, 29, 32–33
  conversion to Quakerism,
    35–37, 40, 42–43, 56, 58
  criticism, 78, 81, 90–91, 98–99,
    114–115, 149–153, 164–166,
    246–248
  death, 225–227
  education, 20–24, 88, 135–137,
    140
  finances, 37, 41, 43, 49, 138,
    156–157, 182–184, 206–207,
    217
  Quaker ministry, 44, 81

religious beliefs, 34, 38–39,
    46–47, 70, 100, 139
  women's rights, 99–106, 141,
    160–161, 173, 220–223,
    240–248
  writings, 88, 94, 99–101,
    243–244
*Grimkes: The Legacy of Slavery
    in an American Family*
    (Greenidge), 20, 246, 248
Grimké, Thomas, 38–39, 72, 76,
    78, 223
  education, 21–23, 33, 58

Harper's Ferry, VA, 191–192
Hartford Female Seminary,
    59–62, 95
Hetty, 19–20
house servants
  education, 19, 215
  jobs, 17, 24, 30, 94, 113, 135,
    138, 162, 164, 203–204
  release from enslavement, 57,
    78, 120, 153
  treatment, 11, 14, 18–20, 24–29,
    37, 50–52, 63, 87, 146–147,
    172–173, 175, 212–215

Kitty, 50, 78

Lee, Robert E., 191, 206
*Letters on the Equality of the Sexes,
    and the Condition of Woman*
    (Sarah Grimké), 99, 183, 224
Letters on the Province of Woman
    (Sarah Grimké), 99
Lewis, Diocletian (Dio), 203–205,
    231
Liberator, 68–69, 73–76, 96, 99,
    166
Lincoln, Abraham, 193–194,
    196–197, 200, 203, 206, 217

Morris, Catherine Wistar, 42, 47, 53, 62, 69–70, 72
   religious beliefs, 55–56, 66, 77–78
Morris, Israel, 37, 39, 41–42, 45, 59
Mott, Lucretia, 77, 133, 186
   abolition, 67, 124, 126, 129, 131, 160–161
   religious beliefs, 44, 91, 121
   women's rights, 67, 158, 173–174, 220–221, 243

National Association for the Advancement of Colored People (NAACP), 238–239

Parker, Mary S., 99, 124
Pease, Elizabeth, 137, 151–152
Pennsylvania Hall, 120, 123–134, 141
Philadelphia, PA, 34, 40–41, 47, 59, 62–64, 71–73, 78–79, 86, 113, 117, 129–130, 173, 202
   society, 35–38, 48–49, 53–57, 66–67, 83, 91–92, 120–123, 133–135, 141, 151, 185, 232
Philadelphia Female Anti-Slavery Society, 67, 72
Philbrick, Samuel, 105, 112, 120
"planter" families, 15, 17, 24, 37–38, 147, 172, 214
Presbyterians, 34, 37, 40, 46, 48, 60, 62, 112, 121, 217, 227–228
   abolition, 53, 72, 85, 89, 208, 238
Protestants, 46, 89, 201
Purvis, Harriet Forten, 68, 120, 176
Purvis, Robert, 68, 120, 133, 176
Purvis, Sarah Forten, 68, 232

Quakers, 35, 37, 64, 72–73, 82, 84, 129, 133, 136, 173, 184
   beliefs, 39, 46, 50, 56–57, 66, 69–70, 93, 151–152
   clothing, 36, 44–45, 83, 105, 110, 139, 189
   customs, 40–43, 48, 52–53, 55–56, 59–60, 78, 81, 89, 119–121, 138, 201
   Hicksite Quakers, 56, 58, 67–68, 91
   Orthodox Quakers, 56–58, 77, 152, 247
   plain speech, 36, 55–56, 83, 105, 139

Rachel (Angelina Weld Grimké), 238–240
Raritan Bay Union, 182, 187–188, 192, 243
reform dress, 180–181, 188–189
Revolutionary War, 15, 155, 204
Roman Catholics, 46, 192

Seneca Falls Convention, 173, 177
Smith, Gerrit, 159, 176
Smith, Jane, 86, 113, 117, 120, 123, 125, 151, 157
   correspondence with Grimké sisters, 138–142, 162, 169
Southern fashion, 30–31, 36, 44, 83, 189, 205
Stanton, Elizabeth Cady, 157, 160–161, 173–176, 197–199, 220, 243
Stanton, Henry, 70, 84, 108, 120–121, 157, 159–160, 173
Stone, Lucy, 189, 198, 225, 231
   abolition, 218, 221
   women's rights, 172–173, 180–181, 208, 220, 242–243
Stowe, Harriet Beecher, 60, 179

Tappan, Arthur, 84, 120, 159–160
Tappan, Lewis, 84, 89, 120, 156, 159–160, 166
Truth, Sojourner, 190, 220, 243
Tubman, Harriet, 190, 193
Turner, Nat, 65

Uncle Tom's Cabin (Stowe), 60, 148, 179, 215

Washington, Booker T., 237–238
Weld, Angelina Emily Grimké
　abolition, 9, 64–66, 68, 72–92, 96–97, 102–106, 108–111, 115, 125–134, 137, 141–153, 158–161, 171–172, 179, 193–209, 217–221, 242–248
　appearance, 105, 110, 119, 157, 180–181, 186, 188–189
　career, 59–63, 175–176, 187, 190, 203–207
　childhood, 23–30, 37, 135
　childhood beliefs on slavery, 24–28, 38–39, 53–54
　conversion to Quakerism, 48–52, 55–58
　criticism, 66, 76–77, 90–91, 95–99, 102–103, 114, 149–150, 166, 246–248
　death, 230–231, 242
　education, 58–62, 84–85, 136, 140
　finances, 49, 138, 156, 168, 183, 206–207, 213, 217
　health, 154–155, 162, 167–169, 177, 216, 223, 227
　lectures, 88–90, 95, 106, 108–111, 115, 126–129, 198–199
　marriage, 107, 112–114, 116–123
　religious beliefs, 45–46, 70, 72, 138–139, 169
　women's rights, 92, 101–105, 158–160, 174, 180, 189, 197–199, 220–223, 242–248
　writings, 75–76, 80–82, 94, 144–154, 244
Weld, Charles (Charley) Stuart Faucheraud, 154–155, 158, 163, 168, 185, 194, 207, 213, 223, 225, 233, 235
Weld, Sarah "Sissy" Grimké, 170–171, 185, 195, 207, 221, 223, 225
Weld, Theodore Dwight, 96–97, 105–108, 111, 154, 177, 218, 226–227, 230, 233–235
　abolition, 70–71, 76–77, 85–86, 88–89, 93, 113–116, 125–126, 129, 138, 158–159, 162–169, 171–172, 175–176, 180–182, 190, 194, 197, 201–203, 205–209, 219
　appearance, 86, 112, 119, 186–187, 189–190
　finances, 156–157, 163–164, 169–170, 183, 187
　lectures, 70–71, 137, 141, 171, 202, 222
　marriage, 116–123, 135–136
　women's rights, 102–103, 158–159
　writings, 141–151, 242–244
Weld, Theodore "Sody" Grimké, 161–164, 168, 185, 194–195, 198, 203, 207, 223, 235
Weston, Nancy, 172, 211–217, 228, 232, 235–236
Whittier, John Greenleaf, 84, 101–102, 119, 121, 159, 208
women's suffrage, 208, 218, 221–224, 229, 235, 242–243
World Anti-Slavery Convention, 160–161
Wright, Elizur, 80–81, 85–86, 159, 176, 208

Photo Acknowledgments

Image credits: Lake Erie Maps and Prints/Alamy, p. 8; North Wind Picture Archives via AP Images, p. 10; Greene, C. O./Library of Congress, p. 15; YA/BOT/Alamy, p. 16; The Illustrated London News, p. 18; Library of Congress, pp. 27, 29, 32, 44, 51, 73, 82, 85, 114, 124, 132, 139, 158, 173, 192, 196, 208; Charles Bayless/Library of Congress, p. 25; The Library Company of Philadelphia, pp. 28, 57, 69, 96; Metropolitan Museum of Art Open Access, p. 31; Sepia Times/Universal Images Group via Getty Images, p. 36; W. Birch & Son, p. 38; Lower Merion Historical Society Archives, p. 43; National Portrait Gallery, Smithsonian Institution, pp. 60, 190; Schlesinger Library on the History of Women in America, p. 61; History of American conspiracies: a record of treason, insurrection, rebellion & c., in the United States of America, from 1760 to 1860 (Public Domain), p. 65; National Portrait Gallery, Smithsonian Institution, gift of Frederick M. Rock, p. 67; National Portrait Gallery, Smithsonian Institution, bequest of Garrison Norton, p. 76; Alchetron, p. 81; The American, January 1910 article by Ida Tarbell, Vol 69, pp. 91, 99, 126, 224; Robert Peckham, p. 102; City of Boston Archives, p. 106; University of Pennsylvania Digital Library, p. 108; Digital Commonwealth, p. 110; Angelina Grimké, p. 118; American Antiquarian Society, p. 122; Friends Historical Library of Swarthmore College (Open Access), p. 134; British Abolition Movement, p. 137; Mathew Brady Studio/National Portrait Gallery, Smithsonian Institution, p. 146; Collection of the Massachusetts Historical Society, pp. 151, 189, 230; Engraving by J. Andrews after a daguerreotype by Bundy & Co. via Wikimedia Commons, p. 156; Archivart/Alamy, p. 161; Mathew Brady, accessed via Wikimedia Commons, p. 165; Corbis via Getty Images, p. 167; Heritage Art/Heritage Images via Getty Images, p. 174; The J. Paul Getty Museum, Los Angeles, p. 178; Blackwell Papers, Library of Congress, p. 181; The Life and Work of Susan B. Anthony (Volume 1 of 2), p. 185; William L. Clements Library, University of Michigan, pp. 186, 229; Bequest of Dr. Paul J. Sartain/The Pennsylvania Academy of the Fine Arts, p. 204; Schomburg Center for Research in Black Culture, Photographs and Prints Division, The New York Public Library, pp. 210, 235, 239; Napoleon Sarony, National Portrait Gallery, Smithsonian Institution, p. 220; The Booklovers Magazine, July 1903, p. 228. Design element: Annie Spratt/Unsplash.

About the Author

Angelica Shirley Carpenter is the author of five biographies for young people, *Frances Hodgson Burnett*, *L. Frank Baum*, *Robert Louis Stevenson*, *Lewis Carroll*, and *Born Criminal: Matilda Joslyn Gage, Radical Suffragist*. She wrote two picture books, *The Voice of Liberty* and *The Secret Gardens of Frances Hodgson Burnett*, and edited a scholarly anthology, *In the Garden: Essays in Honor of Frances Hodgson Burnett*, based on a conference she convened as curator of the Arne Nixon Center for the Study of Children's Literature at California State University, Fresno. A past president of the International Wizard of Oz Club, she is also a member of the Society of Children's Book Writers and Illustrators, the Authors Guild, Biographers' International Organization, the Women's International League for Peace and Freedom, Authors Against Banned Books, and the American Library Association. She lives in Fresno with her husband. Her website is www.angelicacarpenter.com.